MICROECONOMIC APPLICATIONS: UNDERSTANDING THE AMERICAN ECONOMY

Robert Paul Thomas
University of Washington

Wadsworth Publishing Company
Belmont, California
A Division of Wadsworth, Inc.

Economics Editor: Marshall Aronson
Production: Cobb/Dunlop Publisher Services, Inc.

Printed in the United States of America

1 2 3 4 5 6 7 8 9 10—85 84 83 82 81

Library of Congress Cataloging in Publication Data

Thomas, Robert Paul.
  Microeconomic applications.

  Includes index.
  1. Microeconomics. 2. United States—Economic conditions. I. Title.
HB172.T48   338.5'0973   80–29050
ISBN 0–534–00968–9

Contents

CONTENTS

Preface

This book has only one goal: to aid the beginning student in bridging the gap between economic theory and application. Economic theory is abstract. That is the way it should be. The concepts that make up the heart of the principles of economics course must be mastered if a student is to think systematically about economic problems. Such an understanding is as important to the economic way of thinking as mastery of the rules of mathematics is to working algebra and calculus problems. But economics does not stop with a knowledge of economic theory. The ultimate goal is to employ theory to understand the contemporary world. This means application. The theoretical concepts that are presented in the principles textbook must be applied to a real-world situation if the true value of the economic way of thinking is to be appreciated by the student. Application helps the student recognize both the relevance of the principles of economics to his or her life and the way that theory can be used to explain how the world works.

There is, however, potential danger in attempting to apply theory for the beginning student. The example must be selected with great care to ensure that only the concepts the student has mastered are necessary to successfully analyze the problem. Should a student's knowledge be insufficient to understand the application, the result may be confusion rather than enlightenment.

PREFACE

Many current public issues require the simultaneous application of several economic concepts. This is all right, of course, if such issues are used at the end of the course. But in my experience the willingness of many students to learn abstract concepts is directly proportional to their belief in the usefulness of the tools, and much of the usefulness of learning economics through application is lost by delay. For this reason application should begin early in the process of teaching economics. In practice, this means at least one application for each chapter in the textbook and two or more for the core and summary chapters.

For each key concept commonly presented in teaching the principles of economics this book contains an application at the student's level of mastery to demonstrate how the concept can be used to analyze a real-world situation. The applications are presented in approximately the same order as the concepts appear in most textbooks. For textbooks that differ in the order of topic presentation, a correlation table appears at the end of the preface.

Each chapter begins with a preview that introduces the problem to be examined and the major economic concepts to be employed. Following the preview is a list of statements that summarize the important points in the analysis. A list of readings following each application indicates where the student can find additional information about the topic.

The applications in this book were initially developed from classroom presentations. The material was class-tested by the author, and student responses were incorporated into this published edition. The author thus owes his thanks to the countless students whose classroom comments, criticisms, and test scores led to improvements in the level of presentation and in the analysis itself. The author also wishes to thank the reviewers of this book, whose efforts are reflected in the final product: Terry L. Anderson, Montana State University; Harold R. Christensen, Central State University; Charles J. Gallagher, Virginia Commonwealth University.

KEY TO USING MICROECONOMIC APPLICATIONS WITH MAJOR INTRODUCTORY TEXTS

CHAPTERS IN MICROECONOMIC APPLICATIONS

	PART I INTRODUCTION TO ECONOMICS								PART II SUPPLY AND DEMAND				
	1	2	3	4	5	6	7	8	9	10	11	12	13
McConnell *Economics*	1	2	5 33	3	4	5	7	8	24	23	25	25	25
Samuelson *Economics*	1	2	3	3	4	4	6	9	22	20	23	23	24
Spencer, *Contemporary Microeconomics*	In	5 7	2	1	2	2	3	4	5	6	7	8	8
Wonnacott/Wonnacott *Economics*	1	2 19	3 30	3	4	4	6	5	18	17	19	19	19
Mansfield, *Principles of Microeconomics*	1 2	3	19	18	4	4	6	5	7	8	9	10	10
Dolan, *Basic Microeconomics*	1	1	2		3	3	6	4	5	3	7	7	7
Lipsey/Steiner *Economics*	1	1	4	4	5	7	19	25	8 9	6	12	11	10
Gwartney/Stroup *Microeconomics*	1	2	3	4	3	3	11	19	5	5	6	7	6
Miller *Economics Today*	1	1	2	4	3	4	4	6	22	21	23	24	23
Waud *Economics*	1	2	3	3	4	4	24	18	17	17	19	19	19
Baumol/Blinder *Economics*	1	3	30	30	4	4	24	32	19	18	20	21	20
Amacher/Sweeney *Principles of Microeconomics*	1	1	2	2	2	2	12	4	5	3	7	7	7

KEY TO USING MICROECONOMIC APPLICATIONS
WITH MAJOR INTRODUCTORY TEXTS

CHAPTERS IN MICROECONOMIC APPLICATIONS

PART III PRODUCT MARKETS						PART IV FACTOR MARKETS						PART V CURRENT ECONOMIC PROBLEMS							
14	15	16	17	18	19	20	21	22	23	24	25	26	27	28	29	30	31	32	33
26	27	29	28	34	34	31	31	32	32	23	34	31	28	36	36	36	8	8	37
21	25	25	26	26	26	27	27	28	30	20	25	29	26	40	40	3	8	8	5
8	9	10	14	14	14	11	11	12	12	17	14	15	10	18	18	17	4	4	16
20	21	22	22	22	21	27	27	29	29	4	5	28	22	23	24	3	24	5	32
11	12	13 19	13	14	12	9	15	16	16	4	12	15	13	19	18	19	5	5	17
8	9	9 11	12	13	14	15	15	17	17	15	14	16	12	19	19	2	4	4	18
14	15	16	16	18	18	20	21	22	22	7	14	21	16	13	24	25	25	24	23
7	10	9	8	11	11	12	12	12	12	3	11	14	8	18	17	19	19	19	15
24	25	25	26	27	27	28	28	30	30	3	27	29	27	33	33	4	5	5	31
20	21	23	22	24	24	25	26	27	27	18	24	26	22	18	18	18	3	18	28
23	23	23	22	25	26	27	27	28	28	26	26	27	32	31	31	30			29
8	9	11	10	12	12	13	13	13	13	4	12	14	10	15	15	15			15

I

INTRODUCTION TO ECONOMICS

1

Introduction: Application of Economic Principles

Economics is a systematic way of thinking about a wide range of personal and social problems. Once a person has mastered the principles of economics, opportunities to employ them appear everywhere. These principles allow the thinker to sort out sense from nonsense in the daily reports of the news media, in the statements of politicians and special interest groups, and in the conversation of friends and neighbors. The application of these principles allows people to exert more control over their lives by increasing their ability to understand what goes on around them.

It doesn't require a Ph.D. in economics to master the economic way of thinking. In fact, this way of thinking rests upon a set of very simple principles:

1. Economic thinking recognizes that providing scarce goods involves a cost or sacrifice of other goods; scarce goods are not free.
2. Economic decision makers economize; they implicitly recognize that economic goods are scarce and always attempt to obtain a goal at the lowest possible cost.
3. Economic thinking recognizes that incentives matter in decision making. As the personal benefits from choosing an alternative increase, a person is more likely to choose that option or, if the costs increase, reject it.
4. Every economic action has several effects. In addition to the direct result of an action, there are secondary effects that also must be identified and considered.

3

5. Finally, the test of economic thinking is its ability to explain human behavior. This often reduces to the ability to predict future behavior.

Because all economic thinking is little more than the application of these principles to particular problems, the proper way to master this method of thinking is by application. The purpose of this book is to provide a connection that will allow you to proceed from a knowledge of economic principles gained from a textbook to the application of the principles to real problems and issues. The examples in this book thus bridge the gap between theory and application, demonstrating the ability of the economic way of thinking to clarify issues and point the way to purposeful action.

Each application in this book begins with a preview that introduces the problem to be analyzed and identifies the economic concepts that will be employed. Following the preview is a list of key economic points that alert you to what you should learn as you study the application. Then follows the application itself: a description of the problem, phenomenon, or issue to be explored and an analysis that applies the relevant economic concept. The task of explaining the economic concept itself is left to the basic textbook.

The best way to use this book is to first read the assignment in the basic textbook and master the theoretical concepts presented there. Then you should read the application assigned in this book. As you read, keep in mind the key economic points of the analysis. When you have finished, ask yourself if you understand each key economic point discussed.

It is hoped that the more than thirty applications in this book will convince you that (1) economics is widely applicable to contemporary social problems and (2) the discipline has much to contribute toward an understanding of how our modern society operates.

The list of past accomplishments of economics is impressive. The advances in knowledge about economics have guided the intervention of the federal government to moderate business fluctuations. As a consequence of this intervention, the post–World War II economy has been relatively free of economic recessions and another major depression has been avoided. The fact that recessions still occur and inflation has become a major social problem only testifies that work remains for economists to do.

Advances in economic knowledge have also guided government intervention to improve the performance of the economy. Economics has provided the guidelines for the regulation of pollution and the improvement of economic efficiency. Economics has also been in the forefront of the movement to improve the regulation process itself. It was the work of economists that directly led to the deregulation of the airlines, for example.

Private business has also benefited from economic research. Many, if not most, of modern business practices have their foundation in economic

4

analysis. Recent advances in the process of business decision making, such as capital budgeting, inventory control, accounting practices, and business forecasting, were all developed from the initial efforts of economists.

Few public issues are debated today without the application of the principles of economics at some stage of the argument. At the very least economic analysis narrows and defines the issues; at best it allows an efficient and effective public policy to be developed.

During such debates it will be observed that professional economists sometimes disagree. It has become fashionable for the nation's press to focus on these areas of disagreement, but don't be misled. Conflict is interesting, hence newsworthy, while agreement is dull, therefore ignored by the media. Professional economists agree on most things! But they do sometimes disagree, so it is important to understand why.

Economists can disagree because of genuine differences in scientific diagnoses. These differences generally arise when the problem lies on the frontiers of economic knowledge. Economists disagree on the causes of inflation, for example, because the profession does not as yet fully understand the phenomenon of inflation. Just as biological scientists do not as yet understand the causes of cancer and are pursuing different approaches to finding the answer, economists are exploring the inflation problem from different directions. Until a breakthrough is made and a consensus develops among economists, disagreements as to how best to deal with inflation—and other unresolved areas—must be expected.

The opinions of economists may also differ because the basic facts are unclear. A difference of opinion as to the accuracy of economic facts could obviously lead to a difference of opinion among economists, as it would in any profession. Economists disagree on the correct policies to follow to deal with poverty, partially because the facts about the extent of poverty are not known. They disagree on what to do to ensure an adequate supply of energy in the future, in part because some of the basic facts are little more than guesses. Thus, where economic facts are elusive and cause and effect relationships unclear, it should not be surprising that economists disagree.

But even if there were basic agreements to how the economy operates and agreement on the basic facts, economists would still sometimes disagree on some matters of public policy. The basis for this disagreement is not the discipline of economics itself, but rather the differences in social philosophies held by individual economists. Such differences are reflected in the diversity of recommendations as to the appropriate policy the government should adopt. For example, economists could differ on what the government should do about inflation. One group might argue that inflation is such a social evil that the government should take immediate steps to halt it, even at the expense of temporarily increasing the amount of unemployment in the country. Another group of economists could argue that inflation is a social problem but unemployment is even worse. They would argue that the inflation problem must be attacked in a way that will not increase the amount of unemployment. The two groups of economists disagree, but not over the economics of the matter. They disagree on what they value most and on whether the benefits of immediately halting inflation exceed the costs to society. This is partly a matter of fact but also a matter of social conscience.

These possible sources of disagreement may also apply to the applications in this book. The views expressed may not be shared by every other economist. The possibility that disagreement can exist provides you, the student, with another reason to acquire the ability to think like an economist: so that you can analyze problems for yourself.

Preview

The nationwide 55 mph speed limit for highway driving was designed to save gasoline and human lives, but it does so only at the cost of increased driving time. This chapter employs the economic concepts of opportunity cost and efficiency to investigate whether the speed limit is the best way to accomplish these goals. There are always several ways to attain any goal. The best way is the one that does the job at the lowest cost.

Key Economic Points

Obtaining more of certain scarce goods, such as gasoline and human life, requires the sacrifice of other scarce goods, in this case, time.

Is the 55 mph speed limit the most efficient way to achieve the goals of saving gasoline and human life?

How does the employment of positive incentives compare with the negative speed limit as the means of achieving the goals of saving gasoline and human life?

2

The Opportunity Cost of Saving Lives and Gasoline: The 55 mph Speed Limit

By now everyone is familiar with the 55 mph speed limit. The law limiting highway speed to a maximum of 55 mph was passed at the federal level in response to the energy crisis of 1974, with the expectation that reduced highway speed would cut down on our consumption of petroleum. The National Highway Traffic Safety Administration estimates that since that time, besides saving 1 to 2 percent annually on total gasoline consumption, reduced highway speeds have saved 4,500 lives each year. Supporters of the reduced speed limit are now emphasizing the life-saving aspect of the law, relegating the conservation of gasoline to the status of an added benefit. This development has led to bumper stickers that read, "55 mph Speed Limit Is a Law We Can *Live* With."

Not everyone agrees. Bills have been introduced in several state legislatures and in the U.S. Senate to repeal the 55 mph speed limit. While none of these bills has been passed, it is clear that many drivers find the reduced speed limit intolerable. State highway patrols across the nation report writing citations in record numbers (8 million in 1978) in their attempt to enforce the reduced speed limit. Several state patrols have been able to pay for new airplanes and increased numbers of patrolmen out of the receipts from speeding fines. Despite increased efforts, general compliance has not been obtained, as a freeway drive anywhere in the country will attest.

The main reason that people do not voluntarily obey the 55 mph law (fewer than half do) is that it is personally expensive to do so. The principle is simple: time is money. The cost of increased travel time for many individuals is greater than the saving in gasoline and the personal benefits of reduced chances of having an accident. The time saved by exceeding the speed limit is for many also worth the risk of being cited for speeding by the state patrol.

An individual's time is a precious commodity because it is scarce, but life is precious too, and so is gasoline, as supplies become increasingly limited and expensive. It is clear that in the case of the 55 mph speed limit we cannot have more of all three. In this case, to save lives and conserve gasoline we must sacrifice time. But is the time well spent? Economics is particularly well suited to answer this question.

Studies have shown that commuters are willing to pay up to 42 percent of their hourly wage to save an hour of travel time. It is estimated that the 55 mph speed limit forces drivers to spend 2,710 million extra travel hours annually, which, valued at 42 percent of the average hourly wage rate, equals $6 billion worth of travel time per year.

What does this added expense purchase? We have already mentioned the savings in life and in gasoline. Saving a life by reducing highway speeds costs $1.3 million worth of time per life saved. Is this a bargain? How can anyone place a value on human life? As difficult as it seems, it can be done. Indeed, the legislators who passed the lowered speed limit implicitly did just that. For instance, they could have reduced legal highway speeds to 5 mph or to zero. If they had done the latter, the almost 50,000 lives currently lost annually on our nation's highways would be saved. The fact that our government chose 55 mph rather than zero suggests that the overall benefits to the nation of driving at 55 mph is felt to be worth the 47,600 human lives lost in highway accidents in 1977.

We can also look at the cost of saving a life by reducing the speed limit in terms of years of life gained or lost. If we compare the extra travel time to the reduction in traffic fatalities, we find that it costs 102 years spent in extra driving time to save the life of one person who, on average, could be expected to live 35.2 more years. This may suggest that the lower speed limit is an inefficient way to save lives. But society often seems willing to impose such a cost when it is spread, as in this case, in small amounts among millions of persons to avoid the violent early death of a few.

Almost all economists would agree that the value or worth of anything is determined by what a person is willing to pay or sacrifice to obtain the good. The personal valuation of a good, however, may not be the same as its social value or cost. There may be benefits or costs to society that are not included in the individual's valuation. This is certainly the case in highway driving. A driver's personal valuation of the benefits of driving at certain speeds imposes costs on others. A fast driver who has an accident may also harm or kill others. Thus a private determination of the benefits of driving faster than 55 mph may impose significant costs upon society. It would be useful to know whether the public values a human life at more or less than the $1.3 million it costs to save a life by reducing highway speeds to 55 mph.

There have been two serious attempts to estimate the amount the public is willing to pay to reduce the risk of death, which is the figure that a government decision maker would be interested in when evaluating whether the 55 mph speed limit is worthwhile or not. These two investigations both studied the job market. Individuals, since they spend a large part of their lives on the job, have an incentive to find out about job-related risks. Dangerous jobs will be less attractive to workers, so employers will have to pay higher wages to induce employees to accept the risks. One study used injury rates among hourly workers in manufacturing. After correcting for education, experience, and other factors affecting relative wages, the study found that workers in dangerous jobs received 1.5 percent higher wages than workers in jobs where the death rate was half as high. This estimate suggests that collectively workers were willing to accept $1.5 million less if employers took safety steps that might save even one life. The second study found that 1,000 workers in an occupation where the risk of death above the level normal in industry was 1 in 1,000 would each be willing to sacrifice $200 a year if the extra risk were eliminated. This implies that collectively a life was valued at $200,000.

The range between the two estimates is too wide for our purposes. According to the first estimate, the 55 mph speed limit is an efficient way to save lives; according to the second, a life saved by reducing driving speeds costs six and one-half times too much. There is yet another way of determining the willingness to pay, one that can be derived from peoples' driving habits. Buckling a seat belt reduces the risk of death by one in 5 million for the average trip. Even though over 20,000 deaths a year stem directly from not using seat belts, many people appear willing to take the risk rather than experience the minor hassle of "buckling up," and the small probability of death by automobile accident suggests that drivers value their lives at less than $500,000. If the $500,000 figure is accurate, the 55 mph speed limit collectively forces people to spend too much to save a life.

Another way to look at the economics of saving lives by reducing the speed limit is to consider the cost of alternative ways of accomplishing the same goal. What does it cost to save a life by other means? About 2 million Americans die each year, most (over 99 percent) from non-traffic-related causes. For instance, as many people die each year from fires as from motor vehicle accidents. It has been estimated that placing a smoke detector in every home would save almost as many lives as the 55 mph limit at a cost of only $40,000 to $80,000 per life saved. Heart disease presently accounts for 40 percent of all deaths. An additional mobile cardiac care unit costs only $2,000 per life saved. There are numerous opportunities to save lives for $20,000 to $100,000 each by reducing roadside hazards for drivers. In comparison, the cost of $1.3 million in extra travel time per life saved by a reduced speed limit appears to be too expensive a way to save lives.

The true cost of anything is the sacrifice that is involved in obtaining it. Economists call this concept the opportunity or alternative cost. In this case the opportunity cost of resources spent saving lives by reducing the speed limit is too high because there are other means of saving lives that cost much less. Efficiency in this case suggests that the government abandon the 55 mph speed limit and adopt alternative life-saving forms.

The efficiency of a reduced speed limit in saving gasoline can be analyzed in the same way. What is the cost compared with alternatives that would accomplish the same task? The government estimates that the 55 mph speed limit reduces our gasoline consumption by 9 million gallons a day, or 1 to 2 percent. This same amount of gasoline could be saved by switching every car to radial tires when existing tires require replacement, or by changing spark plugs at regular intervals, or by simply keeping tires inflated at the proper pressure. Each of these alternatives would save as much gasoline at a cost that is trivial when compared with the present cost of the 55 mph speed limit. Another alternative would be to convince just 4 percent of the drivers to switch to more fuel-efficient cars. The average car in the United States now runs about 14 miles to the gallon, but automobile manufacturers offer dozens of models that get much better gas mileage, often twice as much.

How can society induce people to drive more fuel-efficient cars? There are two traditional ways to influence human behavior: (1) pass a new law that makes the desired behavior compulsory or (2) increase the personal incentives for the desired behavior. In other words, the government can use either the carrot or the stick to alter public behavior. The carrot is in many cases a more efficient means of changing behavior because it is self-enforcing. If it is in a person's interest to do something, society does not have to check to see if it was done: self-interest takes care of the enforcement. But pass a law prohibiting a certain behavior on pain of punishment, and society not only has to constantly monitor people's behavior but must punish violators as well. The expanded state highway patrols needed to enforce the 55 mph speed limit bear witness to this fact. The cost of enforcing a law prohibiting behavior suggests that alternatives employing the carrot be seriously considered before the government resorts to the stick.

The government, however, has already taken steps that employ the stick. Automobile manufacturers now must produce a fleet of cars that average a certain gasoline mileage. That is, for every car sold that obtains poor gas mileage, a manufacturer must sell enough fuel-efficient cars to maintain a fleet average that complies with the government standard.

Numerous other options could be designed to provide incentives for individuals to voluntarily behave in the desired manner. One way would be to tax fuel-inefficient cars, either when they are first purchased or annually when the owners relicense their vehicles. Fuel-inefficient cars would become more expensive to drive, hence fewer people would be willing to drive them, choosing instead the now relatively cheaper-to-operate smaller cars. A second option, really a variation of the first, is to impose a gasoline tax sufficiently high to encourage individuals to put good gasoline mileage high on their shopping lists when considering the purchase of a new car.

A novel proposal made by Charles Lave (*Newsweek,* October 23, 1978) is to allow drivers of fuel-efficient cars to drive faster than the 55 mph limit, which would still be imposed for "gas guzzlers." That is, allow fuel-efficient cars to travel 65 or 70 mph, and issue two kinds of license plates, so that the state police would have no trouble telling the two classes apart. Would this approach work? The results of economic research on transportation, according to Lave, suggest that the fastest mode of transportation attracts all the commuters. The chance to drive faster would provide the incentive to choose fuel-efficient cars. The point is simple. According to Lave, if we insist on manipulating the speed limit to affect energy consumption, then we should do it in an efficient way. The most effective way to reduce gasoline consumption is to provide an incentive for individuals to drive more fuel-efficient cars. Any of the above incentives would both save more gasoline and cost less than the 55 mph speed limit.

The 55 mph speed limit originally imposed to conserve on gasoline had the additional advantage of saving lives, but only at the cost of additional travel time. The economic question is whether the saving in life and gasoline, both of which are scarce goods, is worth the sacrifice of time lost, which is also a good. The value of anything is determined by the willingness to pay or sacrifice to obtain it. The cost of the resources imposed by the 55 mph speed limit lies between various estimates of what workers are willing to pay to avoid the risk of death, and is substantially above the amount suggested by the behavior of drivers concerning seat belts. The opportunity costs of saving lives by a reduced speed limit is the number of lives that could be saved if the resources were used to save lives in the best alternate way. The 55 mph limit comes out poorly when this comparison is made. Mobile intensive care units, smoke detectors, and the removal of roadside hazards save more lives for the same resource cost. The same approach suggests that switching to radial tires, changing spark plugs regularly, or merely keeping tires inflated would save as much gasoline at much less cost.

The relatively high cost of enforcing the reduced speed limit suggests that alternative means of saving gasoline be explored. In addition to passing laws prohibiting certain behavior, society has the option of creating incentives that will redirect individual behavior in the desired way. The advantage of employing incentives over prohibiting behavior is that the former requires effort for the government to enforce. Taxes, for example, could be used to provide the incentive for drivers to switch to more fuel-efficient cars. A novel approach would be to allow only fuel-efficient cars to exceed the 55 mph speed limit. In any case, changing incentives would probably be a more efficient way to reduce the consumption of gasoline than the continued use of a 55 mph speed limit.

Additional Readings

Lave, Charles A. "The Costs of Going 55." *Newsweek,* October 23, 1978.

Rhoads, Steven E. "How Much Should We Spend to Save a Life." *The Public Interest,* Spring 1978.

Singer, Max. "How to Reduce Risks Rationally." *The Public Interest,* Spring 1978.

Tomerlin, John. "The 55 MPH Myth: Six Years of Speed Prohibition." *Road and Track,* May 1980.

Preview

There exists a widely publicized fear that the world may soon exhaust many of its resources. This fear is allegedly supported by computer studies that predict that within a century "a sudden and uncontrollable decline in both population and industrial capacity" will result from the exhaustion of our nonrenewable resources. There are, however, good reasons to reject these doomsday prophecies. The main defect of these studies is that they ignore the existence of a functioning price system. This chapter demonstrates how the price system can register and respond to the increasing scarcity of nonrenewable resources. When the effects of a functioning price system are taken into account, the future looks quite different from that predicted by the doomsayers.

Key Economic Points

The price system registers and reacts to scarcity.

An increase in price will affect the quantity of a resource demanded and supplied.

A functioning price system is incompatible with the total exhaustion of nonrenewable resources.

The appropriate question to ask about the continued availability of natural resources is not how long will they last but how much will they cost.

3

Function of the Price System: The Doomsday Syndrome

In the past it was not uncommon for persons of fervent religious belief to walk the city streets with sandwich boards proclaiming, "The End of the World Is at Hand." These individuals have recently been replaced by scientists and philosophers who for different reasons believe essentially the same thing. What distinguishes the current "doomsday syndrome" from its predecessors is the claim that predictions are based upon scientific estimates. Modern doomsayers don't merely state that the end of the world is at hand; they can produce a computer printout that demonstrates it!

The most famous of the modern doomsayers is a 1972 publication entitled *The Limits to Growth* sponsored by the Club of Rome. It has sold more than 3 million copies and continues to have a tremendous impact upon public opinion. This study found:

If the present growth trends in world population, industrialization, pollution, food production, and resource depletion continue unchanged, the limits to growth on this planet will be reached sometime within the next one hundred years. The most probable result will be a rather sudden and uncontrollable decline in both population and industrial capacity. (p. 23).

This study thus concludes that continued economic growth into the not too distant future will be impossible. Furthermore, the world as we know it will end with a bang, not a whimper.

The authors tell us why. The end of the world will come like one, two, three because one, the earth's natural resources will soon be exhausted; two, increased output will smother the world in pollution; and, three, growing world population will outstrip the capacity of the planet to produce food. Unless drastic changes are made, the world economy will overshoot the level of output and population that can be sustained by a planet of fixed dimensions and will in the near future suddenly collapse.

In this chapter we examine the conclusion that the world is going to run out of natural resources relatively soon. This dismal conclusion results directly from the assumptions incorporated in the doomsday model. The basic assumptions are (1) that the stock of the world's natural resources is fixed, (2) that the world's economies will tend to consume this fixed stock at an ever increasing rate, and (3) that there are no built-in mechanisms that will reduce the rate of consumption prior to the complete exhaustion of the resource base.

The first two assumptions are questionable and must certainly be qualified, as we shall see below, but the third assumption is simply incorrect, making the conclusion of the doomsayers almost certainly wrong. The theory used in the Club of Rome study ignores the existence of a functioning price system, which is the main social institution for registering and reacting to the existence of scarcity.

There are several ways that the workings of a price system will direct society's behavior to avoid the predicted catastrophe. Economic theory divides market forces into those affecting the supply of a good (or resource) and those affecting the demand. The role of price is to equilibrate the quantity supplied with the quantity demanded. As a resource becomes increasingly scarce, its price will rise relative to other goods. This will cause buyers of the resource to voluntarily reduce the quantity of the good they demand, thereby reducing consumption. On the supply side, a higher price will induce suppliers to offer more of the resource either by mining the reserves more intensively or by finding new sources to exploit. Thus increasing scarcity is translated by the price system into a set of incentives to conserve on the use of the resource, on the one hand, and on the other hand, find and provide more of it.

First let us consider the known stock of existing resources as a limit on the supply side. Almost everyone would argue that the world is fixed in size and contains a fixed amount of resources. Hence it must follow that once we have consumed all of a particular resource, it will be all gone. Luckily for us, when viewed in terms of the demands of human beings the total amounts of the earth's resources are virtually limitless. A cubic kilometer of the earth's crust, on average, contains about 210 million tons of aluminum, 150 million tons of iron, 150,000 tons of chromium, 7,000 tons of uranium, and 80,000 tons of copper whereas a cubic kilometer of seawater contains about 37.5 million tons of solids, mostly sodium and chlorine but also large amounts of magnesium, gold, cobalt, lead, and mercury. These are the amounts of minerals found on the earth's crust—only 4 percent of the total mass of the earth. Beneath the crust the amount of resources available staggers comprehension. While fixed in size, the earth can still provide people with virtually unlimited quantities of resources.

But not without cost. The important question is not the total amount of resources in existence, but how easily (expensively) can resources be obtained for humanity's use? This is the same as asking what it will cost to mine and supply the resource in the markets of the world. The Club of Rome study did not ask this question. Instead, the authors accepted existing estimates of mineral resources and calculated how long they would last at various rates of exploitation. Existing estimates of known resources are those reserves that we know about and that can be exploited profitably at current market prices. They found that known resources of natural gas, for example, were 1.14×10^{15} cubic feet, which they calculated would last 22 years. There were only 13 years resources of silver figured the same way, and 15 years of tin, 20 years of petroleum, 111 years of coal, and 93 years of iron.

But do we know the total amounts of all the existing resources in the world? The world's resources, in truth, remain relatively little explored. Consider the case of crude oil, which is the example that will be used throughout the remainder of this chapter. The known reserves of petroleum in 1970 amounted to 455×10^9 barrels of 55 gallons each. The Club of Rome study estimated that this resource will last 20 years. Does this mean that in 1990 the world's economies will suddenly consume the last drop of oil? Furthermore, is the known estimate today equal to the total world stock of crude oil? The answer to both questions is no for at least two good reasons.

In the first place, most of the drilling for oil has taken place in a very few countries. Fully 75 percent of all oil wells have been drilled in the United States. No geologist believes that 75 percent of the world's oil is or ever was in the United States. There are twice as many oil wells, for example, in Kansas as in all of Africa. Much of the world has simply not yet been systematically explored for oil. When the Club of Rome published its study, proven oil reserves in Mexico were considered to amount to no more than 2.8 billion barrels. Today proven reserves total 50 billion barrels, and private estimates of 160 billion barrels, equal in amount to Saudi Arabia's, have been made. Recent discoveries in China may well amount to 50 billion barrels also. A study recently done for the World Bank estimated total world reserves to be ten times more than the Club of Rome assumed. Actually, nobody really knows how much oil there is.

The world still remains basically unexplored for oil. The reason for the lack of exploration is that until quite recently oil was relatively easy to discover, and was worth more the closer it was located to the regions in which it would be consumed. Naturally, petroleum engineers looked in those places first. When oil was discovered in abundance in the Middle East, that discouraged further efforts to look elsewhere. All that was required in Saudi Arabia was to drill a hole in the sand to find oil that could be produced for less than a penny a gallon. Why look further?

Another factor that explains why much of the world remains to be explored for oil is that it doesn't pay to know about all the oil that exists. The larger the stock of known resources, the less valuable it will be to find more. Is it really worthwhile, for example, to spend resources now searching for oil that won't be sold for 20 years? The larger the known reserves, the less valuable it is to discover more. There is simply an optimal amount of known reserves. Once this amount has been found, it doesn't pay to look further.

There is a second reason that one shouldn't take the existing known resource estimates as seriously as do the authors of *The Limits to Growth*. Known resources are estimated as the stock of resources that can be profitably exploited at the current price for the resource. Under a price system, as a resource becomes increasingly scarcer its price will rise. When that happens, some deposits of the resource that are already known, but were considered too expensive to exploit, become commercially feasible. Known reserves thus expand automatically with increases in the resource price. Furthermore, as the price of oil increases, it will be profitable to find more, and exploration will increase.

There are other sources of oil not currently being exploited. Currently, it pays to abandon an oil field when only 30 to 40 percent of the oil has been extracted. More than half of the oil is left in the ground. As the price of oil increases, it pays to spend more to extract a larger percentage of the resource. As the price of crude oil increases, it will become profitable to extract oil embedded in other material. The tar sands of Canada could be exploited to produce oil, as could oil shale in the United States. There are 40,000 years of oil at present levels of consumption contained in these deposits alone. Coal also can be converted to oil and gas, further increasing the potential supply of oil. Talk about an absolute shortage of oil is therefore unjustifiable as long as the price system is functioning. As oil or any resource becomes scarcer, its price will rise, which provides an incentive to discover and supply more of it. The important question is not the absolute amount of oil or any other resource, but what it will cost to supply. The world will never run out of oil, but oil might become too expensive to use.

The second assumption of the Club of Rome study is that the consumption of resources will continue at an exponential growth rate. For an example of exponential growth, consider what happens to a number that doubles every time period. The exponential sequence 1, 2, 4, 16, 96, 9216, 8534016 will quickly exhaust the spaces available on a desk calculator. Exponential growth generates immense numbers very quickly. Economic growth rates do not often double each time period, but a growth rate of 1 percent doubles consumption in 72 years, a 5 percent rate will double in 14 years, a 10 percent rate in 10 years. A rate of increase in petroleum consumption of 5 percent means that we shall use twice as much oil in 14 years as we are using today.

Consider now the future demand for oil. The use of historical growth rates to predict future consumption ignores the incentives provided by the price system to reduce the rate of consumption. As a resource becomes more scarce, its price will increase, which will discourage its use. As a resource, such as oil, becomes more valuable, people will have a strong incentive to economize on its use. Individuals will insulate their homes. They will purchase smaller automobiles that obtain better gasoline mileage, or they will switch to motorcycles, bicycles, or electric cars, or ride public transit, or even walk more. Goods that use a lot of oil will become relatively more expensive than goods that use relatively little, and consumers will respond to changes in relative prices by buying less of the former and more of the latter.

As the price of oil increases, industrial firms also will conserve on its use. Electricity, coal, and wood will be substituted for oil as sources of energy. Waste heat will be recycled. The reason that so much oil is currently used is that historically oil has been very inexpensive relative to alternative sources of energy. As oil becomes more expensive, it will certainly be used more sparingly. Current estimates state that the demand for oil falls 1 percent for every 4 percent price increase while supply increases 1 percent for every 5 percent price increase. Thus the world is threatened not by the imminent exhaustion of crude oil, but with the prospect of higher prices for petroleum products. The world may well abandon oil, if its price rises too high, in favor of lower cost substitutes. But we will never run out of oil.

In summary, one should not have the slightest confidence in the predictions of a theory that ignores the operation of the price system. Relative prices provide the information for individuals and business firms to make economic decisions. As a good or resource becomes more scarce, its price will rise. The higher price will increase the quantity supplied of the resource. Higher prices will encourage the more intensive exploitation of existing resources and the discovery of new reserves. Conversely, higher prices will discourage the use of the resource, providing an incentive for users to conserve the resource, to employ substitutes, and to purchase less of the goods that use relatively more of the resource. Increasing scarcity will be translated into higher prices well before the resource is totally exhausted.

Additional Readings

Hall, R. E. and R. S. Pindyck. "The Conflicting Goals of National Energy Policy." *The Public Interest,* Spring 1977.

Maddox, John. *The Doomsday Syndrome*. McGraw-Hill, 1972.

Meadows, D. L., et al. *The Limits to Growth*. Universe, 1972.

Solow, Robert M. "Is the End of the World at Hand?" *Challenge*, March–April 1973.

Preview

Labor has always viewed technological change as a potential threat to jobs—with some justification. There is a long list of occupations that have disappeared as the result of technological improvements. So in one sense this fear is justified. But during the past century, which has been characterized by rapid technological change, the overall rate of unemployment has not risen. This paradox can be resolved by the application of the circular flow of economic activity model. This model suggests that developments in one sector have consequences for the other sectors of the economy. In order to accurately assess the impact of technological change in one industry, it is necessary to consider the effects it has in other areas. Within this context it can be seen that if technological change reduces the opportunities for labor in one industry, the increased productivity that results creates offsetting opportunities in other areas.

Key Economic Points

Households and business firms are linked by product and factor markets.
Technological change increases the productivity of the economy.
Economic efficiency requires the periodic transfer of workers from less productive activities to more productive ones.
The effects of technological change upon employment opportunities cannot be evaluated by considering only the industry in which it occurs.
The costs of unemployment to workers affected by technological change are compared with the benefits of increased productivity for the economy as a whole.

4

Circular Flow of Economic Activity: Does Technological Change Cause Unemployment?

Adam Smith, the first great economist, lived through the Industrial Revolution and apparently missed it, so gradual were the changes occurring. Today you don't have to be a great economist to know that we are currently living through the computer revolution, so dramatic are the changes going on all around us. Your college registration and grades, your purchases at the grocery store, your paycheck, and your utility and credit card bills are all processed by computer. The computer now predicts election results when only 2 percent of the votes are counted. The same computer that predicts the outcome of next week's professional sports contests is used to design automobiles and hi-fi equipment. The computer is now moving into the home in personal sizes; one is even called a Pet.

The computer is widely acknowledged to be a laborsaving device. The number of labor-hours saved by the computer in performing the tasks just described staggers one's imagination. It also raises the question: does the widespread substitution of the computer for workers cause unemployment? If it does, will the unemployment be permanent?

In order to understand the effect of technological change on the unemployment rate, it is necessary to understand how the various elements in the economy are related. Often the developments in one sector affect other sectors as well. Technological change is one of these developments. Economists have developed a theoretical construction called a circular flow model of the economy, which shows the relationship between households and business firms. This is a useful tool for analyzing the effects of technological change upon unemployment.

In this model business firms and households are related to one another by their transactions in product and resource markets. Households sell resources to firms in order to obtain income, and the firms use these resources to produce goods and services which are in turn sold back to households. The specter of scarcity haunts these transactions because households have limited amounts of resources to supply to business firms; thus their money incomes will be limited. This will allow the purchase of only some of the things households, as consumers, would like to buy. Also, because the amount of resources that business firms can acquire is limited, the amount of goods and services that can be produced, given the state of technology, is limited.

Technological change allows business firms to produce more goods with the existing amount of resources. Because goods now require fewer resources to produce, they cost less, which provides consumers with the incentive to buy them. Because consumers are never able to satisfy all their wants, there is always a demand for lower priced goods, hence always a demand for labor to produce goods. Therefore, technological change cannot result in a permanent reduction of the demand for labor in general.

But historically the working person has viewed technological change with alarm, if not fear. Technological change may be the introduction of a more productive way of producing goods and services, but it often takes the form of new machines that do the work previously done by several workers and machines. Workers see the machines as taking their jobs. The medieval guilds, which were associations of skilled laborers, had strict rules against employing other than traditional methods. In the 1790s a group of English cloth spinners, called the Luddites, actually destroyed the first multispindle textile-spinning machines which allowed one person to do the work of several.

Such fears on the part of the working person have often been justified. Glassblowers, typesetters, elevator operators, cordwiners, icemen, and puddlers are but a few of the workers whose occupations have all but disappeared; the tasks these people used to do are now performed solely by machines.

The disappearance of these occupations is part of the process of economic growth. The substitution of capital for labor accounts for much of the increased standard of living we enjoy relative to our ancestors and to much of the modern world. The productive capacity of each laborer increases as he or she is provided with more capital equipment with which to work. The increases in labor productivity, upon which increases in the standard of living are based, are in large part tied to the introduction of new technology embodied in new capital equipment.

There is little doubt that technological change has reduced the demand for some kinds of labor. The list of extinct occupations demonstrates this. But does technological change cause an increase in the overall unemployment rate in the economy? After all, what is true of the part is not necessarily true of the whole. It may be a fallacy of composition to argue that because the introduction of a computerized cold type process in printing eliminates the jobs of linotype operators, the widespread use of "smart machines" will increase the national level of unemployment.

Consider the example of American agriculture. In 1870 about 45 percent of our population lived on farms; one farm worker produced enough food to feed roughly five other persons. By 1970 the proportion of the population living on farms had declined to less than 5 percent; the vast majority of Americans lived in urban areas and were employed in nonagricultural pursuits. Despite the fact that the American population had increased from 40 million to 205 million over the century, there were less than half as many farmers in 1970 as there had been 1870, one-third as many as existed at the start of World War II. What caused the relative and absolute decline in employment in agriculture? It was the increased productivity of labor resulting from the development and introduction of new technology—improved seeds, fertilizer, irrigation, and the mechanization of farming. In 1970 one farmer produced enough to supply the food requirements for forty-seven persons.

The increase in productivity in agriculture during the last century significantly increased the amount of food and fiber potentially available. How was this increased availability enjoyed by the American consumer? The increase in productivity increased the supply of foodstuffs, which reduced the price of food relative to other goods. The American consumer could now buy more food with the same budget or could buy the same amount as before and have money left over for other things. Americans were already relatively well fed in 1870, so they tended to use much of their now surplus food budget to buy other things. More labor was required to produce the increased amounts of nonagricultural goods households now demanded. The temporarily technologically unemployed farmer moved to the city to become the employed industrial worker, a process that continued for a century. Despite the migration of millions of farmers out of agriculture, the long-term rate of unemployment did not change appreciably. If technological change causes unemployment, it would be expected that the unemployment rate would have risen significantly over the last century. But it didn't. The rate of unemployment fluctuated, to be sure, but this was the result of the fluctuation in national income as the economy experienced various business cycles, not of the shift away from agriculture by millions of Americans.

Technological change does not always result in the reduction of the demand for labor within the industry in which it occurs. Consider one of the most important industrial developments during the first half of this century: the development of the automobile industry. The rapid growth of the automobile industry was made possible by the introduction of mass production initially by the Ford Motor Company. Between 1909 and 1923 Ford pioneered and developed the techniques of mass production that embodied principles of worker specialization and the substitution of capital for labor in producing the famous Model T. Each person employed on the Ford assembly line repeatedly performed a limited specialized task and was provided with specialized capital goods that allowed the task to be performed more efficiently.

As a consequence, the labor hours required to assemble a Model T declined from 12.5 in 1911 to 1.5 in 1914, a saving of 88 percent in the amount of labor required. But the total number of workers hired by Ford actually increased despite the new labor saving techniques. The reduced cost of producing automobiles allowed Ford to reduce the price of the Model T from $1,000 to less than $400 over the same period. The response of consumers to the lower price was to increase their purchases of Fords by 650 percent. The increase in the quantity of Model T automobiles sold actually required the employment of more labor, not less.

As long as scarcity exists, there will not be a shortage of things for labor to do. The price system functioning through resource and product markets provides the incentives, when technological change occurs, for labor to move from socially less desirable occupations to socially more desirable ones. The argument that since technological change may reduce the demand for labor in a particular industry, the introduction of new technology will result in widespread technologically-induced unemployment is indeed a fallacy of composition.

This does not mean that unemployment is not a serious national problem because from time to time it certainly has been. It does mean that cyclically high rates of unemployment are caused not by technological change, but by forces that lead to business fluctuations in the aggregate economy.

Nor does this mean that the benefits of technological change are without cost to all members of society. The glassblower who after years spent acquiring his skill is replaced by a machine and decides to take a job at a lower wage as a warehouseman is certainly worse off. During the course of the century, labor has tended to become more specialized. Each of us can do fewer things better than ever. If technological change eliminates the demand for a specialty, the next best opportunity may be terrible in comparison. While the benefits of the improved productivity that results will be widespread, the costs may be narrowly imposed upon the few workers unemployed as a result of technological progress.

It is no wonder that skilled labor, when faced with such a threat, resists the change. Stokers are still employed by railroads even though diesel electric trains do not require people to stoke the furnaces. The longshoremen are currently resisting the use of cargo containers which would reduce the demand for their services. This resistance is for good and personally valid reasons, but if it succeeds as it has so far in these two cases, the full benefits of increased productivity will not be available to society. A case could be made for the compensation or retraining of technologically displaced workers provided the costs of such programs are less than the gains from the more rapid introduction of new technology and from the reemployment of retrained workers.

In summary, while individual workers and professions may have reason to fear the employment consequences of technological change, there is little reason to expect that the unemployment rate for the economy as a whole will increase. This becomes apparent when the economy is viewed within the framework of a circular flow model. The process of technological change increases productivity, allowing the prices of some goods in the product markets to fall. The fall in prices has potentially two effects. First, the quantity of the goods demanded will increase, which in the case of the Model T actually increased the demand for labor by the Ford Motor Company in the resource market. Even if the increase in demand for the products with lower prices is not sufficient to offset the reduced demand for the labor, as was the case in American agriculture, it will still increase employment opportunities elsewhere. The lower prices made possible by technological change allow people to satisfy their desires for those goods at lower cost and thus have money left over to satisfy other wants. The increased demand for these other goods creates employment opportunities in other industries for the labor initially displaced by technological change.

The U.S. economy has benefited from substantial technological progress during its history, but there is no evidence that the trend in the unemployment rate has increased. This fact should not be surprising because, since scarcity exists, there will always be a demand for the goods labor produces, and a functioning price system, described by the circular flow model, provides the incentive for labor to move from less productive jobs to more productive ones. Should labor that has been displaced by technology fail in a short time to take up alternative employment, the fault lies not with the introduction of new techniques but with impediments to the allocation of resources within the economic system. It is the removal of these restrictions rather than the attempts to impede the introduction of new technology that society should consider.

Additional Readings

Leontief, Wassily. "Is Technological Unemployment Inevitable?" *Challenge*, September–October 1979.

Mansfield, Edwin. *Technological Change.* Norton, 1971, Chap. 5.

Pauling, W. G. "Some Neglected Areas of Research on the Effects of Automation and Other Technological Change on Workers." *Journal of Business,* July 1964.

Silberman, Charles E. *The Myths of Automation.* Harper and Row, 1966.

Preview

During the 1970s adult Americans took to their bicycles. By the middle of the decade more bicycles than automobiles were sold in the United States. The phenomenon of millions of Americans riding bicycles has been called the "bicycle boom." The purpose of this chapter is to explain the "bicycle boom" by employing the economic tools of supply and demand.

Key Economic Points

Is it a shift in the supply of or the demand for bicycles that accounts for the boom? Which of the forces that could have caused this shift was in fact responsible for it? An expansion of industry output could be caused either by an increase in demand or in supply.

5

Supply and Demand: The Bicycle Boom

Today it is ordinary to see numerous adult bicyclists peddling along city streets and across college campuses. A decade ago it would have been unusual to see an adult on a bicycle. Bicycles were then conveyances for children. The most popular model sold was called the High Riser, a bizarre, garishly decorated vehicle with small wheels, a banana-shaped saddle, and handlebars shaped like the arms of an ape. It was an unglamorous product produced mainly by small, family-owned manufacturers.

Suddenly, as a new decade was dawning, adult Americans went slightly mad over cycling! The number of bicycles sold doubled in 2 years, increasing from 6.9 million in 1970 to 8.7 million in 1971, to 13.9 million in 1972, and to 15.3 million in 1973. The retail price of a basic ten-speed bicycle increased as sales grew during the boom. The average price of a bike in 1970 was $55; in 1971, $62; in 1972, $66, and in 1973, $74. If we employ the consumer price index to factor out the effects of inflation and express the price of bicycles in real terms (in 1967 dollars), we still find that the average price of a bicycle increased over the boom. In 1967 prices, the average price of a bicycle in 1970 was $48; in 1971, $52; in 1972, $55; and in 1973, $60. In 1973, despite higher prices, Americans were buying more bicycles than automobiles.

The bicycle people wanted was not the oddly shaped High Riser but the elegant English style, a lightweight bike with narrow tires and five, ten, or more gears that allowed the rider to mount a hill without great difficulty. American manufacturers had for years produced a few models of the English type. The High Riser, however, had been the best seller because kids had been the ultimate customers for nine out of every ten bikes produced. This situation changed during the 1970s, when "cycling mania" swept through the adult population. Adults, defined as anyone old enough to drive a car, now purchased for their own use half of the bicycles sold. American manufacturers rushed to produce an adult bike in quantity. Meanwhile imports filled the demand. There were more than 100 manufacturers of bicycles in 42 countries selling bicycles in the United States.

Within the United States in 1973, eight major manufacturers produced 76 percent of all bicycles sold domestically. Murray Ohio, Huffman, AMF, and Schwinn were the biggest of these, selling over 1.5 million each. U.S. manufacturers in total produced 10.3 million bikes, and imports accounted for the rest, bringing the total sold during 1973 to 15.3 million. Britain's Raleigh and France's Peugeot were the best sellers among the imports.

The total number of bicycles in America increased over the 4-year bicycle boom from around 20 million to over 65 million, and the presence of vastly increased numbers made itself felt on the urban cityscape. More than 25,000 miles of bike paths from which motor vehicles are excluded have been built or set aside for the use of cyclists. The U.S. Congress in 1973 provided $120 million for more bikeway construction. Bicycle racks, always present at grade schools, became a common sight on college campuses, in shopping centers, and even on Fifth Avenue in New York. One Miami bank installed "pedal-in" teller windows at its suburban branches.

The great bicycle boom took everyone by surprise, including the manufacturers. In retrospect, it is possible, if the principles of supply and demand are applied, to understand what happened. It may seem at first glance that because sales increased by 220 percent in 4 years and prices rose by a quarter, the law of demand (which postulates that higher prices discourage consumption) had been violated, since sales increased in spite of the price increases. But first impressions can be deceiving and in this case would be. Such a conclusion involves confusing a movement along a schedule with a shift of a schedule, a common but often disastrous mistake. A combination of increased output and rising prices is consistent only with a demand schedule that is increasing (shifting) relative to supply. The bicycle boom, then, was generated by a sudden (apparently unforeseen) increase in demand which generated a movement of the demand curve outward along the supply schedule, the increase in output reflecting the increase in consumer demand and the higher prices reflecting the higher unit cost of producing an expanded output. The larger output coupled with higher prices was generated by a demand schedule moving along a fixed supply schedule, verifying the principle of supply which states that more will be offered only at a higher price.

The increase in demand could have resulted from a number of factors. The price of related goods—complements or substitutes—could have changed, causing the demand for bicycles to be affected. The price of substitutes, such as shoes or automobiles, could have increased, or the price of complements, such as locks and chains, reflectors, and backpacks, could have fallen. The income of consumers could have increased or consumers could have suddenly altered their expectations for future prices, fearing that prices in future would significantly increase. Or the tastes of consumers could have changed in favor of the bicycle. Any or a combination of these changes could account for an increase in demand.

There are several reasons to believe that it was the last of the four possible factors—a change in tastes—that accounts for most of the increase in demand. The first reason is that the demand increased so dramatically that it would require a drastic change in the prices of complements or substitutes, a large increase in consumer incomes, or well-publicized information that future prices would be much higher to account for the increases in demand. Significant changes in these parameters did not occur. There are good substitutes for a bicycle as a means of transportation: walking, motorcycles, public transport, and automobiles are examples. Neither the price of shoes nor alternative means of transportation changed very much, certainly not enough to account for a doubling in the demand for bicycles. While the period from 1970 to 1973 was a recovery period of relatively rapid economic growth in the United States, the median incomes of households increased only from $14,465 to $15,437, an increase of less than 7 percent. Such a small increase hardly seems sufficient to account for a large expansion in the demand for bicycles. Nor does it appear that there was any unusual development in the bicycle industry that would lead consumers to change their expectations about future prices. This process of elimination leaves only a dramatic change in the tastes of consumers to explain the bicycle boom.

Economists do not like to resort to taste change to explain an economic phenomenon because taste changes cannot be observed in the same way that changes in income or in the price of substitutes or complements can. It is possible to use changing tastes to explain anything. If demand increases, then tastes change to favor the good; if demand decreases, then tastes alter in the opposite way. Because taste changes cannot be measured, no explanation based upon taste changes can be falsified. Taste change can explain everything, so in fact it explains nothing.

Therefore, economists then will resort to changing tastes to explain a shift in demand only as a last resort. After all the other phenomena that in theory could explain the change in demand have been examined and eliminated, then a change in taste can be considered. We have seen that the prices of related goods (substitutes and complements), income, and expectations probably did not cause the bicycle boom, therefore changes in taste can be considered.

While changing tastes cannot be observed directly, supporting evidence can generally be found. Usually industries experiencing rapid growth have introduced a new product that catches the consumer's fancy, e.g., Frisbees, Hula Hoops, minicalculators, electronic watches, video games, and video recorders. This was not the case in the bicycle boom. The English ten-speed had been available to Americans since the 1930s. A possible inference is that consumers rather suddenly changed their tastes to prefer this product over other goods.

This inference is supported by the radical shift in the age composition of the final user of bicycles from children to adults. During the 1970s adults purchasing bikes for their own use accounted for almost the entire increase in demand for bicycles. An investigation into the uses to which adults put their new bicycles is also revealing. While the bicycle was the primary means of transportation for children, it was not for adults. The automobile remained paramount as a source of adult transportation. Adults used their bicycles for recreation. By 1975 almost half of the adult population exercised regularly, a significant increase from 5 years before. Walking was the most frequently employed exercise, but calisthenics, swimming, and bicycle riding competed for second place. More than twice as many people rode bicycles regularly for exercise than ran or jogged. The American people discovered physical fitness during the 1970s, and the bicycle fit in perfectly with many individuals' exercise programs.

Other evidence for selecting changes in taste as the major explanation of the bicycle boom can be found in the ending of the boom. Sales peaked in 1973 at 15.3 million and fell immediately thereafter to 13.8 million in 1974. The energy crisis, with gasoline in short supply and long waiting times at the pumps, did not spur bicycle sales as might be expected. In fact, bicycle sales fell by 1.5 million, or 10 percent. The rapid rise in energy prices in 1974 caused the worst recession since the 1930s, and the negative effect upon consumers' incomes simply swamped whatever positive stimulus to demand that substituting a bicycle for a car might have encouraged. The demand for bicycles, like the demand for most other goods, declined during the recession. The demand curve shifted in along the supply schedule. The result was as economic theory would predict. The quantity of bicycles sold fell, as did the average price of bikes—from $60 to $56.60 in 1967 dollars.

The recession of 1974–1975 did not in itself end the bicycle boom, which would have slowed down of its own accord. Americans' new proclivity to exercise was a once-and-for-all change, and so was the increase in demand for bicycles that it stimulated. The rapid increase in sales satisfied a virgin demand for bicycles from individuals who did not have one. Between 1970 and 1974, almost 60 million Americans purchased a bike. The size of the potential market of bikeless individuals was in the process reduced significantly. A used bicycle market developed to compete with manufacturers for sales. In the future manufacturers would depend increasingly upon replacement sales for their business. No one knows how long a bicycle will last an adult user. A child's bike lasts betweeen 5 and 8 years, but these vehicles are not very well maintained. An adult willing to periodically spend a few hours and dollars on maintenance can make a bike last a lifetime.

The bicycle boom would probably have ended of its own accord during the middle 1970s as the market for bicycles as exercise machines became saturated. When this occurred both the relative price and quantity of bicycles sold would probably have declined as the economics of supply and demand predicts.

The bicycle boom provides an illustration of how the economics of supply and demand can be used to explain past events. The pattern of rising prices and outputs is only consistent with an increase in demand (a shift of the demand curve) stimulating an increase in the quantity supplied (a movement along the supply curve). It is thus possible to investigate the potential sources of increased demand to identify the forces that caused the bicycle boom. The economic tools of supply and demand can, of course, also be used for prediction by reversing the process and inquiring as to what would be the effect upon the price and output if one of the sources that can cause a change in either supply or demand is itself changed. The basic tools of supply and demand are therefore widely applicable in explaining economic phenomena.

Additional Readings

"Bicycle Boom Still in High Gear." *U.S. News and World Report,* November 5, 1973.

"Boom Goes Flat." *Wall Street Journal,* October 24, 1974.

Louis, Arthur M. "How the Customers Thrust Unexpected Prosperity on the Bicycle Industry." *Fortune,* March 1974.

"Output Increased, But Still Can't Keep Pace with Demand." *Wall Street Journal,* September 2, 1971.

"Wheeling and Dealing." *Barron's,* June 11, 1973.

Preview

It is a common practice for the top rock 'n roll groups to price their concert tickets below the market clearing price. This practice results in a shortage and requires some nonprice means for allocating the available tickets. During the Rolling Stones' 1972 tour, concert tickets were priced below the market clearing price and the concert managers used means other than price to allocate the scarce tickets. The most frequent means was to sell tickets on a first-come, first-served basis. Other methods were also used: friendship passes, a lottery, even violence. Everywhere the Rolling Stones played, a black market appeared. This chapter investigates the efficiency consequences of employing nonprice mechanisms to allocate concert tickets and explores the question of who gains and who loses when a particular nonprice means is employed.

Key Economic Points

When a price is set below the market clearing price a shortage is created.
Some of the ways scarce goods can be allocated when a shortage exists are
    identified.
What are the efficiency consequences of using the various nonprice means of
    allocating resources?
Who benefits and who loses from each nonprice allocation method?

6

Nonprice Allocation of Scarce Resources: Touring with the Rolling Stones

Aside from the music itself, nothing provokes as much emotion in rock music fans as the way tickets for a major concert are distributed. After every ticket sale, concert promoters and local newspapers receive a rash of complaints and anguished protests from people who couldn't get tickets or who could only obtain "lousy seats." The problem is that there are often more people who want to hear a "major" act than there are tickets available at the price promoters set. Promoters of concerts by superstars, it would appear, do not price the tickets they sell so that the quantity supplied (seats available in the auditoriums) equals the quantity demanded.

This has always been the case on Rolling Stones concert tours. During the 1970s the Stones toured the United States roughly every 3 years. These tours were fantastic successes. The 1978 tour, for example, played to 760,000 people and grossed over $9 million. Everywhere the Stones went they played to packed houses, and still many people were turned away. Individual tickets were scalped (resold) for as much as $400 in an active black market. It was much the same on earlier tours.

Nothing, for example, in the summer of 1972 was more scarce than tickets to a Rolling Stones concert. Millions of fans between the ages of 15 and 35 wanted to see them perform. The Stones' business manager, Peter Rudge, was in charge of the tour. He saw that his problem was not to sell tickets, but to ensure that they were distributed "fairly," that they would not fall into scalpers' hands in large numbers, and that there was no counterfeiting and no riots. Tickets were to sell at $6.50 top, and less in smaller cities such as Seattle, where they sold for $6.

The demand for tickets at that price far exceeded the capacity of local auditoriums. Everywhere they played, they could have sold twice or three times the number of tickets actually available. *Life* magazine estimated that the Stones could have played in San Francisco for 3 months and in New York for 6 months to packed houses. In San Francisco there were only 18,000 seats available; in New York, 80,000; in Seattle, 28,000; in Vancouver, B.C., 17,000; and in Washington, D.C., 50,000. The available seats had to be allocated somehow among the considerably higher number of people wanting them. Some ticket seekers got tickets; many more did not.

The nonprice ways scarce resources can be rationed are numerous, and the Stones and their followers apparently tried most of them at one time or another during the tour. If a price less than the market clearing price is set, then scarce resources must be allocated by means other than a simple exchange of money. There are many possible ways this can be done. One way is on a first-come, first-served basis, which requires waiting in line or queuing. Another is friendship. Other means include bribery, violence, the use of some rationing system, or a lottery. Each of these methods, when compared with a price system, discriminates in favor of some groups over others, redistributes wealth, involves some inefficiency, and suggests an interesting investigation into who gained and who lost.

In Vancouver and Seattle, as in most of the thirty-two cities toured, the tickets were available on a first-come, first-served basis. Tickets were sold about 1 month prior to the performance. Each person could purchase a maximum of four tickets. Customers began to appear at both Empire Stadium in Vancouver and Memorial Stadium in Seattle 48 hours prior to the tickets going on sale. Hundreds actually spent the night in front of ticket windows. Hours prior to the windows opening, a crush began to form. In both places, the concerts were all sold out within 5½ hours. Many who had waited in line for hours were disappointed.

In Vancouver some who were disappointed vented their anger on Empire Stadium, attempting to raze the structure and doing several thousands of dollars worth of damage before they were stopped. The night of the performance 2,000 persons attempted to crash the sold-out concert. A riot ensued in which thirty police were injured, and the promoters were presented with a bill for $12,000 to cover the damages. The gate crashers did not succeed in their attempt to get into the theater.

Forewarned by the events in Vancouver, Seattle police took preventive measures and no violence occurred. In Seattle, 28,000 tickets were sold to 7,500 people who waited between 6 and 8 hours in the crush to obtain them. Thus the Stones got the $168,000 paid by buyers, and the ticket purchasers paid an additional $90,000 to $120,000 in time spent waiting. Many persons who stood in the lines expressed anger at the way the tickets were sold. One young man said that tickets should have been sold at normal outlets or at a location with more ticket windows. Another suggestion was that tickets could have gone on sale simultaneously at numerous locations. Some persons grew weary, and some nauseous, from waiting in lines for hours, and many left without tickets.

By the time the tour got to San Francisco the Stones had taken the man's advice. Tickets, 18,000 in number, went on sale via the computer-controlled Ticketron system, which allows tickets to be purchased at over fifty commercial outlets. One person scouted the available outlets and selected a Montgomery Ward store in Oakland. When he arrived at 7:00 a.m., he found the sidewalk jammed with the devoted who had spent the night in sleeping bags. When the store opened at 9:30, there was a rush to the ticket window and a crush formed. Precisely at 10:00 the computer went on-line and at 10:01 stopped working. All fifty outlets were trying to buy at once and had to wait their turns. This amounted to a delay of 12 to 15 minutes between two transactions at one place. Once again, not everyone who waited in line got a ticket.

However, not everyone who got tickets had to stand in line. At each performance, 500 seats were reserved for VIPs. If a person was someone who mattered or knew someone who did, he or she got tickets for free. Queues and friendship passes were used everywhere on the tour except in New York City Everywhere the age of the majority of persons in the queues was between 15 and 17 years.

In Washington, D.C., one giant performance was given in Kennedy Stadium. Forty-five thousand persons, each paying $5.50, attended, and the crowd was handled like a sellout at a professional sports event, with crowd control precautions taken. Nevertheless, a crowd of 30,000 had formed by 4:00 p.m. when the turnstiles opened, 4 hours before the concert. By 5:00 there wasn't a good seat left in the stadium. The age of this crowd was considerably older, mainly in the 18 to 25 age brackets, but there were almost as many in the 25 to 30 group.

The same was true in New York, where a lottery was employed to distribute "fairly" the 80,000 tickets available for the four performances at Madison Square Garden. Winners were allowed to buy four tickets at $6.50 each. Persons who wanted the right to purchase four tickets sent in a postcard with their names and addresses. A CPA firm employed a computer to first check for duplicates and then select 20,000 names. It is reported that 560,000 persons wrote in, requesting the right to purchase tickets. Their chance of getting what they wanted was 35 to 1—a real long shot. The lucky audience was primarily made up of persons in their 20s.

Let's look closely at the Stones' pricing policy. It is clear that at every concert they could have charged higher ticket prices and made more money. They chose not to, and redistributed the additional income they could have had as a gift to some of their fans, those who could get tickets. They reportedly were interested in fair distribution of tickets and in preventing scalping, counterfeiting, and riots. The latter was accomplished with the exception of the disturbance in Vancouver. Counterfeiting was not a serious problem, but it was an everpresent fear.

Scalping, the process of buying a ticket for one price and selling it for a higher price, was present everywhere. The limit of four tickets per customer was an attempt to take the business away from the professional scalper and give it to the kids. In Seattle tickets were offered for $10 to $15; in San Francisco the price was one lid or $15, but one set of four tickets was sold for $120, or $30 each. In Chicago sales were made at $70 a ticket and in Los Angeles at $75. *Time* magazine predicted that tickets for the Madison Square Garden show would fetch $100.

The Rolling Stones thus provided employment for persons of relatively low opportunity costs to wait in line, purchase, and resell the tickets. If, for example, a person valued his or her time at $2 an hour and had to wait for 8 hours to purchase four tickets at $6, then his or her cost is $10 per ticket. If the ticket is sold for more than that, the scalper makes a profit. A person using one ticket and selling three for more than $13.83 would have his or her way to the concert paid.

The above situation also explains why in the cities that allocated tickets by long waiting lines the people in the lines were relatively young. This group has the lowest opportunity cost of waiting. Thus a ticket allocation method that employs waiting lines or queues will have younger people standing in those lines. Many persons who actually attend the concerts, however, would be older because of tickets being resold.

In Washington, D.C., where the lines were short and started near the end of the working day, there was a group in line whose average age was several years older than in other cities. In Washington, where the crowd on average waited for 4 hours, the cost of a ticket was the price in dollars, $5.50, plus the value of 4 hours time lost.

In New York City 560,000 persons tried to obtain tickets by sending in postcards. New York is bigger than Washington, D.C., but not thirteen times bigger. The reason more people tried to obtain tickets in New York was that it was less expensive to do so. Instead of spending hours waiting in line, one simply mailed a postcard. If one was lucky, one gained the right to buy tickets worth several times their cost. It was a giant lottery. This method of allocating tickets does not obviously favor any one age group, so a mixed age group got tickets.

Let's look at the economics of the various ways the Stones used to provide a gift to their fans, since that is precisely what they did when they offered tickets at less than their market value. The waiting in queues resulted in persons paying with time part or all of the potential gain available from tickets priced at less than the market clearing price. We also know that some people waited in vain and actually lost the value of their time. It is quite possible that the total cost of the tickets, the dollars paid plus the time cost of both the lucky and the unlucky, was larger than it would have been had the Stones instead charged the market clearing price. Clearly, society was worse off. Had the Stones charged the market clearing price, the people who wanted the tickets badly enough to pay the price would have had to create goods and services at least equal to the value of the tickets they wished to purchase. Society would have had both the Stones concert and the wealth created to pay for it.

The use of influence or friendship in ticket allocation, although reprehensible to many, is not nearly as socially wasteful as selling tickets below the market clearing price. It is merely a transfer from the Rolling Stones to the favored few. If these privileged persons could sell the tickets, and they could, then the Stones would have given them a present valued at the difference between what they could scalp the tickets for and what they had to pay to become a "favorite." If the tickets to friends were free, then the price a scalper could get is the value of the gift.

The lottery was to each individual less costly than the queues. It is not clear as to whether the social cost of 580,000 postcards, a CPA firm, and a computer's time is more or less than that of several thousand persons standing in line. In both cases resources are spent trying to qualify for the gift.

The scalping or black market was merely a way for people—either those in the queues with lower opportunity costs, or those in the lottery who were more fortunate, or the favored ones who got their tickets for free—to cash in on the gifts. Whenever a person is given the opportunity to purchase a good at less than the market price, an opportunity is also created for that person to gain by exchanging the ticket with persons who value it higher.

The only method the Stones employed of giving the gift that did not impose social costs was the friendship or VIP method. The queues wasted valuable time in waiting and the lottery ate up postcards.

Why do the Rolling Stones and other top groups price concert tickets below the market clearing price? Perhaps they want to share their wealth. It is also possible that they gain more than they lose by pricing their concert tickets below the market clearing price. The crowds and crushes generated caught the attention of the national press. Every major newspaper carried an article on the Stones tour at least once a week, as did many national magazines such as *Time, Life, Newsweek,* and the *Saturday Review.* National television followed their tour. The behavior of Stones fans attempting to get tickets was news, and it provided the Rolling Stones with millions of dollars of free publicity.

It is more than likely that the publicity of a successful tour would, in record sales, more than make up for the loss in ticket sales. A tour by a major rock group such as the Rolling Stones has as its primary purpose stimulation of the group's record sales. Publicity, and the opportunity to hear the group in person, increase record sales. The Stones employed a nonprice means of allocating tickets because the behavior of fans attempting to locate tickets generated publicity.

Most of the money the Rolling Stones, or any rock group, earns is through record sales. One "gorilla" record that sells several million copies easily earns more money with less effort for the group than an entire tour. The majority of records are sold to high school age buyers. This is a group with relatively low opportunity costs for their time, just the group that is favored by the waiting-in-line ticket allocation method. The Stones picked this method to allocate tickets in most of the cities toured. The Stones in effect chose the allocation method that increased the chances of record buyers to see them in concert. This is probably what Peter Rudge meant when he said he wanted to see the tickets distributed fairly. A person is simply more apt to collect the records of a group that he or she has heard live. Everyone in the record business knows this.

A nonprice method of allocating scarce resources is not without its costs—in this case to the Stones, to their fans, and to society. It cost the Stones the difference between the price charged and the market clearing price; fans who were successful in obtaining tickets paid the price of the ticket, plus the cost of the resources used to qualify for the tickets; those who were unsuccessful in obtaining tickets expended resources for nothing; and society lost the value of goods and services that could have been produced with the resources spent to qualify for tickets, plus the resources spent reallocating tickets in the scalper's market.

The problems and costs associated with employing a nonprice means of allocating scarce resources on a Rolling Stones tour are but a microcosm of the problems to be expected whenever some allocation scheme other than a market clearing price is employed, such as the wage and price controls sometimes employed by the government, or the current price controls in the oil and gas industry, or the plans advocated to control rising hospital costs. Whenever a nonprice means is used to allocate scarce resources, some costs, not borne when the market is employed, are imposed, and some groups are favored over others. Furthermore, there is no guarantee that the people who want the goods most (that is, who are willing to sacrifice the most) will obtain them.

Additional Readings

Flippo, Chet. "Life Ain't What It Used to Be on the Road with the Rolling Stones." *Rolling Stone,* September 7, 1978.

Greenfield, Robert. *S.T.P.: A Journey Through America With the Rolling Stones.* Saturday Review Press, 1974.

Lupoff, Dick. "Rolling Stones: Goodbye to All That." *Ramparts,* July 1972.

Preview

The dominant form of business organization in our economy is the corporation. Although there are relatively few corporations, in comparison with individual proprietorships and partnerships, the corporations do a majority of the business in the industrial sector and control most of the assets. Furthermore, their hold on business activity is increasing. Recently, large corporations have chosen to grow larger by merging with other large corporations. This situation raises the question of whether, in the absence of monopoly, giant size is itself undesirable. A number of social critics think it is. Some legislators and the Department of Justice agree and have asked Congress to pass a law prohibiting large corporations from engaging in mergers. This chapter explores the question of whether giant size is in itself bad for our society, considers whether the giant corporation has escaped from the rigors of the competitive marketplace as some critics suggest, and analyzes the efficiency of employing an antimerger law to restrict the further growth of giant corporations.

Key Economic Points

Arguments are evaluated for the claim that the large size of a corporation is itself bad for society.

To what extent does competition in the product markets limit the power of giant corporations?

Personal interests of the management of large corporations may be different from the interests of stockholders.

To what extent does competition in the factor markets, especially in the stock market, limit the power of corporate mergers?

The advantages of an antimerger law are weighed against the disadvantages of the reduced competitive pressures on corporate management.

7

Business Organization: Does Competition Control the Giant Corporation?

The corporation is the dominant form of business organization in our economy. About 55 percent of the nation's output is produced by business firms organized as corporations. The corporate sector is also highly concentrated. In 1974 the 500 largest industrial firms, all corporations, accounted for 66 percent of the total sales of the industrial sector and 72 percent of the profits. The largest corporations are very big indeed. The sales of any of the ten largest corporations are greater than the national income of most of the countries of the world.

The concentration of the nation's assets in the hands of a corporate few has been increasing. Three decades ago the largest 200 industrial companies held 46 percent of the nation's industrial assets. In 1978 the largest 200 held 64 percent. Mergers are one way the largest firms have grown at the expense of the smaller firms. In 1977 there were forty-one mergers that cost the acquiring firm over $100 million. In 1978 there were eighty, and the trend looks as if it will continue into the indefinite future unless stopped in some way.

The growth of corporate giants has alarmed not only social reformers such as Ralph Nader and John Kenneth Galbraith, but also members of the federal government. Senator Edward Kennedy has introduced a bill to limit mergers by giant corporations, and the Justice Department has requested a similar bill. Either bill if enacted into law would effectively prohibit additional mergers by giant corporations.

The rise of the giant corporation and the suggested legal remedy raise at least two questions. Is bigness bad per se, and if so, is a new antimerger law the way to counteract further growth? First, it must be demonstrated that there is a problem. Second, it must be shown that prohibiting mergers by giant corporations is the way to solve the problem.

Social critics feel that it is absurd for economists to analyze the giant corporation as if it were a Ma and Pa grocery store, only bigger. The giant corporation, they contend, is not merely an inflated version of a small firm but a different species entirely. The sheer size of the organization, they contend, allows it to dominate economic and social behavior. Giant corporations, it is alleged, can through advertising convince people to buy things they do not really want while at the same time excluding rivals from markets by predatory tactics or by combination with smaller firms. Stopped by the antitrust laws from forming cartels, the giant corporation has turned to mergers. The road to monopoly, in the words of one critic, has been paved by mergers.

Even when the monopoly of a market is not obtained, the sheer size of the giant corporation alarms many people. This fear is very old. Supreme Court Justice John M. Harlan in 1911 attacked "the aggregation of capital in the hands of a few controlling the production and sale of the necessities of life." Giant size, the concentration of a large part of the nation's assets in the hands of a few, is feared to be inconsistent with democracy. Big business has a political advantage because of the assets that can be brought to bear in any political debate. According to Ralph Nader, "The costs of corporate oligopoly and giantism to the consumer, to the small business man, to the worker, to the economy, are substantial."

This potential for doing ill, according to Nader, would not be so bad if the owners of our industrial corporations exercised their rights to govern these giant firms. There are millions of individual shareholders who come from all walks of American life. They own, but they don't control. Shareholders exert little authority over the corporations they own, leaving the running of the companies to professional managements who do not own what they control. The interests of the managers, who control, and the stockholders, who do not, often diverge. Shareholders would prefer the firm to be efficient and maximize profits, while managers may be more interested in security, power, prestige, personal income, and advancement. The best way for management to achieve its goals may be for the corporation to grow in size even if this implies a sacrifice in efficiency and profitability.

The larger the corporation, the more secure it is against bankruptcy, the higher the salaries that management can command, the more opportunities there are for advancement, and the more prestige, influence, and social recognition the managers will receive. The management of giant corporations are able to pursue these goals because the board of directors, which in theory represents the stockholders' interest, in practice represents the interests of management. Almost half of the directors of a giant corporation typically are employees (management) of the corporation, and another quarter are executives of other corporations who share the goals and values of management.

The critics of the giant corporation feel that bigness is in itself bad. It is possible, however, that large size is necessary to achieve economies of scale in production and management. Large size allows the corporation to produce at lower costs, to ensure the sources of supply, and to borrow money for expansion at lower rates of interest than smaller firms. In short, there may be economies of large size that allow resources to be used more efficiently. Economists have always been more concerned with the size of a firm relative to the market(s) it competes in than with the potential dangers of size itself.

The antitrust laws have been reasonably successful in preventing monopoly and monopolistic practices in particular markets, but they have done little to curb sheer size. Because of the antitrust laws, large firms have often chosen to grow by acquiring firms in different market areas. The result has been the creation of giant conglomerates operating in many different markets.

Bigness itself would be bad only if there were such insufficient social control that management could actually use its potential economic power in socially undesirable ways. The major system of control over business in our society has always been competition. There are two distinct areas in which competition places limits on the exercise of corporate power. The first is competition in the markets that the corporations serve. Giant corporations do not consider their fellows as allies but as rivals standing in the way of the achievement of corporate objectives. The second is competition to acquire the right to manage the corporation. Existing managers have to consider the possibility of being replaced by rivals who would like to have their jobs.

Let's first consider competition in the markets served by giant corporations. Has giant size insulated our largest corporations from the competitive acts of their rivals? It is one thing for a firm to grow with the economy. It is quite another to grow at the expense of its rivals. The increasing concentration of manufacturing assets in the hands of our largest corporations demonstrates that the giant corporation has grown at the expense of smaller firms. But the successful giants must also have grown at the expense of fellow giants.

The summit of corporate America is, in fact, a slippery place. A comparison list of the top 100 in 1977 reveals that 65 of the 100 on the list in 1917 are no longer there today. Armour (4th) and Swift (5th), both meatpackers, were among the top five corporations in 1917 and are not even in the top 100 today. Neither are some companies you may have heard about, such as Asarco (12th), Anaconda Copper (13th), Phelps-Dodge (15th), Singer (16th), B. F. Goodrich (23rd), or Pullman (26th), plus forty-seven others you probably haven't heard about.

Perhaps it would be more appropriate to focus on the period following World War II. Even in this more recent period, a comparison of the top 100 in 1945 with the top 100 in 1977 would find forty-five firms that were on the 1945 list that are absent from the 1977 list. Among them would be Montgomery Ward, then a close competitor of Sears-Roebuck, and Curtiss-Wright, the largest manufacturer of airplanes in 1945. Replacing them, seemingly from out of nowhere, came companies such as Teneco, Litton, Xerox, Boeing, Monsanto, Caterpillar Tractor, and thirty-nine others.

The rise and fall of corporate giants can be ascribed to changes in technology, changes in consumer-spending patterns, to good and bad business decisions, but mostly to competition. This is not to suggest that giant companies are as vulnerable to misfortune as small firms; they are not. But they are far from invulnerable.

If competition places checks on the giant corporation in the marketplace, does it also place limits on the managers' use of the corporation's assets for its own economic and political ends? The management of a giant corporation with a compliant board of directors could, for example, grant to itself large salaries, attractive stock options, perquisites such as the use of company airplanes, fancy offices, extended paid vacations, liberal retirement plans. Such things do happen. The Internal Revenue Service on one occasion found more than seventy corporately owned jets parked at airports near the site of the Kentucky Derby on race day.

A management operating according to its own interests is from the point of view of the stockholder and society inefficient and perhaps dangerous. How can stockholders control the misuse of company assets? They can and have sued the management of companies for the use of company funds for personal purposes. Stockholder suits, however, are rare because they are expensive. A person owning 100 shares in a company with a management that is consciously or unconsciously misallocating the company's resources will probably not sue but will instead sell his or her shares. That is the easiest way out. If management, for one reason or another, performs inefficiently, the profits of the firm will decline and its stock price will fall as its stockholders attempt to get out. If the stock price falls below the level achievable by an efficiently managed firm, the stage is set for a takeover bid. The assets of a poorly run firm are now worth more to someone else, and the inefficient management should be concerned.

It is this concern that society ought to encourage because it promotes efficient management performance. The decline in stock prices that follows inefficient management is one part of the story. The second is the possibility of another, more efficiently managed firm acquiring the assets and profiting by making the assets more productive. An antimerger bill would reduce the potential number of acquiring firms, thus reducing the incentives for managements of giant corporations to operate efficiently.

Studies of recent mergers have found that the stock of firms that were acquired had fallen abnormally low prior to a takeover bid. The lower the price of the stock, the more likely that another corporation will attempt a takeover. The study also found that if the takeover was successful, shareholders of both firms benefited from higher stock prices. The only losers were the managers of the acquired firm, who were apt to lose their jobs. Furthermore, the study determined that the more incompetent the management, as reflected in abnormally low share prices, the more apt they were to resist the takeover. Approximately one-fourth of the firms subject to takeover bids resisted the attempt using the firm's resources to oppose the offer.

The most infamous examples of successful resistance occurred during 1978 when Mead, a forest products firm, resisted the offer of Occidental Petroleum and when McGraw-Hill resisted the attempt by American Express. In both cases the stockholders lost and management kept their jobs. An antimerger law would have the undesirable side effect of improving the job security of inept managements, who would have less to fear from the possibility of a takeover bid.

Furthermore, prohibiting mergers will not stop the growth of large firms, but it will stop some of them from growing in the most efficient manner. The markets of an inefficiently managed firm would still present an attractive target for more efficient firms. But instead of directly acquiring the firm's assets via a takeover bid, the more efficient firms would have to compete in the markets in which the inefficient firm sells. This would require the costly (from society's point of view) duplication of capital investment.

In most mergers it is bigger firms that acquire smaller ones. Therefore, it is the management of relatively small firms that must keep on their toes. But what about the largest companies, such as Exxon, General Motors, and IBM? What keeps their managements efficient? It is inconceivable that as long as the price of their stocks stay up, any other firm could raise the funds to buy any of the top ten. However, it can be argued that it is precisely because they are already efficiently managed that their stock prices stay up. Consider the plight of Chrysler, which in 1966 was the fourteenth largest industrial firm. In the 1970s Chrysler fell on hard times and lost hundreds of millions of dollars, slipping in size to eighteenth by 1977. The price of Chrysler stock fell below the book value of its remaining assets as stockholders attempted to sell out. Chrysler hired new management, which discovered that Volkswagen was secretly purchasing its stock. Chrysler was probably saved from a takeover by the action of the federal government guaranteeing over $1 billion in loans. Even the very large corporation's management is not isolated from competition. Management is secure only as long as it performs relatively efficiently.

This is not to suggest that bigness is good, and we should not be concerned with the continued accumulation of the nation's manufacturing assets in the hands of a relatively few persons. It may well be that giant corporations are inconsistent with democracy. Doubtless giant corporations can exert political power for their own ends. The federal government rescued Lockheed and Chrysler from bankruptcy because they were large employers whereas it did nothing for the thousands of smaller firms that were failing at the same time. Political power does count for some things.

But it would be costly to attempt to limit growth by prohibiting mergers because such a prohibition would reduce the incentives for corporate management to perform efficiently. Nor is a new merger law necessary to halt mergers pursued for purposes of obtaining a monopoly. The federal government already has that power. Section 7 of the Clayton Act allows the public and private prosecution of mergers if it can be demonstrated that there is a "a lessening of competition or a tendency to create monopoly in any line of commerce in any section of the country." So vigorously has this law been enforced that a shoe firm with only 4 percent of the market was prevented from acquiring a competitor one-eighth its size.

If bigness is bad per se, another way of taming the giant corporation other than by prohibiting large mergers should be found. Prohibiting mergers would have the undesirable side effect of reducing the discipline that competition imposes upon the managers of giant corporations. An antimerger law holds out the prospect for insulating incompetent executives from the rigors of the marketplace.

Additional Readings

Johnson, M. Bruce (ed). *The Attack on Corporate America.* McGraw-Hill, 1976.

Nader, Ralph, Mark Green, and Joel Seligman. *Taming the Giant Corporation.* Norton, 1976.

"Sixty Years of Corporate Ups, Downs, and Outs." *Forbes,* September 15, 1977.

Preview

There is a growing interest in tax reform in the United States. The objective of tax reform in this case is to create incentives for economic growth. A value-added tax has been proposed as an alternative to existing taxes, especially the payroll tax currently used to finance the social security program. According to the proponents, a value-added tax is a more effective tax because it creates incentives that promote economic growth whereas the payroll tax generates incentives to reduce the level of employment. This chapter explores the pros and cons of a value-added tax in comparison with the existing tax structure.

Key Economic Points

How would a value-added tax be collected?

Taxes in general, and the value-added tax in particular, will alter economic behavior.

Economic incentives created by a value-added tax are compared with the incentives generated by the existing payroll tax.

Proposed arguments against a value-added tax are weighed.

Is a value-added tax preferable to the payroll tax for financing social security?

8

Functions of Government: The Proposed Value-Added Tax

The major concern of tax reform for the past generation has been to use the tax system to achieve a more equitable distribution of income. There are signs that the times are changing, that concern has shifted to the effect of taxes upon economic incentives. Several years of relatively slow economic growth and lagging capital formation in the mid-1970s has increased interest in stimulating the level of investment and saving. The revenue bill of 1978, which cut the capital gains tax, was weighted toward the affluent, who are the large savers.

The same concern is behind the renewed interest in employing in the United States a value-added tax (or VAT), which is widely used in Europe. In the United States the Nixon administration proposed such a tax in 1972, first as a substitute for the corporate income tax and then as a replacement for the property tax. Neither proposal ever proceeded past the draft stage. In 1979 America's two most important congressmen involved in creating tax policy came out in favor of introducing a value-added tax in the United States: Senator Russell Long, chairman of the Senate Finance Committee, and Representative Al Ullman, chairman of the House Finance Committee. Both supported the VAT, which ensures that this proposed tax will be seriously considered as an alternative to our present tax system.

The current mood in the country, however, is to reduce taxes and government spending, not to introduce a new tax. This means that any proposal for a new tax would be coupled with promises and/or guarantees to eliminate or reduce other existing taxes. Senator Long suggested VAT as a replacement for the unpopular social security tax and/or as a means of reducing the income tax.

We shall consider the proposed value-added tax compared with the current system of taxation, especially the payroll tax. An economist comparing taxes is interested in the incidence of the tax (who actually pays the tax) and in the incentives the tax creates. Economists are also interested in determining whether the tax is progressive or regressive. A progressive tax is one that causes a person with a high income to pay a greater proportion of that income in taxes than a person with a lower income. A regressive tax is the reverse: it forces a person with a low income to pay a higher portion in taxes than a person with a higher income.

Almost all taxes cause some distortion of economic activity. That is, people will behave differently after the tax is imposed than they would in its absence. Most taxes change incentives in some way. It is important to understand the nature of the incentives that a tax creates in order to predict its overall effect upon economic activity.

A value-added tax is a tax on consumption rather than on income. It is a sales tax that is levied at each stage of production and distribution. Instead of a consumer paying a retail sales tax on each purchase, as is now done in many states, the tax is collected from each firm that had a hand in producing the good. Each company when figuring the tax it owes simply takes its gross receipts, subtracts its payments to other firms, and applies the tax rate to what is left. What is left is the value created, or added, by the company.

Let's consider an example. Suppose a bicycle manufacturer spends $30 to obtain the steel, handlebars, grips, pedals, chain, wheels, tires, and brake assembly that are then fashioned into a bicycle and sold to a dealer for $50. The value added is the difference between the revenues a firm receives when it sells the product ($50) and the payments it makes to other firms ($30). If the value-added tax is 10 percent, the bicycle manufacturer in our example must pay $2 (10 percent of $20) to the government. The manufacturer, of course, will add as much of the tax as possible to the price charged the dealer. The dealer, in turn, will be charged VAT on the difference between what he paid for the bicycle and what he sold it for, and will attempt to pass the tax on to the consumer. So VAT functions as a retail sales tax. The only substantive difference is that it is collected in many bits and pieces rather than all at once.

The value-added tax has been claimed to be a neutral tax, its supporters contending that it does not distort economic decisions, which supposedly gives it an advantage over existing taxes such as the payroll tax. The payroll tax, for example, drives a wedge between the cost of employing a worker and the amount the worker receives in take-home pay.

Because it costs more to hire a worker than the worker receives, employment suffers. The corporate income tax and personal income tax also distort economic decisions in similar ways.

The same is also true of the value-added tax, despite claims to the contrary. VAT taxes consumption but not saving, which is the alternative use consumers have for their income. Nor would the interest received from savings be taxed by a VAT. Consumption thus becomes more expensive than saving, so that consumers will consume less and save more than they would in the absence of a value-added tax. This distortion becomes a virtue for supporters of the tax because it encourages saving and investment, hence stimulates economic growth. Similarly, because households have savings as an alternative to consumption, the full cost of the value-added tax cannot be passed on to consumers. Some portion of the tax, probably a small part, will have to be absorbed by producers.

The value-added tax was first proposed in 1918 in Germany but was not introduced until after World War II. In France in the 1960s it was introduced as a tax on manufacturing. Denmark was actually the first European country to install a comprehensive VAT. Thereafter, VAT spread through Western Europe and currently accounts for a major portion of the tax receipts of many countries. VAT rates in Europe range from 8 to 12 percent in Britain to an average of 20 percent in Scandinavia. Value-added taxes account for 12 percent of total government revenues in Great Britain, 19 percent in Denmark, and 24 percent in France.

The proposals to introduce VAT into the U.S. tax system have not gone without criticism. Critics object that VAT is regressive, would be inflationary, would be widely evaded, would be expensive to collect, and would be hidden from consumers, thereby making it difficult for voters to determine the exact amount of taxes they pay.

There is little doubt that VAT, when considered by itself, is a regressive tax. Poorer people spend a higher proportion of their income on consumption than rich people; therefore they would be paying a high proportion of their income in taxes. This argument is somewhat muted if the value-added tax were used to replace payroll taxes, such as the social security tax, which is itself highly regressive. The social security tax rate is currently 11 percent of the national payroll. But this excise tax will have to increase to a hefty 24 percent of wage and salary income by the year 2030 just to support the current level of benefits. It would take a VAT tax rate of 13 percent in the United States to eliminate the payroll tax that supports the social security program. The 13 percent rate would raise sufficient revenues to replace the $130 billion a year payroll tax if it were to be used for that purpose.

The social security tax is highly regressive because it is charged only on a certain amount of income ($17,000 in 1979) and is not charged on incomes earned after that. Also, only wage and salary income is taxed; rental income, interest revenue, and profits are not taxed. VAT is probably less regressive than the social security tax because it taxes consumption, part of which is paid for by nonwage and salary incomes. Increasing the payroll tax to the proposed level would significantly alter economic behavior, discouraging employers from hiring workers and workers from seeking employment.

A value-added tax, if it were to be introduced in the United States, would almost certainly be used in conjunction with the existing personal income tax. This affords the opportunity to make the value-added tax as progressive as Americans desire by allowing the poor a tax credit on their income tax for the amount of the VAT paid yearly. A rebate of the VAT paid could be allowed the very poor, who would not ordinarily pay any income tax. So the potential problem of VAT being regressive could be overcome by a combination of tax credits and rebates.

The charge that VAT would be inflationary confuses a change in relative prices with a change in the absolute level of prices. Inflation is an increase in the absolute price level measured by the tendency for all prices in the economy to rise. A value-added tax would cause the prices of consumer goods that are taxed to rise relative to investment goods and to the consumer goods that would be exempted from the tax. The U.S. Treasury estimates that housing, banking, insurance, and charitable organizations, which account for about 20 percent of consumption expenditures, would be exempted from VAT. A value-added tax would cause the prices of the goods taxed to increase relative to goods and services that escape taxation, but relative price changes are not the same thing as inflation. Once the economy adjusted to the change in relative prices that a value-added tax would cause, no further price changes would be observed.

Another criticism of VAT is that the tax is apt to encourage widespread cheating. Visitors to several of the countries that employ a value-added tax soon discover that an underground economy which functions to avoid taxes does exist. Self-employed tradespeople and professionals often work only for cash and obviously do not pay the value-added tax. In Sweden, France, and Italy tax avoidance has become a serious problem to tax collectors. In Italy it is estimated that as much as one-quarter of the economic activities subject to VAT avoid payment by subterfuge and cheating.

But high tax rates are always an incentive to cheat, and in France and Italy avoiding taxes is considered by many a moral obligation. Even in the United States, where taxpayers readily consent to compute their own income taxes, a subterranean economy exists. Estimates of its size run as high as 10 percent of national income. Widespread tax evasion is more dependent upon the level of taxes than on how taxes are levied.

The proposal to levy VAT at every stage of the production process, rather than imposing a general sales tax, is designed to make it more difficult to evade the tax. The more stages involved, the easier it is for the tax collector to detect cheating by cross-checking. But collecting the tax from every producer is certainly more expensive than levying a sales tax on final consumption. It costs British companies about $1 billion a year to collect the tax, or 12 percent of the total VAT collections, considerably more than the United States spends to collect the income tax.

There are good political reasons to charge the tax at every stage of production. The tax becomes embedded in the price of the goods, and it becomes difficult for consumers to ascertain the total amount of taxes paid. Politicians since Colbert, the great French finance minister, have realized the political benefits of this strategy. Colbert thought the art of taxation lay in plucking the citizen's goose in a way that obtained the largest amount of feathers while provoking as little hissing as possible. Today this same approach is called the "political theory of the squawk."

The current social security tax, which accounts for 30 percent of government tax receipts, has begun to generate "squawks" from the taxpayer. The substantial deduction from each payroll check is painfully visible to the worker. Moreover, this forced contribution, as we saw above, is scheduled to go up substantially in the near future. It is no wonder that politicians are searching for a less visible way to meet the obligations of the social security system. VAT offers the opportunity to make the tax burden politically less visible, even if it is no less burdensome.

Also, the less visible the tax, the easier it is to raise its rates. For example, in 1978, West Germany increased its value-added tax from 12 to 13 percent with scarcely a murmur of protest. A tax with this kind of reception from taxpayers is very appealing to American politicians feeling the effects of the taxpayers' revolt.

VAT is receiving renewed attention by Congress because it appears to offer advantages over the present tax system, some economic, some political. The present tax system, it is widely acknowledged, discourages saving, investment, and employment. A value-added tax could be designed that would alter existing incentives in a way that would reduce consumption and encourage savings.

The value-added tax has been criticized because it is regressive, potentially inflationary, expensive to collect, would be widely evaded, and is a hidden tax. While in its pure form a value-added tax is regressive, it is no more regressive than present payroll taxes. VAT through income tax credits or rebates can be made as progressive as desired. As for inflation, we have seen that a value-added tax is not inflationary. Nor would it be easier to evade a value-added tax than other current taxes. It is true that VAT is less visible than either income or payroll taxes. A value-added tax is a shy tax, burying itself in the purchase price of goods and services, which does make it harder for consumers to determine their true tax bills. This fact alone makes it politically attractive to our elected representatives.

CHAPTER 8

Additional Readings

Hafer, R. W. and M. E. Trebing. "The Value Added Tax—A Review of the Issues." *Review,* Federal Reserve Bank of St. Louis, January 1980.

Lindholm, Richard W. *Value-Added Tax and Other Tax Reforms.* University of Oregon Press, 1978.

Sullivan, Clara K. *The Tax on Value Added.* Columbia University Press, 1966.

Surrey, Stanley S. "Value-Added Tax: The Case Against." *Harvard Business Review,* November 1970.

Ullman, A. "A Tax Policy for the 1980s." *Challenge,* March–April 1980.

II

ECONOMICS OF SUPPLY AND DEMAND

Preview

The rapid rise in the costs of health care in general and of doctor bills in particular has become a matter of national concern. Recently, it was suggested by the Secretary of Health, Education and Welfare that the rising relative price of physicians' fees was due to the repeal of the law of demand: the more doctors there are, suggested the secretary, the higher the fees doctors will charge. The proposed solution was to reduce the number of students in medical schools. This chapter reviews the evidence put forth to support this view and finds that the evidence in fact supports rather than refutes the law of demand. The vindicated law of demand is then applied to analyze rising health care costs in general. The findings suggest that changes in the nature of medical health insurance would improve the efficiency of health care delivery in the United States.

Key Economic Points

How can the claim that physicians have succeeded in repealing the law of demand be evaluated?

What factors have led to the increase in the demand for medical care?

What effects do the current health insurance programs have on the demand for medical care?

What are the consequences for economic efficiency of our current health insurance programs?

9

Demand: Have Physicians Succeeded in Repealing the Law of Demand?

The rising cost of health care has become a national concern. A substantial part of everyone's health care cost is the doctor bill. The income of physicians has increased more rapidly since World War II than practically anyone else's. The purpose of this chapter is to apply the law of demand; first, to see if this law governs the determination of physicians' fees, and second, to explore the forces causing the price of medical care to rise relative to other goods and services.

The cause of the rapid increase in doctors' incomes was widely believed to be an expanding demand for medical care coupled with an inadequate supply of physicians. As late as 1978 the Federal Trade Commission accused various medical groups of attempting to restrict entry into the medical profession.

During 1978, however, there were signs that the federal government's position was changing. The Council on Wage and Price Stability expressed concern about a surplus of physicians. The council was joined by the Secretary of the Department of Health, Education and Welfare, who predicted a severe oversupply of physicians during the 1980s. Instead of seeing this as good news, and expecting the increased supply of physicians to lead to a welcome decline in health care costs, both the council and the secretary predicted the opposite result: "The chief effect of physician oversupply is dramatically rising costs." It was recognized that this conclusion violated the law of demand, but according to these government officials, "the forces of supply and demand have been overturned in the market for physicians' services."

The genesis of the belief that the law of demand had been repealed can be traced to a speech given in 1975 at the Annual Meeting of the National Institute of Medicine. The speaker, a doctor, warned his listeners, also doctors, about the "impending overproduction of physicians." He maintained, "The consequences of a surplus of physicians will be higher not lower cost. . . . When there is a surplus of surgeons, each surgeon does fewer operations and so has to raise fees to continue meeting expenses" (reported in the *Seattle Times*, November 9, 1975, p. A22).

The key to the alleged ability of doctors to repeal the law of demand is the proposition that physicians individually control their own incomes. When a surplus of doctors arises in a local area, physicians can respond by simply raising fees, and they can expand the demand for their services by prescribing unnecessary treatments and tests. In the case of surgeons, an oversupply can result in unnecessary surgery. A congressional subcommittee stated in a report that in 1977 2 million unnecessary surgical procedures were performed, costing more than $4 billion and resulting in the deaths of 10,000 people.

The contention that physicians and surgeons, if they have not repealed the law of demand outright, can at least control the demand for their services, is supposedly supported by several studies. These studies found that a relatively large number of surgeons in an area is accompanied by high per capita surgery rates and high surgical fees. The explanation provided for this phenomenon was that surgeons have responded to a local oversupply, not by moving to a less competitive locale, but by raising fees and performing unnecessary surgery. If these conclusions are correct, then the medical profession has escaped the discipline that competition in the rest of the economy enforces upon an industry or profession. The only alternative to even higher health care costs, then, is closer supervision and more stringent regulation of the health delivery industry by the federal government.

But has the medical profession really been able to repeal the law of demand? Is there perhaps an explanation for the coincidence of high concentrations of doctors and high rates of illness and high doctor bills that is consistent with the law of demand? Consider the following explanation. Physicians, as in every other consumer-oriented business, tend to locate where demand is the greatest. Just as lawyers maintain offices near law courts and automobile dealers line up next to one another on busy arteries, so doctors tend to group in urban areas near major hospitals and related specialists. Furthermore, the more specialized the doctor, the more dependent he or she is upon the support facilities. Few people would be surprised to find that a Montana rancher who needed open heart surgery would choose to travel to Houston or to Stanford to have the operation performed rather than have the local surgeon perform the operation. Specialists and their medical facilities are apt to be immobile compared with their patients.

In addition, the incomes of surgeons are predictably going to be higher in Houston or Stanford than in Montana for at least two reasons. First, while a rancher will travel out of state for heart surgery, he or she probably will be satisfied to have an appendix removed locally. Open heart surgery is a more complex, hence costlier, surgical procedure than removing an appendix, so a comparison of surgeons' incomes will show that Houston surgeons who do relatively more complicated operations have higher incomes than Montana surgeons who do relatively fewer. Second, it is to be expected that the better surgeons will migrate to areas that have a high demand for surgeons and that the better surgeons, like better lawyers and professional athletes, will be paid more for their services. If the better surgeons tend to be located near major medical centers, the average fee will be higher in these areas. The finding that in areas with a high density of physicians doctors do more business and enjoy relatively higher incomes is not evidence that the law of demand has been repealed but, on the contrary, that the laws of demand and supply are still being obeyed. Such findings are similar to discovering that the best paid stockbrokers who do most of the business are located on Wall Street in New York City.

The alleged oversupply of physicians is not responsible for the rising costs of health care. In fact, just the opposite. If the supply of doctors had not significantly increased during the last decade, the fees charged by physicians would be even higher. Compared with the income of the average college graduate, physicians earned relatively less in 1976 than they did in 1970. More can only be sold at a relatively lower price is what the law of demand says and what the facts about doctor bills show. If the supply of physicians is limited in the future, the relative cost of doctor bills will rise, not fall.

Moreover, the rapid rise in the cost of health care is better explained by invoking the law of demand than by charging its repeal. Increasing government concern about inadequate health care led to the passage in 1965 of the Medicare-Medicaid programs. Subsequent government programs subsidized the consumption of medical care for a substantial portion of American families. The result was to increase the demand for health care relative to an inelastic supply of physicians. As a consequence, the price of health care increased dramatically. Physicians' incomes on average increased 50 percent during the first 4 years of the Medicare-Medicaid programs. The forces of demand were clearly at work.

The government attempted to counter the inelastic supply of physicians by providing grants to medical schools to increase their training facilities. These funds, called "capitation" grants, were awarded on the condition that the schools increase their enrollments. Congress appropriated $144 million for this program to increase the supply of physicians for

1979, but the administration planned to spend only $67.6 million. The administration based its case for reducing the grants on the belief that physicians had succeeded in repealing the law of demand. The position was that if the government increased the supply of doctors, the costs of health care would only go up faster as doctors raised their fees to counter declining patient loads. The evidence, as we have seen, does not support this view. Are we to believe that doctors actually chose lower relative incomes between 1970 and 1976, the last year for which data are available? A better explanation is that more doctors' services can only be sold at relatively lower prices. A government decision to reduce the supply of doctors can be good news only for the medical profession. For everyone else it means higher doctor bills.

The basic economic concepts of demand and supply still remain our best tools for understanding the rapid rise in the price of medical care. Consider the influence that health insurance has had upon the demand for medical care. The government has actively encouraged the acquisition of prepaid health insurance by making the premiums tax deductible or by making employer-paid medical care insurance nontaxable. Furthermore, the government through the Medicare and Medicaid programs is itself an insurer for millions. Today approximately 65 percent of all doctors' bills are paid not by patients but by insurers. For millions of Americans the rising cost of medical care has guaranteed that health insurance ranks among their most valuable possessions. Most feel they "couldn't afford" to be without it.

The increasing use of health insurance has had a significant effect upon the cost of delivering health care. Some policies pay all doctors' bills, and many have a small deductible amount after which all subsequent bills are paid. A person with health insurance considers his or her visits to the doctor as relatively costless since they have been prepaid. Whereas formerly the cost of going to a doctor was a substantial doctor's bill for the physician's time, overhead, and tests performed, plus the cost of the patient's time and travel, with health insurance only the cost of the patient's time and travel need be considered. Medical treatment for minor colds, aches and pains, and the flu no longer requires the sacrifice of dinner out or new shoes for the children. As a consequence, the quantity of medical care demanded has increased.

Had the patient suffering from the common flu been forced to pay for the total bill personally, he or she might have chosen not to see the doctor. As a result of prepaid, tax-subsidized insurance, the total medical payments exceed the value of the benefits that patients receive. This situation is similar to going out to dinner with your friends and agreeing to evenly split the check. Each person has the tendency to order a more expensive meal than if he or she were to pay only for the meal ordered. After all, much of the added cost will be paid for by the other diners. But since the other diners also face the same opportunities and probably will respond in the same way, the total bill is greater than it would have been if separate checks had been requested. It doesn't pay for either the diner or the person with health insurance not to take advantage of the opportunity, because if others do, as they surely will, each individual's share of the cost of the meal or of health insurance will still rise.

The nature of our current health insurance programs thus provides an incentive for the insured to consume more health services than he or she would choose if each had to pay only for the cost of personal health care. This individual incentive to consume more than is optimal has probably added substantially to the increase in the costs of health care delivery.

There are some obvious solutions to the situation. The first would be to replace the current prepaid health insurance with catastrophe insurance (major medical). Catastrophe medical insurance would impose fairly large deductibles upon health insurance policies, large enough so that most healthy persons would still personally pay their own bills, but seriously ill persons would be insured against the financial ruin that a serious illness can bring. Second, so that the poor would not be denied health care, their income should be directly increased rather than provide subsidized medical care. The poor would then face the same choice as their more affluent neighbors when deciding whether to see a doctor or not: is the visit worth the sacrifice of new shoes for the children or whatever else the cost of an office call would be for instead?

The law of demand is still very much in force in the health care industry. Its application is the best guide we have to understanding the rapid rise in health care costs. Asserting that it has been repealed and acting contrary to its implications will make the problem of rising health care costs more, not less, serious.

Additional Readings

Behn, Robert D. and Kim Sperduto."Medical Schools and the Entitlement Ethic." *The Public Interest,* Fall 1979.

Feldstein, Martin. "The High Cost of Hospitals—And What to Do About It." *The Public Interest,* Summer 1977.

Friedman, Milton. *Capitalism and Freedom.* University of Chicago Press, 1962, pp. 149–160.

Leffler, Keith B. "Doctors Fees and Health Costs." *Wall Street Journal,* February 2, 1979.

"Soaring Costs of Medical Care." *U.S. News and World Report,* June 16, 1975.

"Too Many Doctors? Califano's Forecast Sets the Stage for a Budget Battle." *Wall Street Journal,* December 26, 1978.

"U.W. Professor Offers Twelve Goals for Health Care." *Seattle Times,* November 9, 1975.

Preview

The social problem created by the existence and spread of heroin addiction has so far escaped solution. The application of the economic concept of the price elasticity of demand reveals the difficulty of employing a single strategy, such as strict law enforcement, to deal with the drug problem. No single strategy can possibly succeed in simultaneously reducing the spread of heroin addiction, reducing the amount of crime committed by addicts, and improving the welfare of addicts. The investigation of the price elasticity of demand for heroin suggests that a combination of programs must be employed if all these objectives are to be met.

Key Economic Points

What factors determine the price elasticity of demand for heroin?

What is the relationship, implied by the price elasticity of demand, between the quantity of heroin supplied and the total revenue demand from sales of the drug?

Price elasticities of demand of the two groups of heroin users are compared.

One strategy, such as strict law enforcement, cannot meet the social objectives for a drug control program.

The relative price that each group of users should be charged to best meet our social objectives is determined.

The combination of drug enforcement programs that best meet the social objectives are identified.

10

Price Elasticity of Demand: Social Control of Heroin

There pictured on "Sixty Minutes," then the most watched television program in the country, was Harry Reasoner openly purchasing heroin in Battery Park in New York City to demonstrate to millions of Americans just how easy it was to obtain drugs. The program went on to point out that it was almost as easy to obtain heroin elsewhere in the city. By all accounts, the illegal use of heroin has grown steadily in recent years, becoming the major killer of young people between the ages of 18 and 35, easily outpacing death from accidents, suicides, and cancer within that age group. It is estimated that nearly 20 percent of the more than half-million addicts are teenagers. Heroin addiction also has become the major cause of property crime in many cities because addicts often resort to theft to sustain their habits.

The use of heroin has been spreading, in the words of a former U.S. president, with "pandemic virulence," despite the injection of massive doses of federal funds to halt the use and trade. The "war on drugs" has run into serious problems compounded by the patchwork of federal and state agencies having jurisdiction over enforcement responsibilities and often working at cross-purposes. Part of the difficulty is that it is impossible for any single policy to meet all the objectives set. Some of the most important objectives are to reduce the use of heroin or at least its spread to new users, to reduce the amount of crime committed by heroin users, and to improve the welfare of existing addicts.

The application of economic theory to this problem reveals the reasons that no single drug policy can simultaneously meet all the social objectives. A consideration of the price elasticity of demand for heroin suggests that a combination of drug programs would best meet these objectives.

Public concern over the heroin problem is rooted in the costs society bears as a result of addiction. Narcotic addiction often prevents the addict from holding a job and increases the risks of premature death, both of which many members of society view as a waste of resources. Addict-committed crime also imposes significant losses on society. Addicts frequently must spend $20 to $30 per day (over $7,000 a year) for drugs, and $100-a-day habits are not unknown. An addict turning to crime to support a habit may need to steal over $100 worth of merchandise a day to net $25 from a fence. Addict-committed (drug-related) crimes are estimated to constitute between one-third and one-half of all property offenses in our major cities. The added expenses of the criminal justice system that result from the high volume of drug-related crime must be added, along with the social costs of the corruption of law enforcement officials that sometimes occurs.

One estimate of the costs of human addiction places the social cost of a labor-year of addiction in 1970 prices at $14,000. These costs include $3,260 for lost employment earnings; $1,890 as the economic cost of premature death; $4,000 in crime costs; $1,640 in added costs to the criminal justice system; and $3,000 in costs resulting from the spread of addiction to others. The number of addicts in the United States is unknown and estimates vary widely, with 500,000 being the most frequently cited figure. If this figure is used, the annual social cost of heroin addiction in 1970 can be calculated as $7 billion. This figure equals the total value of computers sold in 1973.

Heroin is derived from the opium poppy and is grown mainly in Turkey and in an area in Southeast Asia known as the Fertile Crescent. Opium is converted to heroin in secret laboratories around the world. Between the laboratory and the final consumer there are as many as six distribution stages: importer, kilo connection, connection, weight dealers, street dealers, and "jugglers." The fact that dealing in heroin is a serious legal offense accounts for the existence of so many distribution stages. The fewer transactions a drug dealer makes, the less the chance of detection by the authorities. Each participant attempts to decrease the chance of arrest by making as few trades as possible.

The heroin distribution chain resembles a pyramid, with a few operators at the top and many at the bottom. At the base of the pyramid, the street dealers and jugglers are often addicts themselves, dealing to support their own habits. Because of their addiction, there are few things that these people can do as well as sell heroin, so their opportunity cost is low. The main cost they bear is the risk of arrest, and most suppliers attempt to pass the risk along to their customers. Those at the top of the pyramid bear relatively little risk, while those at the bottom are much more exposed.

Heroin suppliers are extremely profit-conscious. Most narcotic enforcement presently is aimed at reducing suppliers' expected profits by increasing the risk of arrest. In practice this policy takes the form of trying to interrupt heroin shipments to interfere with drug sales. As the supply of heroin is successfully interrupted, the price will increase and each dealer will make even fewer transactions. A second drug enforcement strategy is to identify and arrest the street dealer. Federal narcotic agents concentrate on interrupting large shipments whereas local law enforcement officials deal with street drug traffic.

The effect of a higher price upon heroin consumption resulting from a reduced supply depends upon the price elasticity of demand for heroin. The elasticity of demand for any product depends mainly upon the availability of close substitutes. Because heroin is addictive, for addicts there are no good legal substitutes, and this results in the price elasticity of demand for heroin being very inelastic. Of course, there are some substitutes. Using less is always a substitute, and methadone, a manufactured drug, is a potential close substitute, as are other drugs, so that the demand for heroin is not perfectly inelastic. Also, heroin is not instantly addictive; addiction follows repeated use. Some heroin consumers are infrequent users or "dabblers," who are likely to be much more responsive to changes in price than are addicts. So there are two components of the demand for heroin: the addicts, for whom the demand is highly inelastic, and the dabblers, who are likely to be more responsive to price change.

The current law enforcement strategy of reducing the supply of heroin, thus forcing up the price, will reduce the number of dabblers in the market, which reduces the spread of addiction. The increased risk of arrest that results from increased police attention makes it risky for a dealer to sell to new customers, who might be police officers in disguise. Increased police pressure at the bottom of the distribution chain does reinforce the effects of higher prices in reducing the spread of heroin use. The side effects of this policy, however, run counter to the social objective of reducing crime in general. As the price of heroin increases for addicts, the quantity of heroin demanded by this group does not decline proportionally. This means that the total expenditure by addicts for heroin will increase. Since much of the income addicts spend on heroin is derived from crime, each addict will be forced to steal more to meet the increased heroin expenses. Reducing the supply of heroin thus has the side effect of increasing property crimes in general. This suggests that a single-minded commitment by public authorities to reduce the supply of heroin is self-defeating. It may reduce the rate at which addiction is spreading, but it significantly increases the social cost of each existing addict.

This has led some observers to suggest that heroin use be legalized. This would have the effect of drastically reducing the price of the drug, perhaps by as much as 90 percent. The addict would be much better off; the quality of the drugs purchased would improve, reducing drug-caused deaths; and the addicts' dependence on crime for financial support would fall. The latter would certainly benefit the rest of us. It would be difficult to devise any other social program that would so dramatically lower the crime rate.

The main cost of legalizing heroin use is that the lower price for drugs will increase the number of dabblers experimenting with the drug. The number of addicts is bound to increase as a result, and part of the social cost of drug addiction is the waste of human resources. Therefore, legalizing hard drugs is not cost-free to society.

The fact that the demand for heroin is composed of two components with different price elasticities of demand suggests another enforcement policy. If strategies can be formulated that keep the effective price for dabblers high, thus discouraging experimentation, while keeping the price for addicts low, thus increasing their welfare and discouraging property crimes, the social objectives of drug enforcement could be better met than they are at present. Both groups of users would be better off, as would society in general. If such a policy could be adopted, it would represent a form of what economists call "price discrimination"—a practice whereby different customers are charged different prices for the same good.

Price discrimination is currently practiced by heroin dealers, but in the reverse of the kind that is socially desirable. Currently, a profit-conscious dealer attempts to induce nonusers to experiment with the drug by offering a novice a very low price until the experimenter is "hooked." Then the price is increased. Under this practice the nonaddict pays a low price and the addict a relatively high price, which is the opposite of the socially desirable price policy. Certain conditions must exist before price discrimination can be profitably employed. The elasticity of demand must vary between identifiable groups. These groups cannot have alternative sources of supply and cannot easily resell the good to another group. The present existence of price discrimination suggests that these conditions exist in the heroin market.

In order to reverse the present price discrimination policies, a combination of drug enforcement programs is required. The police should continue to use undercover agents and maintain surveillance of known drug transaction locations. When the risk of dealing with unknown persons increases, dealers tend to confine their transactions to persons known to them. They will rationally discriminate in favor of addicts and against dabblers.

Attacks upon higher levels of the distribution chain, made famous by the movie "The French Connection," tend to raise the level of prices both to dabblers, which is desirable, and to addicts, which is not desirable, because higher prices will have an adverse effect upon the general level of crime unless other programs are pursued simultaneously. It is necessary to pursue programs that will increase the price elasticity of demand by addicts. Providing alternative sources of drugs (increasing the range of substitutes) will do this. There are two possible programs that would have the desired effect on the price elasticity of demand for heroin by addicts: the heroin maintenance program and the methadone maintenance program. These two programs, quite similar except for the drug used, provide a legal substitute for illegal street drugs at a low, perhaps zero, price to proven addicts. The doses available are strictly controlled and must be consumed on the premises to prevent resale on the street. The effect of a drug maintenance program is to increase the price elasticity of demand for illegal heroin, causing the price of heroin on the street to fall. This reduces the dependence of addicts on crime to support their habits.

The application of economic theory to the problem of drug addiction suggests that no single policy or program can meet the desired social objectives of reducing the spread of addiction, reducing drug-related crime, and improving the welfare of addicts. A strategy of strict law enforcement will reduce the spread of addiction, but at the cost of increasing the amount of crime and reducing the welfare of addicts. The alternative of legalizing drugs would certainly reduce crime and improve the welfare of addicts, but would also encourage the spread of addiction.

The best way to meet the social objectives would be a combination of strict enforcement with a drug maintenance program for addicts only. The theoretical basis for this policy is to reverse the present pattern of price discrimination that exists in the heroin trade. Currently, dabblers are offered relatively low prices and addicts relatively high prices. The solution to society's drug problem is to strictly enforce the drug laws at the street level to raise the cost to dealers of dealing with experimenters. This would result in a higher price for dabblers and would reduce the spread of addiction. A drug maintenance program operating at the same time would increase the price elasticity of demand on the part of addicts, effecting a fall in the street price of the drug. A fall in the price of heroin for addicts would both increase their welfare and reduce the amount of crime they are forced by their habits to commit. Law enforcement alone cannot meet the objectives of society, nor can the legalization of drugs, but the application of economic reasoning suggests that a combination of strict enforcement with a controlled alternative source of supply would be the best policy.

Additional Readings

Browing, Frank, and editors of *Ramparts. Smack.* Harper and Row, 1972.

Fernandez, Paul A. "The Clandestine Distribution of Heroin, Its Discovery and Suppression: A Comment." *Journal of Political Economy,* Part 1, July–August 1969.

Mehay, Stephen L. "The Use and Control of Heroin: An Economic Perspective." *Business Review,* Federal Reserve Bank of Philadelphia, December 1973.

Moore, Mark H. *Buy or Bust: The Effective Regulation of an Illicit Market in Heroin.* Heath, 1977.

Moore, Mark H. "Policies to Achieve Discrimination on the Effective Price of Heroin." *American Economic Review,* 1973, pp. 263–269.

Rottenberg, Simon. "The Clandestine Distribution of Heroin, Its Discovery and Suppression." *Journal of Political Economy,* No. 1, January–February 1968.

Preview

The U.S. steel industry has suffered through a serious financial crisis since the middle of the 1970s. Record losses have been reported, and thousands of American workers have lost their jobs. Many critics feel that the United States has lost its comparative advantage in producing steel, and these losses, as costly as they are, are part of a necessary reallocation of the nation's resources from less productive to more productive activities. Others disagree, replying that what the privately owned U.S. steel industry cannot compete with is foreign governments that subsidize the export of steel to the United States. Imported steel, they contend, is being "dumped" on the U.S. market, sold at less than the costs of production. Another possible explanation can be found in the differing nature of the costs of production in the United States compared with those in Japan. In this chapter the cost curves of the business firm are employed to explain why it may be rational for a Japanese steel firm to continue to produce at a loss while at the same time a U.S. steel firm would choose to shut down.

Key Economic Points

In the real world the fact of a lower selling price does not always demonstrate the existence of comparative advantage.

What is the difference between the concepts of fixed costs and variable costs?

The various costs of production are categorized into either fixed or variable costs.

There is a relationship between the price at which a firm will cease to produce and the level of variable costs.

11

Fixed Versus Variable Costs of Production: Crisis in the Steel Industry

The U.S. steel industry ran into serious trouble during the second half of the 1970s. Horrendous is the only word to describe the situation, especially during 1976 and 1977. Entire plants were closed down in Youngstown, Ohio; Johnstown, Pennsylvania; and Lackawanna, New York; 60,000 workers lost their jobs in the process. Bethlehem Steel, the country's second largest steel producer, scrapped 10 percent of its capacity and announced what at that time was the largest quarterly loss in U.S. business history ($470 million). Industry spokespersons predicted that 20 percent more of the industry's capacity would in the future have to be shut down in the same painful way. U.S. Steel, the country's largest producer of steel, lost more than half of its stock market value as its stock plunged in price. Other producers generally fared even worse. Bethlehem lost nearly two-thirds, Lykes four-fifths, and Republic nearly half of its market value.

The steel industry is no longer the foundation of the U.S. economy that it once was. In 1978 the industry employed only 471,000 persons out of a total working population of 90 million. The industry has always been highly cyclical in nature, its output expanding during good times and contracting during recessions. Capital goods, such as machinery, buildings, and equipment, account for 70 percent of steel consumption, and capital goods production varies with the state of the economy. But this time steel fell on hard times during the expansion of the economy, not during a recession. The problem was not a lack of domestic demand but competition from foreign imports. Since steel is produced to the customer's specification, there is no way to differentiate, and no reason to favor, steel made domestically from steel produced in Japan, Europe, or anywhere else. Beginning in 1976, imported steel flooded into the country, capturing 17 percent of the total market in 1977. It was worse on the West Coast, which is closer to Japan. Imports there gained 44 percent of the total market in 1977. Despite intervention by the U.S. government (about which more later), the situation worsened in 1978.

The source of the steel industry's troubles was worldwide excess capacity. The world's steel industry had been rapidly expanding its capacity during the previous two decades. Since 1960, Japan's capacity to produce steel has grown by almost 400 percent, Europe's by 38 percent, and the United States' by 30 percent. World capacity to produce steel in 1976 stood at 560 million tons, although only 325 million tons were produced, about 60 percent of capacity. The CIA estimated that 13 percent of the world's steelmaking capacity was excess in 1977. Japan announced that it was reducing its capacity to make steel by 5 to 8 percent. France also announced reductions and, as we have seen, so did steel manufacturers in the United States; but these reductions were more than offset by the growing capacity of developing Third World nations, such as Korea, Venezuela, Taiwan, and the Philippines, which have emphasized steel manufacturing in their development plans.

Operating at 50 to 80 percent of capacity, the foreign steel producers searched the world for markets. The United States became a major competitive battleground, partially because the U.S. market is the world's largest, and partially because other countries protect their steel industry from foreign competition by tariffs, quotas, and trade agreements. Foreign steel producers invaded the United States. Japan, for example, produced about as much steel as the United States did (90 million tons) but exported 37 million tons, much of it to the United States. Meanwhile, Japan imported only about 1 million tons.

The competition from increasing imports kept the price of steel so low in the United States that many producers operated at a loss and those that earned a profit barely did so. The median return on capital invested in the domestic steel industry was 5.4 percent in 1976, 3.5 percent in 1977, and 5.0 percent in 1978. Even with such a low rate of return, the U.S. steel industry was probably the most profitable in the world. The largest steel producer in the world, Nippon Steel (capacity 18 percent larger than second place U.S. Steel), operated its steel facilities in the red and omitted its dividend. The Japanese, according to one estimate, have lost $3.2 billion manufacturing steel between 1976 and 1978.

The threat posed to the U.S. steel industry by low-priced steel imports clearly has both management and union officials worried. The distinct possibility exists that an even larger share of the domestic steel market will be lost to foreign firms, causing the loss of significant capital and thousands of jobs. This prospect is a bitter pill for the industry to swallow. Nevertheless, this is what would be required to efficiently allocate resources if the United States, as many claim, has lost its comparative advantage in producing steel. If this is so, the U.S. economy would be better off importing low-cost steel and reemploying the capital and labor now employed producing steel in some other area in which we have a comparative advantage.

Some observers feel this is what has happened. The domestic steel industry, according to these observers, has been slow to modernize. The industry, for example, employs the basic oxygen furnace to produce only 63 percent of its output, relying on the less efficient, older, open hearth furnaces for the rest, whereas Japan uses the basic oxygen furnace for 80 percent of its output, West Germany for 72 percent, and France for 68 percent. The United States is also behind in employing continuous casting, which transports steel directly from the furnace to rolling mills while still red hot. The United States employs this process for only 11 percent of its output compared with Japan's 31 percent, Germany's 28 percent, and France's 18 percent.

As a consequence, productivity in Japan steelmaking has risen by 100 percent since 1967, whereas the industry in the United States recorded a gain of only 16 percent. The manpower productivity in Japan has been estimated to be anywhere from 18.5 to 50 percent higher than in the United States. One study estimated that the Japanese, because of their modern plants, have a cost advantage of 30 percent over American producers. Another study suggests that the cost advantage is closer to 18 percent.

Representatives of the U.S. steel industry vigorously deny that this country has lost its comparative advantage in manufacturing steel. They reply that what they can't compete with is foreign governments that subsidize the export of steel to the United States, so that any losses suffered by the manufacturer are made good. Foreign producers allegedly are guilty of "dumping" steel (selling below costs) in the U.S. market, a practice which is illegal. The rationale for this seemingly irrational behavior is to keep the mills running to maintain high levels of employment in foreign countries. These foreign nations, according to steel industry officials, are guilty of exporting their unemployment to this country. The U.S. steel industry wants the government to recognize this problem and take appropriate action to offset this "unfair" advantage.

The steel industry may be right. The Treasury Department has found foreign steel manufacturers guilty of dumping in the past. The main advantage of foreign producers may not be greater efficiency when shipping costs are included, but rather greater willingness to absorb a loss. A study by the Council on Wage and Price Stability concluded that European steel producers were selling steel in the United States below their costs of production and that the Japanese may also be guilty of dumping. The U.S. Treasury in 1977 went further. The Treasury found, in a dumping case brought by Gilmore Steel Corporation, that the Japanese had sold steel plate in the United States at prices 32 percent below the costs of production and shipping.

In 1977, *Business Week* (October 17, p. 130) published the following comparison of steel production costs in Japan and in the United States:

	Japanese manuf. price	Export price	U.S. deliv. price	U.S. manuf. cost	U.S. list price
Steel plate	220.51	180.10	227.99	264.00	304.00
Cold-rolled sheets	270.30	220.91	280.03	281.00	318.25

(*Source: Business Week*, October 17, 1977, p. 130.

According to these estimates, the United States is the lowest cost producer of steel for its own market. The cost of Japanese steel plate is $260.40 per ton calculated as manufacturing costs plus transport cost (transport cost equals delivered price minus export price), which is $4.40 more than the estimated U.S. manufacturing cost of $264. The difference in cold-rolled sheets is still greater. Japanese steel delivered in the United States costs $329.42 per ton compared with the U.S. manufacturing cost of $318.25, a difference of more than $11 a ton. If these estimates are correct (Japanese producers deny they are but refuse to provide any cost information), the Japanese are dumping steel in the United States. Japanese manufacturers are pricing both their steel plates and their cold-rolled steel for export 18 percent below the costs of production.

This raises the question of why foreign producers are willing to sell at below cost in the United States and United States producers are not. A senior economist at a major Japanese bank was quoted in *Business Week* as saying, "Japanese business will continue to export, even losing money marginally, until they go broke." But why is it that when world demand is less than capacity, the Japanese are willing to continue to produce at a loss while U.S. manufacturers choose instead to shut down plants and lay off workers? U.S. manufacturers contend that Japanese producers are indirectly subsidized by their government.

Another possible explanation lies in the different nature of the costs of production in the two countries. In the United States, the plant and equipment, interest payments on indebtedness, rental payments, depreciation, insurance, and salaries of key personnel are fixed costs. These costs must be paid whether the firm produces or not, so that these costs do not vary with the level of output. A large part of the total cost of producing steel or anything else in the United States, however, does vary with output. These variable costs are associated with hiring labor and purchasing raw materials, fuel, and transportation. If the firm chooses not to produce any output, it needn't incur these costs. They are avoidable. In the United States, variable costs are typically a larger portion of the total cost than are fixed costs. Labor payments alone, for example, account for three-quarters of the total factor payments in the economy, and most hired labor is a variable cost.

This is not the case in Japan. The rapid economic development of the Japanese economy after World War II was characterized by severe labor shortages. In order to attract and hold labor, Japanese industries guaranteed lifetime employment to the workers they hired. Virtually all new workers then and now come to a company fresh out of school and rarely change jobs until they retire at age 55. Their pay is based upon seniority, and they serve their company loyally. In return the employer provides housing, on-the-job meals, and paychecks uninterrupted by layoffs even during recessions. This system served both employer and employee well for three decades while the Japanese economy was rapidly growing. Japanese products came to be known for high quality and precise delivery and after-purchase service, results of the loyalty employees showed to their companies.

A system of lifetime employment also converts labor costs from a variable cost to a fixed cost. Wages and perquisites have to be paid whether the firm produces or not. In Japan these costs cannot be avoided by shutting down production as they can in the United States. This presented no problem while the Japanese economy was constantly growing. But the oil embargo late in 1973 seriously interrupted the growth of Japan's economy. By the middle of 1978 Japanese industries employed about 1.5 million surplus workers acting as messengers and doorkeepers and performing other trivial functions because there was no productive work to do. Nippon Steel alone maintained on the payroll 5,000 surplus workers who once produced steel, granting them annual pay increases based upon years of service.

The fact that one of the major costs of production, labor, is a variable cost in the United States and a fixed cost in Japan explains the apparent willingness of Japanese steel firms to continue to produce in the face of falling demand and prices, whereas U.S. steel firms shut down. It is rational for a steel firm, or any firm for that matter, to continue to produce as long as the price received is greater than the average variable costs of production. So even if steel firms in the United States and Japan had the same total costs, the Japanese would have lower variable costs because for them labor is a fixed cost. The Japanese will continue to produce steel as long as price is greater than cost of raw materials and energy required, a price well below the point at which U.S. producers began to shut down their plants and lay off workers.

The difference in the nature of production costs provides an explanation for the willingness of Japanese industry to continue to produce and export even at a loss. As long as the price of steel is sufficient to cover the variable costs, as long as selling steel adds more to revenues than to costs, it pays the Japanese to continue to produce, even at a loss. The certain loss suffered is still less than the loss that would be incurred by shutting down and continuing to pay the labor force.

The staggering losses suffered since 1973 by the Japanese industry are finally threatening the system of lifetime employment. In 1976, 18,000 Japanese firms failed, including some very large concerns. A survey by a bank indicated that one out of ten firms listed on the Japanese stock exchange was virtually bankrupt. Nevertheless, the system is not dead yet, and it can still place U.S. firms at a competitive disadvantage, allowing Japan to literally export its unemployment to the United States.

The system of lifetime employment in Japan (perhaps combined with hidden subsidies) provides Japanese steel manufacturers with a competitive advantage in the U.S. market during periods of excess capacity, an edge not based on comparative advantage but on the fact that in Japan labor is a fixed cost whereas in the United States it is a variable cost. The Japanese manufacturer cannot avoid the cost of labor by shutting down, whereas the U.S. manufacturer can. The Japanese, therefore, have a greater incentive to continue producing at a loss. It simply takes a much lower sales price to cause a Japanese steel firm to stop production than it does in the United States. This would be true even if the total costs of production were the same in both countries.

Additional Readings

"Fading Tradition: Economic Woes Spur Firms in Japan to Alter Lifetime Job Security." *Wall Street Journal,* December 20, 1977.

"Japan: The End of Lifetime Jobs." *Business Week,* September 19, 1977.

"Japan's Economy Tomorrow." *Business Week,* January 30, 1978.

"Nippon Steel: Zen and Yen." *Forbes,* March 6, 1978.

"Steel Builds Its Dumping Case." *Business Week,* October 17, 1977.

"Steel's Sea of Troubles." *Business Week,* September 19, 1977.

Preview

One of the most basic principles of price theory is that only marginal costs should be considered when a firm is making price and output decisions. In this chapter, the success of three business firms that sold part of their output at prices below the average costs of production are traced. Two of the firms found this to be a profitable practice; the third suffered losses and went bankrupt. The crucial difference between success and failure in these cases was that the successful firms employed marginal cost pricing and the failed firm average cost pricing.

Key Economic Points

Only marginal costs are relevant to a firm's pricing decision.
The results from marginal cost pricing are compared with the results from average cost pricing.
A firm can maximize profits only by employing marginal cost pricing.

12

Only Marginal Costs Count: Success and Failure in the Business World

In 1974 the biggest bank failure in the nation's history occurred. The Franklin National Bank, once the twentieth largest commercial bank in the United States, was declared insolvent by the U.S. Treasury, and the Federal Deposit Insurance Corporation was named the receiver. Franklin's cardinal sin was that it loaned money at rates less than the rates it paid for those funds. This may appear to be a foolish thing to do, a sure way to lose money and end up bankrupt. But consider the case of Continental Airlines, which continues to operate flights that lose money and yet finds it profitable. Or consider the example set in the nineteenth century by Thomas A. Edison, the man who some say invented modern America. In the 1880s Edison found a way to make money by selling electric lamps below the costs of production, a discovery that should rank among his great inventions along with the electric light and the phonograph.

Edison discovered that when pricing a product, it is the marginal costs of production that count. As long as any activity adds more to revenues than it does to costs, it is profitable. A firm should not limit output to the quantities whose returns cover the average or fully allocated costs, but should produce the quantity that ensures that the returns from the last unit sold just equal the costs of producing that unit. Edison found that he was not making much money producing electric lamps. His manufacturing plant was not operating at capacity because he could not sell enough lamps domestically. So he decided to operate his factory at full tilt and sell the extra lamp bulbs at less than their full cost of production (the average total cost) in foreign markets. Every one of his associates thought this a foolish thing to do.

Nevertheless, Edison asked his accountant to figure out how much it would add to costs to increase production. It added only 2 percent to costs to increase output 25 percent. Acting on this information, Edison increased production and sent a salesperson to Europe who sold lamps there for less than the costs of production, but for much more than the added manufacturing costs incurred. Edison Electric thus made money by selling at less than the average costs of production but at more than the marginal costs.

Edison thought that he was the first manufacturer in the United States to adopt the idea of "dumping" surplus goods in foreign markets, of profiting by practicing price discrimination. In fact, he had discovered the much more basic concept of marginal cost pricing.

In more recent times, Continental Airlines has received much favorable publicity for following this same approach. Continental bolsters its profits by deliberately running flights that are not expected to cover the full costs of operation. Such flights are profitable as long as the value of tickets sold exceeds the out-of-pocket or marginal costs incurred because they add more to revenues than to expenses.

The costs of operation for Continental or any other business firm can be broken down into fixed and variable costs. Fixed costs are those that must be paid whether the airline operates or not. Such costs include overhead, depreciation, and insurance. Variable costs are the costs that must be borne only if the airline operates its planes. Variable costs include the flight and ground crews, fuel, landing fees, and maintenance. Continental's management refers to variable costs as out-of-pocket expenses and to the total of fixed-plus-variable expenses as fully allocated costs.

Neither of these costs, however, are relevant in deciding whether or not to add another flight from, say, Denver to Seattle. Suppose the fully allocated costs (the total costs) of this proposed flight would be $10,000 and the expected revenues $6,000. On this basis it would appear that another flight would lose $4,000, but that would be incorrect. The portion of the fully allocated costs that would have to be incurred whether the flight is flown or not is irrelevant to making a proper decision. Suppose that overhead (a fixed cost) accounts for $7,000 of the $10,000 in total costs. The extra out-of-pocket costs of the proposed flight (the marginal costs) are only $3,000. Therefore, creating the flight adds $6,000 to revenues and only $3,000 to costs, thereby increasing profits or reducing losses by $3,000. Thus, the fully allocated or total costs are irrelevant to deciding whether to operate an additional flight or not. Only the extra out-of-pocket or marginal costs count.

Both Edison Electric and Continental Airlines sold some of their output at below the total costs of production and profited thereby. Franklin National Bank did the same thing, lost money, and became insolvent as a result. Where did Franklin go wrong? Both Edison and Continental employed marginal cost pricing whereas Franklin chose to follow a policy of average cost pricing.

Franklin generally approved a loan if the rate of interest charged was at least 1 percent above the average cost of the funds lent. At first glance this may appear a reasonable thing to do. After all, if a bank lends at more than it costs to borrow, it should make money. But it won't make as much money as it could if it practiced marginal cost pricing, and the practice can lead, as it did in Franklin's case, to actual losses. Franklin in the year prior to its failure earned only one-eighth as much on its assets as the average commercial bank. The managers of the bank felt forced to search for profits by speculating in foreign exchange because the bank earned virtually nothing on normal operations. When the speculation in foreign exchange suffered losses ($39 million) instead of profits, the bank was finished. Had Franklin instead followed marginal cost pricing when lending, it would have, like other banks, profited from loaning money. Perhaps it would not have felt forced to seek profits by speculating in foreign currencies. Even if it had chosen to speculate, had it been profitably operated in the first place, the bank would probably have been able to suffer the foreign exchange losses and remain solvent.

Franklin, like other banks, obtained most of the money it loaned by borrowing. Besides the capital invested by stockholders, a bank has three sources of borrowed money. The first source is the demand deposits that individuals leave with banks for the convenience of maintaining checking accounts. While banks do not pay interest on demand deposits, neither do they charge their customers the full cost of servicing checking accounts. A typical checking account annually costs the bank about 2.25 percent of the funds deposited. In the year Franklin failed, it had about $2 billion in demand deposits.

A second source of loanable funds is the passbook savings account, on which banks do pay interest. Franklin, which had about $1 billion in savings accounts, was paying 4 percent annually for these funds.

A third source of loanable money is the federal funds market. In this market banks with excess funds to lend loan them for short periods of time, perhaps only a day, to other banks. If a bank finds itself temporarily with more deposits than loans, it lends the surplus to banks with more loans than deposits. Franklin was a heavy borrower in this market. From 1973 to 1974, Franklin borrowed and reborrowed as much as $1.7 billion, or 50 percent more than its total deposits. The cost of federal funds is always greater than the cost of deposits, and the rates charged fluctuate rapidly. Between 1973 and 1974, the federal funds rate rose from 6 to 11 percent. As a result, Franklin found itself, as we shall see below, with loans that earned less interest than the bank was forced to pay to attract federal funds.

But it wasn't the unforeseen rise in federal funds that caused the bank to fail; it was what the bank did with the money it borrowed to reloan. The bank's pricing policy was to loan money if the loan would return 1 percent more than the bank's average cost of obtaining the money. It was this policy of average cost pricing that put the bank into financial trouble.

Franklin could easily calculate its average cost of borrowing money in the following way:

$$\frac{\overset{\text{demand deposits}}{(\$2 \text{ billion at } 2.25\%)} + \overset{\text{passbook savings}}{(\$1 \text{ billion at } 4\%)} + \overset{\text{federal funds}}{(\$1.7 \text{ billion at } 10\%)}}{\text{total funds } (\$4.7 \text{ billion})}$$

$$= 5.42 \text{ percent average cost of money}$$

When other banks charged a prime rate of more than 10 percent, reportedly Franklin made loans at 6.5 percent. It is no wonder that Franklin was swamped with loan applications.

Consider how much money Franklin made by following its pricing policy. By loaning out its demand deposits, Franklin earned a spread, the difference between what it received from its loans and what it paid for the money it lent, of 4.25 percent (6.5 percent − 2.25 percent), or $85 million a year. The spread on the savings accounts was 1.5 percent (6.5 percent − 4.0 percent), or $15 million on the $1 billion in savings deposits. But on the loans it made of funds acquired in the federal funds market, it actually lost 3.5 percent (6.5 percent − 10.0 percent) on the $1.7 billion it borrowed for this purpose, or over $59 million a year.

Franklin, by relying on the average cost of borrowed money, was misled as to the true cost of the money it was lending. The average cost, because of the availability of relatively inexpensive deposits, was less than the cost of the money Franklin borrowed in the federal funds market to make additional loans. Because of the rapid increase in the cost of federal funds during 1973 and 1974, average cost was substantially less than marginal cost. The bank found itself in the position of lending money at rates of interest less than it cost to borrow, a situation in which additional cost exceeded the added revenue earned on the loans. These loans reduced profits. Although Franklin grossed $41 million on its loans, when it deducted its overhead costs and loan losses for bad debts, it earned virtually nothing.

If Franklin had instead followed marginal cost pricing, it would never have made new loans that didn't cover the additional cost (marginal cost) of obtaining the funds. Franklin, instead of losing $59 million on its additional loans, could have loaned out less money but profited more. If

Franklin had loaned all of its deposits to other banks in the federal funds market, it could have made $300 million a year on its $3 billion in deposits while the federal funds rate was 10 percent, instead of the virtually nothing it in fact earned. Franklin would have been a smaller but a much more profitable bank.

Franklin failed because it followed an average cost pricing policy, and Edison and Continental Airlines profited because they employed a marginal cost pricing policy. It is simply irrelevant as to whether the price received is greater or less than average costs as long as the extra revenue received is greater than the extra costs incurred. When allocating resources, it is marginal, not average, costs that count.

Additional Readings

"An Airline Takes the Marginal Route." *Business Week*, April 20, 1963.

Edison, Thomas. "On Average and Marginal Costs." *Wall Street Journal*, December 20, 1911.

"The Numbers Game—The Franklin National Bank Situation." *Forbes*, July 1, 1974.

Rose, Stanford. "What Really Went Wrong at Franklin National." *Fortune*, October 1974.

Watson, Ronald D. "Estimating the Cost of Your Bank's Funds." *Business Review*, Federal Reserve of Philadelphia, May–June 1978.

Preview

A few years ago physicians in California went on strike protesting a large increase in medical malpractice insurance rates. The striking doctors stated that higher costs for them meant higher prices for their patients. But physicians' malpractice insurance is a fixed cost, and a basic concept of microeconomics is that fixed costs do not enter into the pricing decision. This chapter applies this concept to the physicians' malpractice insurance controversy to determine whether higher insurance rates meant higher doctor bills or just lower profits for doctors.

Key Economic Points

Fixed costs are sunk costs and do not enter into the pricing decision of a firm. What are the circumstances under which an increase in medical malpractice insurance costs would lead to higher doctor bills for patients?

A way is given to evaluate the doctor's statements that higher physician costs would in this case necessarily lead to higher prices.

13

Fixed Costs Don't Count: The Medical Malpractice Insurance Controversy

A few years ago doctors in California went on strike. Physicians in other states, especially New York, Indiana, and Minnesota, vowed support for their striking colleagues, and some even staged sympathetic slowdowns and brief walkouts. Doctors in these states were rallying to a common cause: the rates charged for malpractice insurance had just been drastically increased. Outraged doctors called on the public for support, pointing out that higher costs for them would have to be passed on to their patients in higher doctor bills.

The striking doctors wanted the rate increases rolled back. How this could be accomplished was not clear. What was clear from their public statements was that doctors did not want their patients to bear these added costs, preferring that the insurance companies absorb them instead. Failing that, the public in general should bear the added costs. Many Americans were sympathetic to the doctors' plight, because they had already suffered medical costs rising faster than any other element in the cost of living for a decade.

The insurance companies were thrown on the defensive. Directly responsible for increasing their prices, the companies argued that increased rates were necessary to cover the increased costs of issuing malpractice insurance. In their public statements, they pointed to the increasing frequency of malpractice suits and to the large settlements awarded by sympathetic juries when malpractice was proven. In 1969, for instance, there was one claim for every twenty-three doctors insured; 5 years later the companies had to deal with one claim for every ten doctors. When the companies had to pay a claim, they had to pay ever larger amounts. In the state of California in 1969, there were only three awards of over $300,000 in malpractice suits. In 1974, there were over thirty. One insurance company that issued malpractice insurance claimed to have lost $102 million during 1974. Faced with mounting losses, the insurance companies increased their rates substantially, sometimes by as much as 300 percent, and some doctors responded by locking their offices and walking out of the hospitals. Perhaps it was more show than substance, but the public and their elected officials were alarmed.

The law holds that anyone damaged by someone else's negligence is entitled to compensation for his or her loss. If in the course of treating a patient a doctor could have prevented an injury, but did not, the doctor is liable and must pay for the damage incurred. Physicians deny that the rapid increase in the number of malpractice claims is due to increasing negligence on the part of doctors. Instead, they attribute it to the increasing practice of ambulance chasing by hungry lawyers and to an increased willingness on the part of the general public to sue in the courts. Lawyers reply that the cause of malpractice suits is physician malpractice. Whatever the explanation, the probability of any doctor facing a malpractice suit has increased, and few doctors are willing to practice at all without being insured.

The phenomenon of hundreds of physicians joining together to stage a public protest was certainly a newsworthy event. The well-heeled doctor is thought of as a pillar of the community and not the type of person who takes to the streets to protest professional grievances. Throughout the period of protest the leaders of the striking physicians repeatedly made public statements designed to win public support.

Many observers remained skeptical of the physicians' motives. After all, the cost of medical care had been rising for some time without engendering much in the way of a protest from physicians. The cost of having an appendix out had increased from $600 in 1965 to $1200 a decade later. The cost of having a baby had increased even more, from $425 to $1150 during the same period; and the cost of having tonsils removed rose from $200 to $500. These cost increases did not cause a doctors' strike, but the increase in malpractice insurance rates, which, according to the doctors' own estimates, would increase the fees they would have to charge by 10 percent, did get a reaction.

The skeptics in this case were right. The reason doctors took the increased insurance rates to heart was that, despite their statements to the contrary, they could not immediately pass along to their patients the full amount of their increased costs. Whether increases in costs can be passed on to patients or consumers depends upon whether the costs that increase alter the supply of the service or product. Only marginal costs affect supply, and only variable costs affect marginal costs. Fixed costs do not affect marginal costs. So when fixed costs increase, they are absorbed by the firm and cannot be passed on to consumers by price increases.

Malpractice insurance is a fixed cost that cannot immediately be passed on to patients. In many states physicians are required by law to have malpractice insurance, and even where they are not, financial prudence ensures that they acquire such coverage. When doctors purchase a malpractice insurance policy, they agree to pay the price charged in return for the insurance company's agreement to assume the doctors' liability for any and all claims of malpractice by the doctors' patients. Doctors agree to pay a known fixed cost to avoid the possibility of a much larger loss if malpractice is shown. Malpractice insurance covers a fixed time period, usually 1 year, and costs a fixed amount that does not vary whether the doctor treats one patient or 10,000 patients. The cost of insurance for a physician is a fixed cost for the time period over which he or she is insured.

Fixed costs do not affect prices that doctors or any other business firms charge; only marginal costs do that. The price any firm charges is affected by the demand and supply of its services. The supply of medical services which an increase in costs might affect depends upon the marginal cost of practicing medicine. Variable costs, which are costs that increase by treating another patient, affect marginal cost. But fixed costs, such as malpractice insurance, that must be incurred whether another patient is treated or not do not affect marginal costs. Hence, changes in fixed costs cannot affect the prices doctors charge.

Consider the decision of whether a physician will treat another patient or not. Sometimes this question is put in the context of deciding whether to take Thursday afternoon off to play golf. The doctor will consider how much he or she stands to gain in fees from one or more patients and will calculate how much it will cost in his or her time, in assistants' time, and in materials. If the additional income is sufficiently greater than the additional costs to compensate the doctor for not playing golf, the doctor will practice medicine instead; if it is less, the office will be closed Thursday afternoons. Note that the physician considers only the added costs and revenues from treating one more patient, not the cost of renting the office for one more afternoon. The office is already rented for that time. Whether the office is open or closed on Thursday afternoons, the rest still has to be paid. Office rent is a fixed cost and does not enter into the decisions about how much medical service a physician will supply during a week. Fixed costs do not affect the supply of anything.

Malpractice insurance is analogous to the rent on a doctor's office. If a doctor is in business at all, he or she must be insured, just as he or she will need an office. And just as the doctor does not consider the cost of the office rent when considering whether to take off Thursday afternoons, he or she will not consider the cost of malpractice insurance. Since the cost of insurance is not considered when deciding how much medical service a physician will offer, the cost of malpractice insurance will not affect the fees that doctors charge.

As long as malpractice insurance is treated as a fixed cost, the individual doctor will have to absorb any increase in rates and will not be able to transfer the higher insurance costs to the patient in the form of higher fees. No wonder that physicians as a group were incensed by the large increase in malpractice insurance rates. The increase in costs meant a reduced income for doctors.

How long will the new, higher malpractice rates remain as fixed costs? In the long run all costs are variable costs and can be avoided by no longer doing business. Because the usual time period covered by insurance is 1 year, at the very least doctors paying the new rates are locked in for 1 year. Because the rates for anesthesiologists, surgeons, and obstetricians in California increased from $5,377 in 1974 to $21,506 in 1975, these doctors suffered quite a drop in their income, even considering that they were on average earning over $60,000 a year. A fall in income of more than one-fourth would make nearly anyone unhappy, even if viewed as temporary.

There are, however, reasons to think that this decline in income might last for years and not be confined to the 1 year over which insurance coverage lasts. Entry into the medical profession has been limited for a number of years. Not everyone who is willing and able to be a doctor has been allowed admittance to a medical school. The number of physicians has not grown as fast over the years as would be expected given the increase in demand for medical care in the United States. As a consequence, the income of physicians has risen more rapidly than that of any other professional group. The average income of self-employed physicians in 1976 was $37,000, whereas the average income of college and university professors who had similar educational backgrounds was $18,500, or about half that of self-employed physicians.

Physicians thus earn a considerable income solely from their right to practice medicine. Should they stop practicing medicine and turn to their next best alternative, they would sacrifice considerable income. Malpractice insurance can be viewed as the cost of obtaining this extra income. An increase in insurance rates would not affect a doctor's choice to continue to practice medicine unless the insurance premiums exceeded the extra income a doctor receives over the next best opportunity, which so far has not happened. Malpractice insurance, then, can be considered as remaining a fixed cost, or perhaps as a fixed charge against profits, neither of which will affect the marginal cost of treating patients. Doctors, in this case, will not be able to pass the increased costs along to their patients, but must absorb the costs and earn lower, although still substantial, incomes.

This view is probably a bit extreme, since some doctors will quit the profession because of the higher insurance costs. Some doctors nearing retirement and previously considering practicing only part-time may choose permanent retirement instead of paying the higher insurance premium. Others may decide to teach, work for government, or do research. The supply schedule of doctors will be somewhat adversely affected by such decisions. As a consequence of a decline in supply, physicians will be able to pass part of the increase in insurance costs to their patients in the long run.

The substantial extraordinary income earned by physicians from their legal right to practice medicine will probably keep such increases to a minimum. As a consequence of higher malpractice insurance costs, doctors will have lower incomes for a number of years, which may be reason enough for them to stage public protest, but little reason for their patients to support their efforts to have the public bear the costs in one form or another.

Additional Readings

Herman, Tom, and Barry Kramer. "States Act to Avert a 'Malpractice Crisis,' Keep Doctors on Job." *Wall Street Journal,* May 15, 1975.

"Malpractice Crisis: How It's Hurting Medical Care." *U.S. News and World Report,* May 26, 1975.

"Soaring Costs of Medical Care." *U.S. News and World Report,* June 16, 1975.

III

PRODUCT MARKETS

Preview

The supertanker, the largest ship afloat, was specifically designed to transport crude oil. Prior to 1974, the amount of oil transported by tankship had been increasing at the rate of almost 10 percent a year. The oil tanker industry expanded in anticipation of the continued growth of demand. The 1973 oil embargo and subsequent price hikes for crude oil temporarily interrupted and permanently reduced the rate of growth of Mideast oil exports. As a consequence, the demand for the services of oil tankers was drastically reduced. The result was instant depression for the tanker industry: prices fell by almost 90 percent and remained at a depressed level for years, causing losses for owners that were measured in billions of dollars. In retrospect, the overexpansion of the industry was free enterprise's biggest mistake. This chapter applies the theory of perfect competition to the oil tanker industry in order to explain the spectacular booms and busts that have characterized the industry's history.

Key Economic Points

What conditions must be met in order for an industry to be classified as perfectly competitive?

The development of the supertanker was affected by certain economic factors.

Economic profits play a role in allocating resources in a competitive industry.

The elasticities of demand and supply determine the price and quantity of oil tanker services.

Sometimes it is rational to operate when the revenues received are less than the total costs of production.

There are both short-run and long-run adjustments to changes in demand.

How can we evaluate, in the light of the enormous losses suffered by the owners of oil tankers, the claims economists make for the economic efficiency of a perfectly competitive industry?

14

Perfect Competition Among the Supertankers: Free Enterprise's Greatest Mistake

Many of the large individual fortunes made since World War II have been made by the owners of oil tankers. The most famous tanker owner was Aristotle Onassis, whose opulent life style and famous wife made him an international celebrity. The fortunes of more circumspect tanker owners, Greeks such as Niarchos, Goulandres, Colocutronis, and Karageorgis; Scandinavians such as Sigval Bergeson and Hilmar Reksten; C. Y. Tun and Y. K. Pao from Hong Kong; the Indian Ravi Tikkoo; and the American Daniel Ludwig, rivaled and perhaps exceeded the fabled success of Onassis.

The past successes of these men allowed them during the early 1970s to tap the world's capital markets for more than $35 billion to finance the construction of the world's fleet of supertankers, the largest ships afloat. The sole purpose of supertankers is to transport crude oil from locations where it is produced, mainly in the Mideast, to parts of the world where it is refined and consumed. The supertanker, displacing over 200,000 tons, is very good at doing this job; a 200,000-ton supertanker is reported to be four times more efficient than a 50,000-ton tanker.

During the late 1960s and early 1970s, the West became increasingly dependent upon world trade to supply oil for its industrial activities. The sales of oil-exporting countries grew at a rate of 9.6 percent a year, doubling roughly every 8 years. The demand for the services of oil tankers expanded at more or less the same rate. The supertanker was developed as a means of more efficiently transporting the ever increasing quantities of crude oil. The oil tanker industry launched its first supertanker during 1967; by 1969, 63 were afloat; by 1971 there were 287; and by 1973, 393. Orders for 500 more had been placed with the world's shipyards to accommodate the expected future increases in demand.

But the expected increases in the demand for oil tankers failed to materialize. Beginning late in 1973 and continuing during 1974, oil exports ceased increasing at the anticipated rate. Exports of oil during 1975, for the first time in a quarter of a century, actually declined by 13 percent, which is fully 27 percent below the anticipated rate for which the oil tanker industry had purchased capacity. The result was an instant depression for the tankership industry. Half of the world's supertankers became unemployed, which ruined many of the owners. Excess capacity characterized the industry well into the next decade. Free enterprise had made its biggest single mistake: the $35 billion invested in supertankers became worth only a fraction of that amount and over $10 billion in tanker mortgage debt became uncollectable.

This chapter traces the developments that led individual tanker owners to collectively overinvest in the industry. The analysis employs the theory of a competitive industry to explain the allocation of resources in the oil tanker industry. It may appear somewhat surprising that an industry in which the average investment may approach $100 million could qualify as purely competitive, but it does. At any one time there may be 100 oil companies, wholesalers, and speculators bidding for the services of oil tankers that are supplied by over 600 independent shipping firms. The largest buyer and the largest seller do not account for even 10 percent of total, so that no individual participant has any effect upon the market-determined price.

Prospective buyers and sellers of tankship services are brought together by brokers, who, for the commission they earn, create a market arranging charters. There are several ways for an owner to charter a ship. He or she can lease the ship to a customer for a period of time, generally a year or more, for a mutually agreeable sum; or lease the ship in the so-called spot market for a single voyage. The price of a charter is quoted at what the industry calls worldscale, a complex index of charges that uses 100 as a base. Worldscale has historically fluctuated rapidly and widely in the spot market, from below 30, which is considered sufficient to barely cover the operating costs of the most efficient vessels, to over 450, a rate that is fantastically profitable for any size tanker.

In 1973, for example, the spot rate at the beginning of the year stood at 40. Then it soared to 450, then fell again by the end of the year to 70. The experience of one vessel during the year, the Sir Charles Hambro, illustrates the changing fortunes in the spot market. The Hambro, a 285,000-ton supertanker, was launched on July 4, 1973, and immediately proceeded to the Persian Gulf, arriving 1 month later to load a cargo at worldscale 250, which earned a profit of $3 million for the 2-month voyage. The Hambro, after discharging its cargo, immediately returned to the Gulf and found a cargo at worldscale 350, which meant a profit of $7 million. Upon completing this voyage, the ship returned and waited in the Gulf for 7 months, which cost the owners the $3 million it had earned from the first voyage, before finding a cargo at worldscale 53, which barely covered operating costs. After a few more unprofitable voyages, the ship was laid up in a Norwegian harbor.

Rapidly fluctuating prices in a competitive market suggest very inelastic supply and demand conditions. Small changes in supply or demand lead to relatively large changes in price. Such is certainly the case in the oil tanker industry.

The demand for tankership services is derived from the world trade in crude oil. A small percentage change in the amount of oil imported by the United States, Japan, or Western Europe leads to a large increase in the demand for oil tankers. Because the price elasticity of demand for crude oil is inelastic, the demand for tankers is even less elastic. A very large increase in the worldscale will increase the price of crude oil very little because the cost of transport is a small part of the total price of delivered crude oil. Furthermore, there are few substitutes for oil tankers when bringing crude oil out of the Mideast to the West. An underwater pipeline has not yet been seriously proposed.

The elasticity of supply of tankers in the short run is also very inelastic. The size of the fleet in the short run is fixed, and the output can be altered only by steaming faster or slower as the conditions demand. A tanker is a very specialized vessel good only for carrying petroleum products; an ordinary cargo vessel cannot be easily converted to an oil carrier. Supertankers do have limited alternative uses as marine storage vessels, a use to which the Japanese reportedly have put a few of them.

A supertanker has a physical life, barring accidents, of at least two decades. Most of the total cost of owning and operating the vessel is in the initial capital or acquisition cost. Operating costs for crew, fuel, and supplies are only a small part of total costs. Owners will therefore continue to offer their ships for charter at rates that are well below the total operating costs as long as the revenues cover the variable costs and add something toward defraying the fixed costs of the investment. In 1975, for example, a Japanese owner chartered a tanker to Exxon for $900,000 a year; the tanker cost the owners $2 million a year to own. A loss of $1.1 million a year was preferable to a loss of the full $2 million. Japanese ship owners, unlike the owners from other countries, must pay the crew whether the ship is operated or not due to the custom of lifetime employment in Japan.

Even when a depressed market forces some owners into bankruptcy, the excess capacity does not go away. The ship is seized by creditors and resold to the highest bidder. The vessel continues to compete for the available business until it is ready to be sold to a salvage yard for scrap. The size of the fleet at any given moment, the time it takes to expand or contract the fleet, the limited uses to which a supertanker can be put, and the limited substitutes for supertankers are all factors that severely restrict the ability of the industry to quickly vary output in response to price changes.

Exactly the opposite is the case in the long run. Oil tankers are built in shipyards mostly out of labor, capital, and steel. Given enough time, there is nothing that limits the construction of these ships. It took the shipyards of the world only 5 years (between 1973 and 1978) to roughly double the number of supertankers. Reducing the size of the fleet in response to declining demand is apt to take longer because of the physical durability of the vessels and the initial high fixed-to-total cost ratio mentioned above. The long-run supply elasticity is probably asymmetrical with respect to time. The fleet can be significantly expanded in 4 to 6 years at constant costs, whereas contraction takes somewhat longer.

These particular economic characteristics of the oil tanker market, along with political events, account for the boom-or-bust history of the industry. The tanker industry has known depressions before. The middle 1960s also experienced depressed freight rates as a result of previous industry overexpansion. Hilmar Reksten (the man, incidentally, who owns the Sir Charles Hambro discussed earlier) was by 1967 rumored to be near bankruptcy. Legend has him on his way to tell his bankers the bad news when he learned that the Suez Canal had been closed during the Six-Day War between Egypt and Israel. Suddenly the demand for oil tankers was dramatically increased. "People called me broke," Reksten is quoted as saying (*Fortune*, August, 1974, p. 146) "but I was in the best position of any owner. I had 1.7 million tons on the starting line."

Prior to the closing of the canal it had taken a tanker 44 days to make the round trip from the Persian Gulf to Western Europe. After the closing, the trip around the southern tip of Africa required 70 days, or 37 percent longer. The effect of the canal's closing upon the tanker market was to suddenly increase the demand for oil tankers by 37 percent. Worldscale immediately went from around 20 to over 300. Reksten probably made more money in a short time than anyone in the history of the business ever had. Such good fortune was not to last. Tanker owners rushed to order more vessels. Within 2 years the capacity of the fleet had increased substantially and worldscale had fallen to around 100.

The industry looked forward to continued growth as the importance of Mideastern oil to Europe increased during the late 1960s and early 1970s. Tankship operators let contracts for new vessels to fulfill the anticipated growth in demand, and charter rates remained profitable. During the first half of 1973 oil exports expanded significantly, driving up charter rates to more than worldscale 400. Profits of over $11 million were made on single voyages. Shipyards were beseiged with new orders for over 400 supertankers, double the tonnage of any previous year. Premiums were paid for priority delivery dates, and the price of used tankers tripled in 3 months.

Then for the second time in 6 years political events upset the industry, this time for the worse. The 1973 Yom Kippur, or October, War provided the Organization of Petroleum Exporting Countries the opportunity to unilaterally increase the price of crude oil. The result was a fourfold increase in the price of crude oil coupled with an outright temporary embargo on sales to the United States and the Netherlands, the consequence of which was to substantially reduce OPEC's exports and with them the demand for oil tankers. The price of tanker charters fell in a matter of months from worldscale record highs to the point where only variable costs were covered. Still, half of the tanker fleet operating in the spot market were unable to find cargoes. The combination of price inelastic short-run supply and demand schedules means that relatively small percentage changes in supply or demand result in large percentage changes in price.

This sharp reduction in charter rates was not temporary. OPEC's price increase stuck, and with it came a decline in the quantity of oil exported. The decline in demand for tanker services was made worse by the periodic launching of new supertankers ordered during the early 1970s in anticipation of increased demand. During 1974 alone the capacity of the world's tanker fleet increased by 18 percent. Approximately seven new ships were launched every week during 1975. Most immediately streamed to join other laid-up supertankers awaiting better times. More than 400 unfinished but already surplus supertankers remained on order. Almost half of these were cancelled, their owners sacrificing the substantial down payments that were paid when the orders were placed. Other owners simply defaulted on their payments and awaited the inevitable damage suits that followed. Still others took delivery of ships for which there was little possibility of profitable employment. The number of supertankers in the world's fleet increased from 587 in 1975 to 618 in 1977, and to 760 in 1979.

The low charter prices were reflected in the market value of supertankers. By the end of June 1975, used tankers sold for only 10 percent of what they had commanded during the peak months of 1973. Indeed, the price of oil tankers fell to about what the vessels were worth sold as scrap, a fate that claimed increasing numbers of ships. During 1975 more than 200 tankers were scrapped, twice as many as the year before. During 1977 8 million tons were scrapped and in 1978 over 13 million.

Many of the people who had become super rich as tanker owners lost much of their wealth. Colocutronis announced in 1977 that he had reached a new arrangement with his bankers. Helmar Reksten by 1978 was probably broke again. Two of his supertankers were seized for back payments, a court ordered him to pay $67 million in damages to a shipyard for cancelling an order for four 400,000-ton supertankers, and his entire fleet was laid up in Norwegian fiords.

Eventually prosperity will return to the oil tanker industry, but not for several years. A reserve navy of unemployed, brand-new supertankers waits (in 1978, 300 supertankers were still laid up, down from over 500 in 1976) for the revival of demand or the decline in supply due to scrapping that will increase charter rates until all costs are covered. Meanwhile, the owners and their bankers have suffered the largest capital loss in the history of business.

The economic characteristics of the oil tanker industry account for its boom-or-bust history. The industry is competitive, being composed of a large number of independent buyers and sellers. An oil tanker produces a standardized product, transporting crude oil by sea from exporting countries to importing ones. Entry into the industry is relatively easy. Any increase in charter rates in the past that led to extraordinary profits also eventually led to an expansion of the fleet and to a fall in rates until the profits were eliminated.

The demand for the services of oil tankers in the spot market is highly price-inelastic. The demand for oil tankers is derived from the demand for crude oil, which is itself very inelastic. Since there are few alternatives to tankers for transporting oil internationally, and since the cost of the service even at peak rates is a small part of the total cost of imported crude oil, the demand for oil tankers' services is bound to be price-inelastic, a change in the quantity leading to a larger percentage change in price.

The short-run price elasticity of supply is also very inelastic. Built for transporting oil, the existing fleet has few alternative uses. Furthermore, the fleet will continue to be employed at very low charter rates because variable costs are only a small part of total costs. A small change in the quantity supplied will be accompanied by relatively large changes in price. Coupling a very inelastic demand with a highly inelastic short-run supply schedule creates a situation whereby prices will fluctuate widely with small changes in supply or demand.

Given the short-run characteristics of the industry, politically prompted developments such as the closing of the Suez Canal or the 1973 energy crisis will have a major effect upon the price of tanker charters. Because these events can seldom be anticipated with perfect certainty, they inevitably lead to either windfall profits or significant losses for tanker owners.

These short-run effects are eliminated in the long run by the expansion or contraction of the industry. Again, the nature of the industry affects the amount of time required for the long-run adjustment to take place. It takes relatively little time, perhaps 2 years, to build new tankers in response to an increase in demand, but since a tanker has a life expectancy of 20 years, it takes substantially longer to contract the industry. Thus booms are relatively short-lived compared with enduring depressions. Nevertheless, in an industry in which the elasticity of both demand and supply are very inelastic, the short run is long enough to make a fortune or to lose one, as the financial history of oil tanker owners reveals.

Additional Readings

Beman, Lewis. "Betting $20 Billion in the Tanker Game." *Fortune,* August 1974.

Zannetos, Zenon S. *The Theory of Oil Tankship Rates.* MIT Press, 1966.

Preview

For almost a century, DeBeers Consolidated Mines has maintained a monopoly over the supply of new diamonds entering the market. DeBeers has succeeded in monopolizing the new diamond market by the ownership of key mines in South Africa and by exclusive purchase agreements with other diamond mines. This control of the source of supply has allowed DeBeers to achieve the goal of every monopoly: monopoly profits. In the pursuit of this goal, DeBeers, as this chapter demonstrates, has behaved as the theory of monopoly predicts, withholding supply in order to escalate the price of diamonds. Despite this behavior, DeBeers has also gained widespread public support for its practices. This chapter, besides applying the theory of monopoly to explain DeBeers' behavior, also explores the contention that this monopoly operates in the public interest.

Key Economic Points

The conditions that allow DeBeers to behave as a monopoly are identified.

A monopolist will always charge a price higher than the marginal costs of production.

How does DeBeers decide the price and quantity of the new diamonds that it will offer to buyers?

Market forces place limits on DeBeers' freedom to determine the price of diamonds.

What are the social costs that monopoly generates?

The contention that DeBeers monopolistic behavior is actually in the public interest is evaluated.

15

Monopoly: DeBeers and the Diamond Market

It is customary in the Anglo-Saxon world when two people agree to be married for the man to present his intended with a diamond engagement ring as a pledge of good faith. Nearly three-quarters of the new brides in Canada, Australia, and the United States receive a diamond engagement ring, as do two-thirds of the brides in Great Britain. As important as the engagement ring is in the West, most diamonds are used in other types of women's jewelry. Cocktail cluster rings, wedding rings, necklaces, pendants, pins, brooches, and earrings accounted for 47 percent of all diamonds sold in 1975, while engagement rings accounted for 37 percent. Male jewelry contained only 14 percent of all diamonds sold in that year, and investment unmounted diamonds accounted for only slightly more than 2 percent.

The investment aspect of the demand for diamonds has grown in importance in recent years as diamonds have become a hedge against inflation. Investment purchases may account for as much as 20 percent of sales during the last years of the 1970s. People buy diamonds not only because they are very beautiful, but also because they are widely valued. The price of diamonds has been rising rapidly of late, and unlike gold or other reputed inflation hedges, diamonds have not declined in price since the Great Depression of the 1930s. The rise in the price of diamonds since 1960 has also been four times greater than the average of all stock prices.

Diamonds appear to be a unique commodity for which no good substitutes exist, combining great decorative value with solid investment potential. In 1969, for instance, Richard Burton astonished the world when he gave Elizabeth Taylor a spectacular 69-carat stone for which he paid about $1 million. Ten years and a divorce later she reportedly sold it for $4 million.

What is not widely known or appreciated about the diamond market is that the supply of new diamonds has been effectively monopolized by a single firm, DeBeers Consolidated Mines Ltd., for over three-quarters of a century. DeBeers controls between 80 and 85 percent of the world's diamond supply through the ownership of all South African diamond mines, which produce about 40 percent of the world output, and by purchase agreements for 40 to 45 percent more with Russia, Zaire, Liberia, Sierra Leone, Tanzania, Brazil, Botswana, and Angola. DeBeers markets these diamonds through its London-based subsidiary, the Central Selling Organization (CSO). Pure unregulated monopoly is as scarce in the economic world as diamonds are in nature. DeBeers' control over the diamond market, stemming from its control of the sources of supply, provides a rare example of a pure monopoly in action. DeBeers itself refuses to describe the CSO as a monopoly, preferring to call its activities "controlled marketing through a single outlet." Nevertheless, a monopoly is a monopoly, whatever its owners call it.

This chapter explores how DeBeers has been able to monopolize the diamond market and examines the practices that allow it to maximize profits. Remarkably, DeBeers, while behaving exactly as economic theory suggests a monopoly would behave, has at the same time gained considerable public support for its practices. This unexpected reaction suggests an investigation into who benefits and who loses from DeBeers' diamond monopoly.

Monopoly agreements, such as the ones that form the basis of DeBeers' market control, are illegal in the United States, but DeBeers is a foreign company that has agreed since 1945 not to do business in the United States and is thus exempt from the law. Still, DeBeers controls the polished diamond market in the United States as elsewhere by controlling the world's supply of uncut stones. The thousands of Dutch and Israeli diamond cutters who sell to the United States have no other source for rough stones than DeBeers.

The CSO controls the supply of diamonds in two ways. The first is to limit the output of the individual mines. Reportedly the CSO offers each independent supplier a choice between accepting a minimum guaranteed price at which the entire mine's output will be purchased or of accepting a percentage of current CSO sales and the corresponding percentage of the resulting monopoly profits. Most, if not all, diamond producers reportedly opt for the percentage over the guaranteed minimum. The CSO itself maintains a large inventory of rough stones. When sales increase, it is out of this inventory that the diamonds are taken. As the inventory is reduced, it is replenished by increased mine output.

The second mechanism for controlling the market is through its periodic sales, or "sights," as they are called. Ten times a year 220 selected clients are invited to submit a list of their requirements of stone sizes, qualities, and so on, and the amount of money they are willing to spend. These clients are generally in the business of cutting and polishing diamonds or selling to people who do. The CSO then makes up a package of diamonds DeBeers is willing to sell for that amount. On the day of the sight the buyer is shown the package and has 3 hours to examine the stones and to take the package or leave it. No bargaining or haggling is allowed. The CSO frowns on a client rejecting its offer; to do so is to risk not being invited back.

The package selected by the CSO represents the monopolist's response to market conditions, which the organization closely watches, and its current inventory of stones. Buyers are often in the position of having to accept some stones they do not want and must in turn resell later. Buyers seeking large, perfect stones, for instance, must sometimes purchase several flawed small diamonds also. DeBeers, through this novel "all-or-nothing" marketing scheme, is able to practice a form of price discrimination and extract much of the profit potential from selling cut and polished diamonds. DeBeers evidently does not succeed in exacting all the profits from being a "client," since this remains a valued position.

DeBeers' major management problem is that, although it can control the supply of new rough diamonds, the firm cannot control the final demand for diamonds nor the supply of cut and polished stones in the hands of dealers and private persons. DeBeers is in effect the residual diamond supplier, deciding how many new diamonds to put on the market after taking into account the stocks of cutters and polishers and the state of the resale market. The resale market is often called the "estate" market, a euphemism suggesting (incorrectly) that only death separates a woman from her diamonds.

The CSO maintains constant on-the-spot surveillance of the world's diamond-cutting centers, gathering information about the prices and quantity traded in these markets. This information allows DeBeers to estimate the demand for diamonds on the part of its 220 clients, which in turn allows the monopoly to supply the quantity of stones at its next sight that will maximize monopoly profits. A sure identification of monopoly is to find that price exceeds marginal cost. Although it is impossible to give precise figures, it appears that the price at which the CSO sells its rough diamonds is between four and six times the marginal cost of obtaining them. The CSO alone has averaged a sales profit of 27 percent during the 1970s and almost 22 percent on assets. The 500 largest industrial firms in the United States earned about 12 percent in assets during the same period of time. These figures do not include the profits earned by the individual mines themselves, which must have been substantial.

The price and output decision has proven a difficult one for DeBeers to make because the demand for diamonds has in the past been highly erratic. Because, as the head of DeBeers states, "owning a diamond ring is nice, but it is not necessary," the demand for diamonds has proven to be very income-elastic. When the United States, the major purchaser of diamonds, suffers a recession, the demand for diamonds declines. During the 1970 recession, for example, sales by the CSO fell by 27 percent, between 1974 and 1975 by 14 percent, and during the Depression decade of the 1930s to almost zero. Furthermore, because diamonds are widely considered to be a hedge against inflation, years of rapid inflation such as 1967–1969 and 1976–1979 have seen large increases in the demand for diamonds.

DeBeers reportedly believes that a large part of the demand for diamonds is based upon the confidence of buyers that diamonds have permanent value. The monopolist believes that it is extremely important to maintain this confidence, and that the price of diamonds never be allowed to fall and not be allowed to fluctuate widely. When a new supply of diamonds was discovered in Brazil in 1724, the price of diamonds plummeted and didn't recover for years, which ruined many gem dealers. And when vast deposits were discovered in South Africa in the 1870s, the same scenario occurred. It was this diamond depression that led Cecil Rhodes to form DeBeers. So successful has this monopoly been at stabilizing prices that the discovery of vast Russian diamond deposits during the last two decades has not adversely affected diamond prices. The Russians, who may supply 15 percent of the free world's rough diamond output, even chose to market their output through the CSO.

DeBeers uses the price stability argument as the major defense for its monopoly. H. F. Oppenheimer, Chairman of DeBeers Consolidated Mines Ltd., wrote in the firm's 1971 annual report, p. 3:

A degree of control is necessary for the well-being of the industry, not because production is excessive or demand is falling, but simply because wide fluctuations in price which have, rightly or wrongly been accepted as normal in the case of most raw materials would be destructive of public confidence in the case of a pure luxury such as gem diamonds of which large stocks are held in the form of jewelry by the general public.
Whether this measure of control amounts to be monopoly I would not know, but if it does it is certainly a monopoly of a most unusual kind. There is no one concerned with diamonds, whether as producer, dealer, cutter, jeweler or customer, who does not benefit from it.

DeBeers, by controlling the world diamond market, thus avowedly seeks to protect the investment of all the people in the trade from miner to retail jeweler, as well as the millions of individuals who own diamonds. It is estimated that more than 25 million American women possess diamonds. Unlike most existing or potential monopolies, DeBeers apparently benefits not only its stockholders but numerous other people as well. It is widely considered to be, if not a benevolent, at least a benign monopoly.

So widespread is this opinion of DeBeers that it would be useful to examine whether DeBeers' reputation for benevolence is justified and to ascertain if anyone is harmed by the monopoly that supposedly benefits so many. The advent of a rapid unexpected inflation in 1977 led to an increase in the demand for diamonds to serve as a store of value as the dollar depreciated both at home and abroad. Israeli diamond cutters began to import more stones than they processed for export. Israel in 1977 imported 11.2 million carats of rough stones and exported only 3.35 million, hoarding the rest. The shortage of polished stones led to rapid price increases at retail. A one-carat top-quality stone that had cost $12,500 the year before now went for $20,000.

The activities of speculators alarmed the entire industry as sales of finished diamonds fell while prices rose due to the limited supply of cut and polished stones. Tiffany and Company even went so far as to take out an advertisement in the *New York Times* warning prospective diamond purchasers (reprinted in *Forbes*, April 17, 1978, p. 39). The ad read:

DIAMONDS ARE TOO HIGH

This may be an unusual statement by an organization like Tiffany and Co.

But some speculators have driven diamond prices too high.

We suggest you look before you leap.

The response of DeBeers to the widespread speculation is instructive. If DeBeers were interested in eliminating the existing speculative "fever," one would expect that it would announce a substantial increase in the quantity of diamonds it was offering for sale at current prices. If DeBeers stood ready to supply more diamonds at existing prices, this would dampen speculators' expectations that prices would increase further. Instead of hoarding more, they would begin to sell what they had, and prices would return to normal levels.

Read what DeBeers actually did as reported in the *Wall Street Journal*, March 3, 1978:

DeBeers charges that speculation in diamonds is driving prices up to a much higher level than is warranted by consumer demand. This is due to speculative hoarding. In order to protect the interests of the consumer and the producer DeBeers imposes a 40% surcharge at its recent "sight" and cuts the quantity of diamonds offered for sale by 10%. All diamonds presented at the sight were sold.

DeBeers' action was not the action of a benign protector of the diamond market but of a profit-maximizing monopoly. It may well have been in the interest of producers, but it definitely wasn't in the interest of consumers. DeBeers raised its prices to share in the speculators' profits, which it in effect guaranteed by reducing the supply of new diamonds. No wonder that all diamonds presented at the sight were sold. This is the action not of a benevolent monopoly, but of one strictly interested in profits.

The persons who are harmed by the existence of the monopoly are the persons who purchase diamond jewelry or who are priced out of the market by the monopoly prices. Fewer persons are able to enjoy the ownership of very beautiful diamonds, and those who can are forced to sacrifice more for the opportunity than they would have to if a competitive market existed. Ask yourself if gold and silver have ceased to be used in jewelry because a competitive market exists in the production and distribution of these precious metals. The next time you admire a friend's new engagement ring, you might ask yourself whether the groom made a good investment. That depends upon a number of things. If the courtship ends and the woman returns the ring, the man will find that a jeweler will offer him about half of what he recently paid for it. That would be the wholesale cost. If the price of diamonds goes up by its historical average over the last 30 years, which is 7 percent annually, then he can get his money back in about 10 years. Gem diamonds, after all, have no utility save their beauty and little value save the scarcity that the DeBeers' monopoly can bring them.

Although DeBeers does not like to be referred to as a monopoly, there is little doubt that it is in fact one; both the market structure of the diamond industry and the firm's behavior demonstrate unmistakably that it is. The firm owns all the mines in South Africa and markets output of most other producers, controlling in all 80 to 85 percent of the supply of rough cut stones. Furthermore, the firm prices its diamonds at four to six times their marginal cost, which is a sure sign of monopoly behavior. The result is extraordinary profits roughly twice as large as those earned by the average of the 500 largest U.S. industrial corporations. DeBeers' marketing strategy of offering a package of stones for a nonnegotiable price on an all-or-nothing basis could only be employed if the firm had no competitors. When DeBeers' reaction to changes in the demand for diamonds is examined, it is consistent with the behavior predicted by the economic theory of monopoly. There can be little doubt that DeBeers, without the aid of government, has succeeded in monopolizing the diamond market by controlling the source of supply, a rather rare event in the modern economic world.

Additional Readings

DeBeers is a very secretive firm in an industry not given to providing information about its operations. Information can be found in:

Beerman Financial Yearbook of South Africa

DeBeers Consolidated Mines Ltd. Annual Report

The Mineral Yearbook

Moody Industrial Manual

United Nations Statistical Yearbook

Preview

The Organization of Petroleum Exporting Countries (OPEC) is surely the most successful cartel in world history. Every year, hundreds of billions of dollars are transferred from the rest of the world to the countries that make up OPEC. A cartel is a group of producers that agree to act as a monopoly. In order to ensure a successful cartel all of its members must abide by the agreement. This chapter traces the events and specifies the conditions that were necessary to allow OPEC to behave as a cartel. The theory of monopoly is applied to analyze OPEC's pricing policy and to point out why it is always difficult for OPEC members to agree on the price of oil. The reasons that cartels tend to break up are explored, and the steps a cartel can take to avoid this fate are examined. Finally, some steps the United States could take to hasten the demise of OPEC are considered.

Key Economic Points

The conditions necessary for a single producer to behave as a monopolist are specified.

How, in principle, would a monopoly select the best price to charge?

Why is a cartel basically an unstable agreement?

What are the methods that a cartel can employ to avoid having members cheat on the basic agreement?

The possibilities that OPEC will cease in the future to function as a cartel are evaluated.

16

Cartels: OPEC

The world every year pays a tribute of almost $200 billion to the thirteen sovereign nations who are members of OPEC. The most important members of OPEC, Saudi Arabia, Iran, and the Arab Emirates (Kuwait, Qatar, Abu Dhabi), are in the Middle East. Members in 1980 could sell a 42-gallon barrel of oil, which costs 25 cents to produce, for over $30—better than 100 times the marginal cost of production. Furthermore, members are able to sell over 10 billion barrels at this price each year. Surely OPEC must rank in history as the world's most successful monopoly.

It wasn't always thus. Prior to 1973, OPEC, which was founded in 1960, was mainly a debating society. It was considered by outsiders to be a vociferous, pretentious, but largely innocuous organization. The world was therefore little prepared for the actions the organization took during October of 1973. Rejecting offers of nominal increases from the then-current $3 a barrel, OPEC unilaterally increased its price 70 percent to $5.11. Four months later the posted price went to $11.65, and a year later up another 6 percent to $12.38, a fourfold increase in a little more than 2 years. The world's press reported the initial increases using the words "staggering," "unprecedented," "explosive," "massive," and "huge," all of which accurately described the price hikes.

If these higher prices were to be effective, the OPEC countries had to reduce output, in accordance with the law of demand, which states that a higher price can only be obtained by reducing the quantity sold. The October War between the Arabs and Israelis provided the required political glue for OPEC's Arab members, Saudi Arabia, Iraq, Kuwait, Abu Dhabi, Qatar, Libya, and Algeria, to cut production in support of the war. The Arabs declared an embargo. The United States and the Netherlands, conspicuous friends of Israel, were to be cut off altogether. Other nations were to receive less oil than they had previously. The Arabs were serious; combined production fell during the fourth quarter of 1973 by over 15 percent. The U.S. government responded by allocating petroleum in this country. You may remember the long waiting lines for gasoline in late 1973 and early 1974.

The political glue of wartime Arab solidarity caused, or at least provided the excuse for, the major producers in OPEC to curtail production in the absence of a formal agreement. Output restriction continued during 1974 and 1975, as a result of its success in increasing oil revenues even after the political crisis had abated. During 1974 the production of the five Mideastern countries in OPEC remained physically constant, which was a reduction of 10.24 percent below the historical growth rate. In 1975 output was actually curtailed, partially in response to the worldwide recession of that year, but mostly in support of the cartel's monopoly price. During 1975 oil production fell by 13 percent, which was 27 percent below the level expected by the historical growth rate.

In a very real sense, during 1973 and 1974 OPEC stumbled onto its monopoly power. OPEC announced higher prices without any internal agreement as to how much each country would curtail output. The cartel still doesn't have such an agreement or even a way to enforce an agreement if one existed. The Yom Kippur War provided the reason to reduce output, which was necessary to make the higher list price for oil the actual transaction price. The Arab states, especially Saudi Arabia and Kuwait, are still relied upon to restrict output by the non-Arab members, which appear at times to produce at near capacity.

There are several reasons that 1973 was the ideal time for OPEC to flex its economic muscles. The availability of low-cost Mideastern oil had for some years discouraged exploration anywhere else. Seemingly all one had to do to strike oil in the Middle East was drill a hole in the sand. The Vietnam War had discouraged the Western world from further foreign interventions. The U.S. oil import quota system had ensured that the United States would consume its own oil reserves first before turning to cheaper foreign sources. By the middle 1960s the United States was consuming domestically produced oil more rapidly than new reserves were being discovered. As a consequence, by the late 1960s the United States was becoming even more dependent upon imported oil. This seemed nothing to become concerned about as long as the international trade in oil was competitively supplied. Oil in the Middle East cost about one-half cent a gallon to produce, there were many years of proven reserves, and the three-fourths of the world that remained basically unexplored would surely produce alternative sources when the Middle East was pumped dry. Oil, it appeared, was unlikely to become substantially more scarce in the future than it had always been.

Early in the 1970s it looked as if the supply of crude oil would always be competitively determined. Crude oil is available in many places throughout the world. As important as Saudi Arabia is in the world's oil market, in 1975 it produced less than 13 percent of the world's supply. It would not pay, with such a small market share, for Saudi Arabia to go it alone and try to increase the world's oil price by curtailing output. It only pays a producing country to take unilateral action by holding a commodity, such as oil, off the market if its share of the market is greater than the price elasticity of demand facing the industry. The short-run price elasticity of demand for crude oil is widely considered to be fairly inelastic. There is some dispute as to the actual value, but estimates range from -0.2 to -0.5, with -0.37 being used by some experts. All the estimates exceed Saudi Arabia's share of the market.

No one, not even the cartel members themselves, foresaw the success of their efforts to transform OPEC from a debating society into the most successful monopoly in history. However, if we look at the combined market share of the member countries of OPEC, we can see that the conditions that would make a monopoly a paying proposition for OPEC existed by 1973. During 1975 OPEC members produced almost 50 percent of the world's oil output, well in excess of most estimates of the price elasticity of demand. It clearly paid then, and pays today, for OPEC to restrict output to increase the world's price of oil.

However, it is one thing for the necessary conditions for a cartel to exist and quite another to successfully establish one. The members of the cartel obviously have a mutual interest in obtaining a higher price than would exist in a competitive market. But the members are bound to disagree on how high the price should be set and will certainly disagree about who must sacrifice, how much in sales, to bring it about. The question of the optimal price to charge is thus a difficult one for any cartel to decide.

Consider first the best price for OPEC to charge if it were a pure monopoly instead of a multimember cartel. The best price is one that maximizes profits, but the important question is over what time span this should occur. In the immediate short run, for instance, the best price would be the one that maximizes revenue because production costs are so small. Thus, all that OPEC's economists must do is to calculate the price at which the elasticity of demand becomes unitary.

The best cartel price, however, is not the short-run revenue-maximizing price, but the price that maximizes the discounted value of the income over the time span that OPEC's reserves will last. OPEC will thus endeavor to set prices that will maximize the asset value of its oil reserves. If OPEC were tempted to make a "quick killing" by raising prices above this price, profits would soar for 2 years or so, and then the demand for oil would begin to decline significantly as the world's economies conserved on oil consumption and switched to alternative sources of energy. OPEC would find its sales falling even more than the decline in demand as alternative sources of oil (new fields, tar sands, oil shale) were developed and brought into production. The price of oil would fall in the future as the combined result of these developments, and OPEC's future earnings would consequently suffer. A quick killing is undesirable because it destroys the value of OPEC's remaining oil reserves.

The fact that OPEC's oil reserves are unequally distributed among members is the source of conflict within the cartel when it attempts to set the best price. Saudi Arabia, Kuwait, and the Emirates have higher percentages of reserves to annual production than the other members of OPEC. Oil production can be expected to last longer before exhaustion on the Saudi Arabian peninsula than elsewhere, hence future prices are more important to these states than to other OPEC members. The best price for Saudi Arabia and its neighbors, because of their larger reserves, is lower than the best price for other OPEC members, such as Iran. This is consistent with the struggles that occur during OPEC meetings, with Saudi Arabia always seemingly in the position of resisting the demands of other members for higher prices.

The best price for Saudi Arabia, because of its importance within the cartel, is the price that probably will prevail unless political pressures dominate. This price can be easily calculated by OPEC's economists, or they can read the *Wall Street Journal,* which, prior to OPEC price meetings, regularly runs an article by economist Robert S. Pindyck, who provides the calculations. Employing a computer model that quantitatively describes the characteristics of the world's oil market, Pindyck predicted that the best price in 1978 was between $12.50 and $13. OPEC set a price of $12.70. Furthermore, according to Pindyck, the best price is apt to change little in future years in real terms. The dollar price of oil will change more to adjust to inflation and depreciation in the international value of the dollar than to changes in the best price.

The predictions of this model assume the stability of the cartel. Political instability in the Middle East, such as that existing in Iran, whether caused by war or revolution, may lead to production cutbacks and higher prices or perhaps to the actual break-up of the cartel itself and lower prices. A severe decline in the demand for oil as the result of a world recession might also cause the cartel to break up internally and, even if it didn't, would certainly alter the best price.

The break-up of OPEC, however, has been prematurely predicted many times in the past. When world demand began to fall in 1974, for instance, the *Economist* magazine, a Nobel-Prize-winning economist, and the U.S. Secretary of the Treasury all predicted the imminent demise of the cartel. They were joined by other experts in 1975, but all were proven wrong.

Nevertheless, OPEC suffers from several defects that suggest that the organization is fragile at best. A cartel must have not only a firm agreement on price but also related agreements on production control and market sharing to make the price agreement effective. A means of monitoring the behavior for members is also necessary because individual members have an incentive to cheat on the agreement. A means of penalizing violators is also required. OPEC has none of these; it is a purely voluntary organization.

Any cartel, precisely because it does create a situation whereby price is above marginal or incremental cost, generates a powerful incentive for each member to cheat. Secretly cutting price slightly below the cartel price will greatly increase a member's sales, adding more to revenue than to costs. Hence it is profitable to cheat if cheating cannot be detected by other members of the cartel or if they do not punish the offending member. OPEC has already experienced secret price cutting. This occurred late in 1975, and again during the first half of 1978 during declining cartel sales. Aside from warnings by Saudi Arabia that it might increase output if the cuts continued, no action was taken by the cartel on these occasions to deter future price cutting.

A cartel that can detect a member cheating can certainly deter further price cutting. All that is needed is an agreed-upon way, and there are several available. One is the fine. The cartel can levy a fine on the offending member steep enough to eliminate the incentive to cheat. Better than the fine is the revenue pool. Members of the cartel agree to pool their oil sales and distribute revenues according to the agreed-upon market share. Because any extra income gained by cheating must be shared, but any member breaking the cartel agreement has to bear all the costs of producing the increased output, there is less incentive to cheat. Even more effective in reducing the incentive to cheat, but more expensive, is retaliation in kind, each member agreeing to increase its output by the same percentage as the cheater, thus reducing along with cartel profits the profits of the cheater. OPEC as yet does not have any agreed-upon method for punishing price cutters.

Even if it did, deterrence depends upon prompt detection, and OPEC has no formal means of speedily detecting price cutting. As price cutting becomes more common it is to be expected that OPEC will establish some formal means for detection and deterrence. There are three possibilities. The first is to form a pool, as mentioned above, so that all oil sales by members are made through OPEC. As long as each nation surrendered its right to sell oil itself, no cheating could occur. A second possibility is the formation of an exclusive purchasing agent—a countervailing power—to represent customers. The organization would have information about all sales and prices, which would ultimately be available to OPEC. Provided with this information, OPEC could punish cheaters in one of the ways mentioned above. A third deterrent is an international commodity agreement in oil, in which both importing and exporting countries agree on a narrow range in which price can move. The cartel's right to a monopoly profit would be recognized by all, and those who bought and sold above and below the set maximum and minimum prices would become outlaws. The U.S. State Department views favorably some type of a commodity agreement. If price cutting becomes a problem and threatens the existence of the cartel, you can expect OPEC to move in one of these directions.

Rather than legally recognize OPEC through a commodity agreement that would ensure the continued annual payment of billions of dollars in tribute to the monoply, most economists feel that steps should be taken to break up the cartel or, at very least, reduce its profitability. Professor M. A. Adelman of MIT, who is widely considered to be among the foremost petroleum economists, regards the breaking up of OPEC as both necessary and possible. His method would be to make it as easy as possible for an OPEC member to secretly cut prices.

Adelman suggests that the United States establish a sealed bid auction of oil import authorization tickets that would be required to import oil into the United States. The government would estimate the number of tickets to be put up for auction to the highest bidders. The tickets would have no scarcity value because there would always be just enough, but they would have a convenience value because they would be required for the import of oil. The identity of the real buyer would be concealed by letting anyone bid for the tickets—individuals, brokers, agents, companies, or nations. Tickets could also be resold.

A member of OPEC that wished to secretly sell more oil in the United States would simply have an agent buy the tickets. Existing cartel members who now sell to the United States would find their sales declining because of a lack of tickets and would have to match the current ticket price or lose their market share in the United States. Libya, Indonesia, Venezuela, Algeria, and Nigeria, which sell, respectively, 31, 36, 45, 72, and 49 percent of their output to the United States, would have to bid for the tickets or suffer large sudden losses in income. Nor could they sell their oil elsewhere without destroying the cartel price.

Since all sales in the United States would be at the OPEC price and the cartel does not have a monitoring system to measure the production of its members, any member desiring to increase its sales secretly could easily do so. The secret purchase of oil import tickets would simply rebate part of the existing monopoly price to the U.S. Treasury. These revenues in turn could be refunded in some way to U.S. consumers.

As it became less profitable to sell in the U.S. market, cartel members previously selling to the United States would attempt, by various means, to sell more elsewhere. The inelastic price elasticity of demand would sharply reduce the price of oil in these areas as sales increased. The oil import authorization ticket system would put the cartel under great stress as soon as any member attempted to secretly increase its sales to the United States. This proposal, because it facilitates cheating on the OPEC price agreement, encourages individual members of OPEC to expand their sales to the United States, the ultimate consequence of which is to threaten the cartel's continued existence.

Should OPEC survive despite its internal organizational weakness, its importance will continually be reduced by competitive forces outside its control. The artificially high price of crude oil has since 1973 reduced the rate of growth in the demand for oil, increased the rate of expansion of non-OPEC sources of oil, as well as stimulated the development of alternative energy sources. The U.S. government reports that Mexico, a non-OPEC member, could be producing as much per day in 1990 as Saudi Arabia is today. Furthermore, most of the world remains little explored for oil. After all, the extent of the Mexican fields, almost as large as Saudi Arabia, were unknown when OPEC first began to flex its economic muscle, and China is beginning to develop resources reportedly bigger than Iran's. The proliferation of alternative sources of oil will, by reducing the West's dependence upon Middle Eastern oil, eventually spell the quiet death of the cartel itself.

Additional Readings

Adelman, M. A. *The World Petroleum Market.* Johns Hopkins University Press, 1972.

Blair, John M. *The Control of Oil.* Vintage, 1978.

Karpel, Craig S. "Ten Ways to Break OPEC." *Harpers,* January 1979.

Osborne, D. K. "Prospects for the OPEC Cartel." *Review,* Federal Reserve of Dallas, January 1977.

Pindyck, Robert S. "Gains to Producers from the Cartelization of Exhaustable Resources." *Review of Economics and Statistics,* May 1978.

Pindyck, Robert S. "OPEC's Dilemma: How to Control Production Levels." *Wall Street Journal,* December 13, 1978.

Preview

The wearing apparel, or garment, industry produces the clothing that we as consumers spend almost 8 percent of our disposable income buying. Fashion is the hallmark of the industry, which is populated by some very large firms and many small ones, each producing garments differentiated by style. Life is precarious in this industry. A significant portion of firms fail financially each year, but their places are generally quickly taken by others. The garment industry is an excellent example of monopolistic competition, combining some elements of monopoly with elements of perfect competition. Like a monopoly, the firm because it produces a differentiated product must decide the price to charge for that product. Like a competitive industry, entry into the industry is easy to effect. In this chapter the theory of monopolistic competition is employed to explain the economic organization and functioning of the wearing apparel industry.

Key Economic Points

What conditions must be met for an industry to be classified as monopolistically competitive?

Product differentiation plays a role in a monopolistically competitive industry.

Profit plays a role in the allocation of resources within this kind of industry.

The efficiency with which resources are allocated in a monopolistically competitive industry is compared with the efficiency of a perfectly competitive industry.

The losses resulting from inefficient allocation of resources are weighed against the benefits of differentiated products.

17

Monopolistic Competition: The "Rag" Trade

The "rag" trade is industry jargon for the wearing apparel industry, which produces the pants, shirts, tops, suits, sportswear, coats, and gloves that clothe us all. Consumers spend almost 8 percent of their disposable income on clothing, making the wearing apparel industry an $80 billion a year business.

Fashion is the hallmark of the industry. Each of the thousands of clothing manufacturers attempts to anticipate the desires of the consumer and produce attractive styles at a price the buyer will pay. Fashion is fickle, however, and to be in the garment trade is to be in a risky business. A firm whose designer correctly anticipates the consumer mood by putting buttons on collars or taking them off, by putting belts on the back of pants or taking them off, or by flaring the legs of pants or making them stovepipe straight can make a lot of money. Conversely, to be behind the fashion is probably to lose everything. According to the International Ladies Garment Workers Union statistics, one company in five changes its name or nature every year. In short, each year 20 percent of the industry goes broke. Firms that fail are quickly replaced by new entrants, each of which feels its designers are in touch with the public's buying pulse.

Economists refer to industries with the characteristics of the wearing apparel industry as monopolistic competition. The industry combines characteristics of both monopoly and competition. The industry, because each firm produces a differentiated product, faces a downward sloping demand curve for its product. Each firm, like a monopolist, must search out the best price to charge for its products. But unlike a monopoly, entry into a monopolistically competitive industry is easy to achieve, so that any monopoly profits a firm might make will be short-lived as rivals offering close substitutes enter the industry. Economic profits, therefore, cannot exist in the long run in a monopolistically competitive industry.

A new firm can easily enter the wearing apparel industry, especially in New York City. All that is needed is several thousand dollars and a few unique clothing designs. A loft left vacant by an unsuccessful firm can be rented on Seventh Avenue and the required capital equipment leased. The Garment Workers Union will supply the skilled labor. All a new entrant into the industry must do is produce a few samples, put a price on them, and exhibit them at the regional shows for buyers which periodically occur in Dallas, Los Angeles, Chicago, and New York.

The price a firm sets is as important as the style. If too high a price is set, the best look in the world won't sell enough to keep the firm in business. If too low a price is set, the firm will not be able to cover manufacturing costs and overhead. The novelty of each firm's designs differentiates its products from the garments of rival firms; therefore, each firm's demand schedule slopes downward. Although each firm's garments may be unique, a thousand other manufacturers are offering very close substitutes. The closeness of numerous rivals' designs ensures that the demand curve faced by each firm in the industry is very elastic.

If enough of the 12,000 buyers who attend fashion shows like the goods and their prices well enough to place sufficient orders, the firm is in business. A bank will lend the money to produce the garments for which there are firm orders. If insufficient orders are received, the firm takes its place, along with some more experienced firms, among those that fail each year.

In short, the rag trade is a gamble. A manufacturer who was struggling to survive last year can be flourishing this year. And next season, who knows? Although entry into the industry is easy, it is even easier for existing firms to copy success. A "hot" new look or style introduced by one firm can be copied by others within a month. Competition is fierce, which is reflected in the low profits earned in the industry. The median return is less than 3 percent on sales or 9 percent on invested capital, barely a normal rate of return.

While the median rate of return in the industry is not attractive, the fact that 20 percent of the industry's firms make nothing at all (given the nature of a median with half above and half below) suggests that some firms also do well. These firms are the ones that have anticipated (guessed) the buying public's current taste in fashion. The rag trade has learned through experience that the public's taste in fashion is not made in Paris or anywhere else. The *haute couture* houses such as Dior, Balenciaga, Chanel, and St. Laurent influence style, but they do not dictate it. Women's wear manufacturers still remember the "midi" fiasco. After the Paris showings in 1970, *Women's Wear Daily* decreed that the miniskirt was out and the midi length was in. It wasn't, to the sorrow of thousands of manufacturers and retailers who tried to sell the midi length to the women of America. Women bought pants suits and jeans instead. It was the *New York Times'* turn to be wrong in 1976, when it proclaimed Yves St. Laurent's "peasant" look a fashion revolution that would pry women out of their pants and back into skirts. It didn't. High fashion designers propose, but women dispose.

No one knows where fashion comes from. The miniskirt originated in London boutiques, such as Mary Quant's, not on the runways of the high fashion houses of Paris. Jeans came from the anti-Vietnam War protesters. Fashion, it seems, is neither a law nor an order, but a mood that stems from unknown sources. It is like the common cold. No one knows what causes it, but once it is started the symptoms can often be recognized fairly early.

New times and new technologies create new possibilities for the designer. Polyester double-knits and panty hose allowed the pants suit or sportswear revolution. Never before had women en masse worn pants in public. Fashion remains unpredictable. Betting is all any manufacturer can do. The garment industry is the only major industry left where intuitive management still gets the credit for business success. A London designer and manufacturer was quoted in the industry press as saying, "I go to Paris for reaffirmation of what I'm doing. It's nice to step off the cliff hand in hand."

Success does come to some manufacturers. Halston introduced a basic shirtdress in 1972 made out of a new material, ultrasuede. Very simple and very nice to touch. Despite the material being hot to wear indoors, the dress stimulated $2.5 million in retail sales. Diane Von Furstenberg during 1976 managed a similar feat, selling 750,000 wrap-around dresses featuring distinctive, elegant print materials.

Designers may make their names as dress designers, but they make their fortunes elsewhere. A monopolistically competitive industry does not lead to long-run profits. When Halston sold out to Norton Simon, it was revealed that the cornerstone of Halston's business was perfumes. Similarly with Chanel, who reportedly lost $500,000 a year with her salon but more than made up the losses with fragrance sales.

The nonexclusive nature of the business keeps profits down. Because dress designs cannot be patented or copyrighted, once a design is shown it can be copied. Indeed, most of the designs shown in *haute couture* houses are sold to manufacturers who copy them for resale. Many of St. Laurent's 1976 peasant look designs were purchased for $4,500 each and copied in New York for sale at one-tenth the price. But it isn't even necessary to purchase the original; a photograph or a sketch is enough to allow copies to be produced. A couturier can make a style and not cash in on it. A volume dressmaker, for example, can sell wholesale for $40 a silk shirt-dress that is almost indistinguishable from a $200 Mollie Parnis Boutique dress.

Even trademarks which can be registered to a single owner may prove difficult for the owner to protect. Levi Strauss, the most famous and the largest manufacturer of blue jeans, has had trouble with counterfeiters. The fashion trend to blue jeans has made Levi Strauss, Bluebill (Wrangler), and V. F. (H. D. Lee) big businesses in an industry previously characterized by small firms. Levi Strauss' sales have topped 1 billion a year, which ranks it among the 200 largest firms in the country. But even its size has not guaranteed continued profitability. In 1973 the firm lost $14 million on its European operation, which reduced its overall profits by 53 percent. Should jeans fade from fashion, even these firms may be in trouble.

Why do it at all, if trouble lurks around every corner in this feast-or-famine industry? Some people may like the gamble, and in the words of George Stigler, a famous economist, "the short run is long enough to make a fortune." Certainly Halston and Diane Von Furstenberg have done well in the industry. More typical is the short-lived success of a New York firm that listened to a buyer and produced a particular kind of women's pants. They were able to sell 50,000 at a handsome profit in the time it took rivals to gear up for the production of that particular item.

Other firms are able to carve out a niche in the market. Take Jantzen, for example, a Portland, Oregon manufacturer located thousands of miles away from New York's garment district. By 1975 the firm had been able to ring up more than twenty quarterly earnings increases. Not much of a record as a growth stock, but certainly atypical in the rag business. Jantzen, originally famous for its swimsuits (it is still the biggest supplier in the market), has expanded into sportswear. Jantzen does not try to dictate fashion, but prefers instead to listen to its customers. The company attempts to find out what its customers—retailers and consumers—want and then sell it to them at a reasonable price. Jantzen delivers on time and as ordered merchandise that is properly coordinated as to size and color and conforming to rigid quality standards. The goods are nearly always well accepted by customers. The company has earned a great deal of retailer loyalty in an industry famous for the absence of such loyalty.

The rag trade is a good example of what economists call a monopolistically competitive industry. Product differentiation in terms of fashion and style dominate every aspect of the business. Each firm faces a very elastic downward sloping demand curve because its products, although unique, are not much different from those offered by numerous others. This market structure has been criticized by economists because the profit-maximizing price, as in a monopoly, involves restricting output, which is not the case in a competitive industry. The differentiated product produced allows each firm some control over price, so that price will always be above marginal cost.

In the rag trade this objection, although true, is probably of minor importance. It is the price consumers are willing to pay for variety. Because the exact desires of consumers are unknown, the industry offers, like pellets from a shotgun, many alternative styles, hoping that some will hit the target. It is the way a market economy overcomes the lack of information about consumer tastes. Styles that hit the mark are quickly copied by rivals, increasing quantity and lowering the price consumers must pay. The fact that the equilibrium price is greater than the marginal cost of production is the cost that must be paid for variety of choice. This cost (marginal cost less than price) could easily be avoided if everyone wore the same uniform. The closest we have come to this state was (is) the blue jeans look. Almost everyone in college, even on occasion in the White House, wears jeans. But what a variety of jeans there is: flared or stovepipe legs; Western style or saddle back; a star or no stars on the pockets; embossed, contrast-stitched, or riveted; indigo, navy blue, or bleached in color; brushed or plain denim; all cotton or part polyester cloth in various weights. And prices that range from $10 to $40, with most selling for less than $30.

We could all, if we chose to, wear standard work jeans such as the ones produced to specification for Sears that sold for $8.99 in the 1979 catalog. This product would be produced under competitive conditions (a standardized product, many competitors, easy entry). If we all did that, no efficiency loss would occur. We obviously choose not to all dress alike. Since the value of anything is determined by the willingness to pay for it, collectively we feel that variety in our clothing is worth the costs a monopolistically competitive industry imposes.

Additional Readings

"Anatomy of a Garment-Center Firm." *New York Times,* September 14, 1975.

"The New Look Is 'Peasant' but Will the Peasants Buy It?" *Forbes,* October 15, 1976.

"We Treat Our Inventory Like Lettuce." *Forbes,* June 15, 1976.

"The Year of the Dress." *Forbes,* March 15, 1974.

Preview

Section 1 of the Sherman Antitrust Act makes price fixing illegal. During the 1950s firms in the heavy electrical equipment industry broke this law and got caught. Business executives were fined and some sent to jail. Their firms were subjected to losses of millions of dollars as a result of triple-damage suits. This chapter employs the theory of oligopoly to explore the conditions that led the executives of these firms to conspire to fix prices, to examine how the conspiracy was designed to work, and to determine whether the conspiracy actually functioned as intended and at what social cost.

Key Economic Points

The conditions necessary for forming an illegal cartel to fix product prices are identified.

What economic conditions lead to the formation of price-fixing conspiracies?

Within an oligopoly a mutual interdependence exists with respect to price decisions.

Why are price wars costly for the heavy electrical equipment industry?

Did the conspiracy to fix prices actually work in this industry?

18

Antitrust Laws: The Electrical Conspiracy

In 1776 Adam Smith warned that "people of the same trade seldom meet together even for merriment and diversion, but the conversation ends in a conspiracy against the public, or in some contrivance to raise prices." Such was the case in the heavy electrical equipment industry during much of the 1950s, if not earlier. This industry manufactures the turbines, generators, transformers, and switchgears required by private companies and electrical utilities to generate electricity. Two large firms, General Electric and Westinghouse, dominate the industry, but a dozen and a half smaller firms such as Allis-Chalmers, Federal Pacific, and I.T.E. compete with the giants. Executives of these firms used to regularly get together at expensive hotels for trade association meetings, to play golf together, and to exchange Christmas cards. Just as Smith had warned, it was perfectly natural when having drinks with a rival to converse about common concerns—product specifications, labor problems, the state of the business, even prices. In time it was easy enough to drift from general talk about prices into what should or could be done about their deplorable state. Finally, such friendly meetings among rivals evolved into separate meetings called specifically to fix prices for everyone's mutual benefit. What had started as legitimate meetings to exchange information turned into a full-fledged conspiracy to cartelize the industry.

What makes the electrical conspiracy particularly interesting is that the conspirators were caught and convicted, and some executives who were pillars of their communities were sent to jail. Price fixing is illegal; Section 1 of the Sherman Antitrust Act is explicit about that. Any person engaging in such a combination or conspiracy was at that time guilty of a misdemeanor, subject to fine or imprisonment. Altogether, $1,924,500 worth of fines were levied, seven jail terms imposed, and twenty-four suspended sentences handed down. The convicted firms were subject to triple-damage suits by their wronged customers, which cost millions of dollars more before the issue was settled.

The Justice Department eventually found nineteen separate cartels, some of which had been in existence for at least 8 years prior to their discovery. Many had roots going back much further in time. For a number of years the executives of various electrical companies had periodically met to fix prices, divide up markets, and cartelize their industry. Price fixing had become the way of life in the industry. The fact that the conspirators got caught has placed in the public record the information necessary to answer economists' questions about cartels. What were the conditions that led "honest men" to engage in this patently illegal behavior? How were the cartels designed to work? Did they work? What were the consequences for society? How did the conspirators get caught? These are the questions we shall consider.

A necessary condition for forming a cartel is that a limited number of competitors exists in the industry. Economists refer to an industry with few competitors as an oligopoly. The heavy equipment industry is composed of several market segments. General Electric and Westinghouse accounted for 50 to 60 percent of the business in each segment; the remainder, depending upon which segment it was, went to as few as two or as many as twenty other small firms. The product produced by the industry is built to specifications of the buyer or to general industry specifications, so heavy electrical equipment, for all practical purposes, is identical no matter which firm actually produces it. Price is the central selling point in obtaining business. The lowest price receives the business.

In every segment of this oligopoly there existed a mutual interdependence between competitors. The final effect of any price or output decision by one firm depended upon the reaction of its rivals. If a firm raised its price and all other rivals went along, then its share of the business would decline according to the elasticity of the industry demand schedule, but if other firms held to their prices, then the firm that increased its price would suffer a serious loss of business to its rivals. Conversely, if one firm lowered its offer price and everyone went along, the business would increase according to the industry demand schedule, but if other firms held their prices constant, the firm lowering its prices would gain a substantial increase in business. Every industry executive who testified about the conspiracy stated that this was so. Either you met or bettered the lowest bid or you lost the business.

Heavy electrical equipment is a producer-durable good, and as such the demand is highly cyclical. The demand for electrical equipment is derived almost equally from industrial firms and electric utility companies. Much of the demand is generated by new construction. Investment, as is well known, is the most cyclical of the major components of gross national product. It can be delayed during bad times, awaiting better economic conditions. One of the conspirators summed up the conditions of industry demand: "This is a feast or famine business."

The production of heavy electrical equipment requires great deal of capital. Rival firms had built expensive plants to deal with peak industry demand; consequently, each was saddled with heavy overhead costs. When the expected business did not materialize at existing price levels, as during a recession, the tendency was to attempt to attract business away from rivals by lowering prices. According to a former general manager of General Electric's switchgear division, "Everybody has their plant in shape. They have the facility. They have the organization. But they have no business. So, they are out grabbing."

But lower prices, if they are matched by rivals, will not solve either the firm's or the industry's problem. The price elasticity of demand for heavy electrical equipment is inelastic. The problem of too little business is caused by a high income elasticity of demand for these capital goods responding to falling national income. No amount of price cutting, if it is matched by rivals, will generate the business needed to operate each firm in the industry near capacity. What price cutting will do is to destroy the profitability of whatever business does exist. Rival firms, because much of their costs are fixed, will continue to meet a price cut until price falls to the point at which variable costs are no longer covered before a firm withdraws from the industry. Because variable costs are a small part of total costs, discounts of as much as 60 percent of list prices were at times recorded in the industry. Yet all the rivals stayed in business, "grabbing" for what they could get.

The situation was ripe for a collusive agreement to make whatever business did exist as profitable as possible and to allow all the firms to survive until good times returned. That is what happened. Collusive arrangements during bad times sprang up or were revived throughout the various segments of the industry. During good times, firms within the industry were content to follow the price leader, which was generally General Electric. GE and its rivals published catalogs listing the equipment offered and their prices. GE's book was the industry's price guide. When industry demand declined, individual firms were tempted to offer discounts off book to attract whatever business was available.

The most detailed information we have concerns the switchgear conspiracy because an executive of I.T.E. kept detailed records that he turned over intact to the Justice Department. The switchgear and circuit breaker segment of the heavy electrical equipment market produces components that interrupt and reroute electricity. Industrial switchgear is much like its household counterparts—light switches, fuses, and circuit breakers—but built to giant scale. An industrial circuit breaker, for instance, can be 40 feet long, 26 feet high, and weigh 85 tons. The switchgear conspiracy was the oldest in existence, having been in operation for over a quarter of a century before it was discovered.

Roughly $75 million in business was done annually by this market segment, broken down into two categories: sealed bids and open bids. The sealed bid business accounted for between $15 and $18 million annually. The objective of the conspiracy was to avoid "price wars" by rotating the business on a fixed percentage basis so that GE obtained 45 percent, Westinghouse 35 percent, Allis-Chalmers 10 percent, and Federal Pacific 10 percent. Every 10 days or so, meetings were held to decide whose turn it was to secure the business. Turns were determined from the results of "bidding" during past weeks. Then a "winning bid," or price, was established. A complex schedule of alternative bids was developed, so that if GE was to be the winner at, say, 5 percent below list or book price, then Westinghouse and the other two firms would consult the table to see how much higher they were to bid to ensure that they lost, but to avoid submitting identical bids which might attract attention. Other cartels in other segments of the industry were not as sophisticated and did submit identical losing bids, which came to the attention of the Antitrust Division of the Justice Department, eventually leading to the downfall of all.

How well did this well-organized conspiracy to fix prices work in practice? Surprisingly enough, not very well. The conspiracy to fix prices didn't succeed in suppressing the desire to compete. Rivals agreed and then proceeded to immediately cheat on the agreements. One of the convicted conspirators stated, "No one was living up to the agreements and we at GE were being made suckers. On every job some one would cut our throat; we lost confidence in the group." Executives in the other cartels had similar experiences: "It might be one day, it might be two days, after a meeting before jobs would be bid all over the place"; or, in another case, the agreements "were only as good as the distance to the closest telephone before they were broken."

Broken agreements sometimes led to giant price wars. The so-called white sale developed in 1954–1955 during a national recession, with prices falling as much as 40 to 45 percent off book. Again, during the recession of 1958, a price war broke out with discounts of up to 60 percent quoted. Once executives in the industry felt their firms had suffered enough from a price war, a move would be made to revive the cartel, apparently always with poor results.

It is difficult to determine what consequences these unstable cartels had for society. Had the cartels been enforceable and chiseling eliminated, no doubt they could have been extremely profitable. Perhaps they were, for the executives who participated had a record of merit promotions within their individual firms. The Bureau of Labor Statistics (BLS) price index for switchgear increased 7 percent faster during the decade of the 1950s than the price index for machinery and equipment in general. But the BLS index was based upon list or book prices, not upon actual transaction prices, so that it actually recorded increases during the white sale, when transaction prices were tumbling down. Probably the most serious consequence of the cartel, had it been successful, would have been to delay the reallocation of resources out of the overinvested heavy electrical equipment industry into other areas where capital would have been more socially profitable. But there is serious question as to whether any of the conspiracies to fix prices were ever successful for very long.

The periodic meetings did, however, provide attending executives with information as to how their rivals felt about business conditions and gave them an idea of how their rivals would react to different situations should they develop. In an industry with such extreme mutual interdependence, this in itself was valuable information. Furthermore, the potential gains for each firm in the conspiracy, if the cartel had worked, would have been great. The chances of being caught were judged to be small; since all the conspirators were in it together, no one would talk, so how could they ever be caught?

But they did get caught. The Justice Department received complaints from the industry's customers about high and often identical sealed bids and began to investigate. Many of the buyers of heavy electrical equipment suspected price fixing and said so. A grand jury was impaneled and began to subpoena executives as witnesses to testify under oath.

Executives who had conspired began to run scared, offering, as John Dean would later do in the Watergate coverup, to testify if granted immunity from prosecution. The smaller firms such as Allis-Chalmers and I.T.E. decided to play ball with the government, and the case was made when I.T.E.'s sales manager for switchgear turned over all the records of the cartel for which he had served as secretary. He had taken his job seriously, recording all that had transpired. This evidence provided the Justice Department with its case.

American industry had learned a lesson. Price fixing was now more dangerous than ever. Nevertheless, the conditions that led to the conspiracy are present in many industries: few rivals, identical products, production requiring extensive capital, and highly cyclical demand. When these conditions exist, a powerful incentive also exists to find some way to avoid drastic price reductions.

The lesson of the incredible electrical conspiracy is that even explicit agreements may not be able to stifle competitive rivalry among business firms. Certainly price conspiracies such as those in the heavy electrical industry are potentially dangerous and expensive. Executives caught and convicted are likely to be sent to jail and their firms fined and subjected to triple-damage suits by their customers. One executive, quoted by *Fortune*

(May, 1961, p. 224), stated: "One thing I've learned out of all this is to talk to only one other person, not to go to meetings where there are lots of people." Perhaps he was reminded of Will Roger's famous statement about political corruption: "Either these fellers must stop doin' it, or stop getting caught." Extreme mutual interdependence such as exists in the electrical equipment industry and in many other industries today creates the desire among the industry executives for a means to increase price stability and profitability. Adam Smith's dictum, quoted at the beginning of this chapter, about what happens when "people of the same trade meet together" still may be operative, but after the incredible electrical conspiracy, the meetings are certainly smaller.

Additional Readings

Backman, Jules. *The Economics of the Electrical Machinery Industry.* New York University Press, 1962, Chaps. 5 and 6.

Fuller, John. *The Gentlemen Conspirators.* Grove, 1962.

Hearings on Administered Price by the U.S. Senate Committee on the Judiciary, Subcommittee on Antitrust and Monopoly. *Price-fixing and Bid-rigging in the Electrical Manufacturing Industry,* Parts 27 and 28. 87th Congress, 1st session, April, May, and June 1961.

Herling, John. *The Great Price Conspiracy: The Story of the Antitrust Violations in the Electrical Industry.* Robert B. Luce, 1962.

Smith, Richard Austin. "The Incredible Electrical Conspiracy." *Fortune,* April –May 1961.

Wall Street Journal. January 10 and 12, 1962.

Walton, Clarence C. and Frederick W. Cleaveland, Jr. *Corporations on Trial: The Electric Cases.* Wadsworth, 1964.

Preview

The New York Stock Exchange used to be organized as a cartel. A limited number of seats were available, which allowed only the owners, called members, to trade stocks on the exchange, and members of the exchange could only trade stocks at a fixed commission rate. The results were high profits and high prices for seats on the exchange. During 1975, the Securities and Exchange Commission ruled that fixed commission rates were illegal, reviving price competition and lowering commission rates charged to customers. The result was also a drastic fall in the price of a seat on the New York Stock Exchange, reflecting the decline in monopoly profits.

Key Economic Points

A cartel is a group of firms that agree to act as if they were a single firm (a monopoly) in making price and output decisions.

Rules and regulations for membership behavior are necessary for the New York Stock Exchange to function as a cartel.

The extent of potential monopoly profits available to members of the cartel is measured by the price of seats.

Competition within the cartel was not eliminated by price fixing but was directed to nonprice methods (such as free services).

The elimination of price fixing led to lower costs for trading stocks and to the demise of free services.

Benefits and costs of a competitive market are compared with the benefits and costs of a cartel.

19

Regulation: The Demise of a Cartel—The New York Stock Exchange

Once upon a time, not so long ago, being a member of the New York Stock Exchange was synonymous with having great wealth. Individuals who owned seats on the exchange reportedly had it made. They earned large incomes, lived on Long Island estates, and arrived on Wall Street in chauffeur-driven limousines. Perhaps this was once so, but it is true no longer. The world of the stockbroker has recently undergone a radical change.

There is still a lot of public misunderstanding about the New York Stock Exchange. Most people think the stock exchange sells stock. It doesn't. It doesn't buy stock either. It is simply a marketplace where thousands of individuals, through their agents, the brokers, buy and sell shares in publicly held corporations. The broker, who is a member of the exchange, arranges the purchase or sale of the customer's stock at the best price currently offered in an auction market. These trades take place in a big building at the corner of Wall and Broad Streets in New York City. The trading room looks like a big basketball arena, with a trading floor about half the size of a football field. There brokers acting on their customers' behalf offer and bid for millions of shares of stock daily. The brokers make their living on the commissions charged when a purchase or sale is completed.

A keen observer would note that there are no chairs or seats to be found anywhere on the trading floor; the brokers all stand to transact their business. Nevertheless, membership in the New York Stock Exchange is referred to as "owning a seat" on the exchange, a phrase carried over from the past. The owner of a seat shares with other members the exclusive right to trade the stocks listed on the exchange. The firms listed by the exchange are the biggest and most important in the nation. In fact, over 80 percent of all stock trading takes place on the New York Stock Exchange, or "Big Board," as it is sometimes known. In the early 1970s more than 4 billion shares of stock worth about $150 trillion were annually exchanged for the public by members of the exchange. Until 1975, brokers charged a fixed fee set by the exchange for this service. The fee averaged out to about 1 percent of the value of the shares exchanged. One percent of $150 trillion, even when split in some fashion among 1,366 seats on the exchange, was a goodly sum, enough to make a healthy income for each member.

In the "good old days," to own a seat on the exchange was to be a member of a highly organized cartel. A cartel is an organization of several individual decision makers who agree to act as if they were a single firm in making price and output decisions. The purpose of any cartel is to secure supernormal profits for its members, profits that would be lost if the individual firms competed among themselves for business. The Big Board secured such profits for its members in the past by a series of rules that each member had to obey or be fined or even expelled from the membership.

The following regulations were the most important in ensuring the profitable operation of the cartel. Shares of listed companies could only be traded on the floor of the New York Stock Exchange by members of the exchange. Every member (broker) had to charge customers a fixed commission set by the exchange for this service. The number of members or seats was limited to 1,366. The exchange maintained a committee to oversee the operations of its members in order to detect and punish any violations of these rules.

As long as these rules were followed, membership in the exchange was very profitable. The exchange set prices well above the cost of providing the service. Because access to this profitable market was limited to members only, there was no way an outsider could share in these profits. It is true that seats on the exchange could be and were sold, but the price at which an owner would sell the seat reflected the future potential profits of membership in the cartel. The value of a seat was thus equal to the discounted value of the monopoly profits to be earned by membership. If a buyer didn't think that membership produced monopoly profits, he or she wouldn't pay anything for a seat on the exchange. Yet an active market in memberships existed, for in any one year about 10 percent of the seats changed hands. The price at which seats themselves are traded is therefore an excellent guide to the extent of the cartel monopoly profits.

The price at which seats themselves are traded used to be a function of the volume of trading on the exchange. Because the commission price was fixed, the monopoly profit earned depended upon the number of shares a member could expect to trade. As the volume of trading on the stock exchange increased, so did the price of a seat; when volume receded, so did the price of a membership. The value of membership in the exchange reached its zenith in late 1968 and early 1969, when seats sold for $515,000 each. Thereafter, despite the fact that the volume of shares traded continued to grow, the price of a seat fell steadily. In 1976, a year in which the exchange traded a record 5 billion shares, a seat sold for only $40,000. The price of membership on the New York Stock Exchange had fallen 92 percent in 7 years.

The decline in the price of a seat on the exchange reflected the decline in monopoly profits gained by exchange membership. What destroyed the cartel? The answer is increased competition among members. In 1965 an individual investor instituted a lawsuit alleging that the New York Stock Exchange violated the antitrust laws. The lawsuit charged that, by enforcing its fixed minimum commission schedule, the exchange was engaging in illegal price fixing. The next year the exchange approached the Securities and Exchange Commission (SEC) with what it regarded as a routine request to increase the fixed minimum commission rates on exchanges of stock. Much to its surprise, the U.S. Department of Justice, agreeing in substance with the lawsuit, submitted an extensive legal brief to the SEC questioning the legality of fixed rates per se. A long debate between the exchange and the two governmental agencies ensued.

The exchange argued that eliminating fixed rates would eventually lead to the destruction of the exchange itself, to the detriment of the nation's capital market. It argued that, in the absence of fixed rates, destructive price competition would result in a highly concentrated industry, in price discrimination in favor of large institutional investors, in a decline in membership, and, finally, in fewer transactions on the exchange, leading to a more inefficient capital market.

Proponents of eliminating fixed minimum commissions argued that none of these results would occur. Breaking up the cartel, they predicted, would lead to more trades on the exchange, not fewer, because higher transaction costs resulting from fixed rates discourage the trading of stocks. Nor would the industry become highly concentrated because the cost conditions involved in trading stocks do not lead to large economies of scale. Large firms could not produce trades at lower costs than smaller firms. Furthermore, any differences in rates between those charged the large institutional trader and those charged the small investor would be the result of cost differences in serving the two types of traders, rather than to price discrimination. The New York Stock Exchange lost the argument, and on May 1, 1975, in accordance with an SEC ruling, fixed minimum commissions became illegal.

The proponents of competitive rate setting were generally correct in predicting the effects of eliminating fixed rates. The New York Stock Exchange, 3 years after the advent of competitive rates, did more business than ever, exchanging almost 6 billion shares which accounted for over 85 percent of all stock traded in the country, up almost 5 percent from pre-1975 levels. The cost for an investor of trading stock has fallen. The cost for institutional customers declined nearly 50 percent between May 1975, and December 1977, or over 65 percent in real terms considering the effects of inflation. The aggregate decline for individuals has been less but is still substantial at over 30 percent. Even small investors have benefited, their real costs declining by 12 percent.

While it is true that the purchaser of 200 shares or less at a time now pays a higher commission rate than the institutional investor trading thousands of shares, the difference is due to costs of trading, not to price discrimination. A broker simply does not incur 200 times as much expense when arranging the purchase or sale of $1 million worth of IBM stock as when arranging a $5,000 transaction. With more than 350 brokerage firms competing for business, you would expect a lower commission rate on the exchange of large blocks of stock than on small trades.

Nor has the brokerage industry become significantly more concentrated since the demise of fixed rates. In 1975, the largest 25 firms did 51.7 percent of the brokerage business; the largest 10, 32.6 percent. By the end of 1977, the largest 25 firms had increased their share of the brokerage business to 56.4 and the top 10 to 33.4. It appears that middle-size firms have not expanded their share of the market by very much. Despite a few well-publicized mergers, the structure of the brokerage industry has not become highly concentrated and still qualifies as highly competitive.

What has changed is the nature of competition in the brokerage industry. Prior to May Day, 1975, a brokerage firm could not attract customers by offering a lower price for services. But it could increase the quality of the services. Each individual broker could be provided with instant quotations by computer and with the results of the research department's recommendations to pass along free to investors. Brokers often offered to manage the customer's money at below cost, published monthly newsletters, and provided comfortable areas where investors could pass the time watching ticker tape results of the day's trading on the exchange. Fixed minimum commission rates led to various nonprice forms of competition as the member firms of the New York Stock Exchange competed for customers in nonprice ways.

The end of fixed commissions led to a change in the competitive behavior of brokerage firms. Price could now be used to attract customers. Most firms reduced both the price they charged for trading stocks and the amount of free service they provided to their customers. Some firms began to charge for formerly free services. Special discount brokerage firms came into existence, offering nothing but the ability to trade stocks, but at discounts of up to 80 percent of the fees charged by the full-service brokerage houses. After May Day, 1975, the investor in the stock market was offered more alternatives by the brokerage houses than were available when fixed commission rates were the rule.

The SEC decision to outlaw fixed minimum commission rates effectively destroyed the cartel. The results were much as economic theory would predict: lower commission rates and a higher volume of stock trades. None of the adverse developments predicted by the exchange occurred, but one which the members had not mentioned did occur. The value of the seats they held fell with the decline of their cartel and the advent of competition between members. As competition developed, the supernormal profits once gained by the cartel disappeared and so did the premium an outsider was willing to pay to obtain exchange membership. By 1977, the price of a seat on the exchange was less than the price of purchasing the medallion required to legally operate one taxicab on the streets of New York City. So far had the mighty fallen, that a taxicab medallion represented greater wealth than did a seat on the New York Stock Exchange.

Additional Readings

Flaherty, Robert J. "Comes the Revolution." *Forbes,* November 1, 1977.

New York Stock Exchange Fact Book. New York Stock Exchange, annual.

West, Richard R. "Broker's Fortunes Since 'May Day.' " *Wall Street Journal,* November 24, 1978.

IV

FACTOR MARKETS

Preview

There is an often expressed fear among sports fans that the richest professional teams, such as the New York Yankees baseball team, will buy all the best players to ensure winning the championship. Economic theory provides good reasons that this will not happen. In this chapter the economic theory of the demand for a factor of production is applied to reveal why it would not pay any single team to acquire all the best players.

Key Economic Points

The demand for superstars is derived from the demand for game tickets by fans.

The best athletes can increase the demand for tickets by demonstrating superior skills and by helping teams to win more games.

The addition of another good athlete on a team, like any factor of production, is subject to diminishing marginal factor productivity.

Profit-seeking professional teams will be interested in both the productivity of an athlete and the acquisition price.

Demand for a Factor of Production: Will the Yankees Buy All the Best Baseball Players?

The New York Yankees have been called, among other things, "the best team that money can buy" because of the manner in which the team was assembled. The star players on the Yankees were acquired by trades with other teams for players and money, and more recently by direct purchase in the free agent draft. By contrast, their frequent World Series rivals, the Kansas City Royals, are mostly composed of players signed out of high school or college and developed on farm teams. This latter method has been the traditional way to build a pennant winner ever since Branch Rickey used it to make the St. Louis Cardinals a dominant team in the 1920s.

The Yankee approach of directly purchasing the talent needed to field a winning team has been quite successful. The Yankees won the American League Pennant in 1976, 1977, and 1978, and were also World Champions in 1977 and 1978. Prior to that, the team had not won a pennant since 1964 and had not been World Champions since 1962. The success of the Yankees "new" approach to building a winning team has come in for its share of criticism. In the view of the non-Yankee fans, the Yankees are the personification of all that is wrong with championship by checkbook. There is also the often-expressed fear that the Yankees will continue to dominate the league play by buying all the best players. Something must be done, so the argument goes, to keep the Yankees from stockpiling all the best players.

Is it true that the Yankees will buy all the best players? What principles guide a business person in deciding how much of a factor of production to purchase? After all, the owner of the Yankees, George Steinbrenner, is a successful shipbuilder. Steinbrenner knows that a firm demanding a factor of production, whether it is the American Shipbuilding Company or the New York Yankees, derives its demand from the demand for the final product. The shipbuilding company's demand for steel depends upon the demand for ships. The Yankees' demand for star players depends upon the fans' demand to attend the baseball games.

The Yankees or any other ball team's demand for star players depends upon the contribution another star will make to attendance at ball games and upon the price that can be charged for tickets. Whether the Yankees will acquire another star player also depends upon the price of the star relative to the prices of substitute factors, in this case existing or available ball players. The Yankees, like any other business firm, will consider the benefit–cost ratio of adding another star with the existing benefit–cost ratio of employing an average ball player. If contracting another star will add more to profits than employing the current team member, the Yankees will attempt to obtain him.

The season's attendance for a major league baseball team is determined by a number of factors, such as the size of the population in the team's location, the personal income of the fans, the ticket price, and the size, location, and condition of the stadium. Generally, the most important factor is the size of population in the team's urban area. Larger cities such as New York, with a population of almost 10 million, will see more fans attend baseball games than will Minneapolis/St. Paul with a population of 2 million, all other things being equal. Other things are seldom equal, however. The Yankees have to compete directly for the sports fan's dollar with the baseball Mets and less directly with the football Giants and Jets and the basketball Nets and Knicks. The Minnesota Twins face only the football Vikings. Competition for the sports fans' dollars causes more professional teams to locate in the large urban areas, which tends to equalize the drawing power of all professional teams wherever they are located.

The quality of the competition also affects attendance. The closer the pennant race and the more uncertain its outcome, the more fan interest will be generated. All teams in the league have an interest in competitive balance, close pennant races being good for attendance. The Yankees would not wish to again dominate the American League the way their teams did in the 1950s and early 1960s. When that happened, the National League outdrew the American League substantially because of the closeness of the pennant races in the senior league.

Nevertheless, it is always better for attendance to win a pennant than to finish second. It is even better to win a World Championship. A pennant or World Championship will increase attendance for the next several years. Winning a pennant is reported to be twice as important in determining next year's attendance than merely engaging in a close pennant race. While it is best to win as the Yankees did in 1978 in a do-or-die playoff game, it is still better to win than lose the pennant, even if it takes ten games.

Teams usually win by fielding the best baseball talent—not always, but often enough to make it a rule for the general managers of each team to seriously seek out talented players. As a consequence, competition between rival teams, each seeking to win the pennant, bids up the prices of talented ball players to the point where baseball teams must economize on their use. Baseball teams, like any other business firm, will acquire talented players up to the point where the value of the additional attendance just equals the cost of the ball player.

Talented ball players add to attendance by winning ball games and by athletic achievement superior enough to warrant the label "superstar." Superstars such as American League players Jim Rice, Rod Carew, and Reggie Jackson add to attendance in their own right. It has been estimated that the first superstar on a team playing in a city of 3.5 million will increase attendance by an estimated 150,000 fans. That's worth $750,000 in increased revenues to ball teams. The first superstar on a team playing in a larger market area such as New York is worth even more, perhaps increasing attendance by 500,000 fans. The superstar will also help his team win more games and make the pennant race closer, which will also boost attendance. In 1977, when Oakland lost six of its better players in the free agent draft, attendance fell by 285,000 fans. Likewise, when the New York Mets traded superstar Tom Seaver, attendance fell by 406,000. In contrast, when the California Angels signed Joe Rudi, Bobby Grich, and Don Baylor as free agents for the 1977 season, despite the fact that these men were not true superstars and that the team did substantially worse in winning games than it had in 1976, it drew 400,000 more people.

A second superstar will not add as much to attendance as did the first. In fact, one estimate suggests that a second superstar adds only half as much to attendance as the first one. The reason for this is obvious. Some of the fans who would have been attracted to see the second superstar already were attracted to see the first. A second superstar will also not help the team win as many more games as the first.

The contribution of the second superstar may at times merely duplicate the efforts of the first, causing the team to win by a larger number of runs games that would have been won anyway. Reggie Jackson was credited with seventeen game-winning hits in 1977, but the Yankees won only three more games than they had the previous season without Jackson. The productivity of the second superstar is simply less than that of the first because of the inevitable duplication of efforts, so that the value of a second superstar to the Yankees decreases. At some point the value of an additional superstar to the Yankees will decline below the value of the first superstar to a team such as Seattle or Minnesota. The Yankees will then drop out of the bidding and Seattle will obtain the player. This does suggest that the Yankees will always have more of the better players and will win proportionally more pennants than will teams located in smaller cities. But they will not acquire all the best players, and they have not. Rod Carew, the best hitter in baseball, went to the California Angels in 1979, not to the Yankees, and most of the starting players for the American League in the annual All-Star Game are not New York Yankees.

In some cases, especially for a pitcher, it is not very difficult to roughly calculate the contribution an individual player makes to a club's total revenues. Vida Blue's agent pointed out to Charlie Finley, the Oakland Athletics' owner, that whenever Vida pitched the attendance at a game increased over the average game attendance. The same was true during 1976 whenever Mark Fidrych pitched for the Detroit Tigers, and in 1978 and 1979 whenever Ron Guidry pitched for the Yanks. Whenever Guidry pitched the Yanks averaged 34,000 persons in attendance, but whenever he didn't pitch the average was only 25,000. Thus Guidry was responsible for increasing attendance over 180,000, which is worth over $900,000 in added revenue to the team. This probably overrates Guidry's contribution to the Yankees' treasury because some people who would have attended another Yankee game may have postponed going until Guidry was scheduled to pitch.

In other cases it is not as easy to calculate the marginal contribution of a professional athlete. Most professional sports are team games, so it is difficult to precisely calculate the contribution of one player relative to another. Professional teams overcome this difficulty by employing a manager or coach and a general manager whose job it is to judge the talent of players and fit them into a winning program, acquiring talent as it is needed. If they succeed, they are rewarded; if they fail, they are fired. The turnover among the coaches and managers of big league teams has approached 50 percent during recent seasons in some sports.

The best team money can buy provides one example of how this can be done. Attempting to produce a winner, like anything else, entails risks. The Yankees recognized this fact. The general manager of the team was quoted as saying: "There's no substitute for talent. The club's got the money, and we can afford the luxury of making mistakes on players." The 1975 signing of pioneer free agent "Catfish" Hunter may have been a mistake. Hunter as a Yankee did not live up to his past performance. But the Yankees perservered. In 1976 they won the pennant, but lost the World Series in four straight games. Against the Cincinnati Reds in the World Series they scored only eight runs while surrendering twenty-two. In order to become World Champion, the Yankees' management figured that they needed more pitching and more batting power. The free agent draft was the vehicle chosen to acquire the needed talent. The Yankees signed pitcher Don Gullett and outfielder Reggie Jackson. Jackson, an outfielder, was signed to provide the needed batting power. The Yankees, who were relatively weak in the outfield, agreed to pay Jackson $2.9 million over 5 years. They could have acquired Sol Bando instead for half the price. Bando possessed almost equally impressive statistics as a power hitter, but was a third baseman. The Yankees already had Craig Nettles at third base, and Nettles, who was then paid only $100,000 a year, had even better statistics than Bando. Nettles' ability relative to his price was a better deal than Bando, and Jackson relative to existing Yankee outfielders was, even at $600,000 a year, a good deal if his acquisition would ensure a world championship. It did.

The Yankees have been successful in acquiring the players that have enabled the team to become World Champions (1977 and 1978), but they have not acquired all the best players available. Both Rod Carew and Pete Rose became available at the end of the 1978 season. The Yankees acquired neither, and not because they couldn't afford the multimillion dollar contracts. The Yankees in 1977 took in $13 million from ticket sales at the gate and concession stands and another $3 million from broadcast rights. The total payroll for players was just $3.5 million. Nor was it because Carew refused to play for the Yankees. He was quoted as being willing if the Yankees would pay the most money. The Yankees chose not to add another superstar because it would not have been profitable to do so.

The increase in attendance to be gained by adding Rod Carew or Pete Rose to the lineup of World Champions who were already attracting over 2 million fans a season would not be as great as their contribution to ticket sales of most other teams. When Carew, for example, signed a $4 million contract for 5 years with the California Angels, the team the very next day sold 147 season tickets to new customers, adding over $50,000 to revenues. Sports writers following the Carew story felt that signing the superstar might well repay the expense in season ticket sales alone. The Yankees, already possessing a number of superstars, probably would not have found Carew's ability to attract new fans anywhere near as great in New York City as it was in the Los Angeles area, not because Carew is less popular among New Yorkers than among Californians, but because the Yankees already possess several superstars.

What these examples illustrate is that adding more of a factor of production, even a superstar, will at some point result in diminishing returns. Thereafter, adding another unit will add less to output than previous units did.

The New York Yankees reached this point late in the 1970s after 3 years of buying talent. George Steinbrenner, reflecting upon the Yankees' past, stated in 1977: "I had to go into the market and buy and make trades. I didn't have time to develop young players then. But now, within the next two years, we'll really be feeding great young players into the Yankee system." The Yankees haven't acquired all the best players in baseball and won't in the future because it simply doesn't pay to do so. The law of diminishing returns sees to that.

Additional Readings

Durso, Joe. "Success Can't Stop Steinbrenner." *New York Times,* October 24, 1977.

Jacobson, Steven. *The Best Team Money Could Buy.* Atheneum, 1978.

Noll, Roger G. "The U.S. Team Sports Industry: An Introduction" and "Attendance and Price Setting." *Government and the Sports Business.* Brookings Institution, 1974.

Preview

The federal minimum wage law has been on the books for more than 40 years. This law requires business firms engaged in interstate commerce to pay their employees at least a minimum wage. Most workers are paid substantially more than that, but more than 4 million workers are directly affected. In this chapter, the effects of the minimum wage on the U.S. economy are explored in terms of the factors that influence a firm's demand for labor. The results of a minimum wage are found to be mixed. For some, the result is as the law intended—a higher wage; for others, however, the result is the loss of a job. The latter result was certainly not intended by the supporters of minimum wage legislation.

Key Economic Points

What effect does low labor productivity have on low wages?
Why increasing the minimum wage cannot cure poverty for everyone.
Which groups will be most adversely affected by a minimum wage?
How much has the unemployment rate among the young been affected by the minimum wage?
The benefits and costs of the proposals to modify the minimum wage law are weighed.

21

Demand For Labor: The Federal Minimum Wage

During 1977 executives in the fast food industry tried to forestall the increase in the minimum wage legislated for the beginning of 1978 by warning that many workers would have to be laid off. Their warnings were ignored, the minimum wage increased from $2.30 an hour to $2.65 an hour right on schedule, and the predicted "mass layoffs" did not happen. Union leaders who lobbied for the increase had predicted that thousands of workers in the fast food industry would get a well-deserved pay increase. That generally did not happen either. In this chapter we explore the effects of the legal minimum wage on the U.S. economy. By considering the forces that influence a business firm's demand for labor, we will be able to determine who gains and who loses when the minimum wage is increased.

The federal minimum wage was established during the depths of the Great Depression to bolster the paychecks of low-wage workers. In the 40 years since the initial legislation was passed, the law has not only been continued but has been expanded. When the legal minimum wage was raised by 15 percent at the beginning of 1978, more than 4.5 million workers were directly affected. Some, perhaps most, of these workers received an increase in their wages; others saw their hourly pay increase, but the total number of hours they could work each week declined; and some lost their jobs altogether. Among the unfortunate ones in the last category, teenagers, especially minority teenagers, were especially hard hit. The benefits of higher wages for some were acquired at the expense of reduced employment opportunities for others.

The reasons for this are straightforward. Although Congress and the President can increase the legal minimum wage they cannot legislate labor productivity. Business firms will hire workers only as long as the value of the output the worker produces is at least equal to the wage rate. The legal requirement that higher wages be paid implies that some workers—those whose output is worth less than the minimum wage—will be let go. When the price of low-wage labor increases relative to the prices of other factors in the production process, business firms react by conserving on the now relatively more expensive factor, substituting, where economical, other inputs into the production process.

The fast food industry responded to the higher minimum wage in 1978 by conserving on labor, which had become more expensive. Some workers who quit were not replaced. Others found their work hours reduced. The *Wall Street Journal,* December 9, 1977, reported one instance in which a worker who usually worked 23 hours a week was reduced to 18 hours, her earnings actually falling from $53 a week to $48. She also had 5 more hours of spare time a week. One fast food chain introduced new overnight roast beef cookers in response to the higher legal minimum wage and started their early shift workers at 7 a.m. rather than 6 a.m., cutting the work week of employees by 5 hours. As a result, the employees' take home pay increased by only 2.4 percent rather than the expected 13 percent. Employment opportunities in the fast food industry were reduced in response to the increase in the minimum wage. While the predicted massive layoffs did not occur, neither did employees benefit as much as a simple reading of the law would suggest.

Who bears the burden of a higher minimum wage when its effects on the overall economy are considered? It will surely be the least productive, least skilled workers, those whose hourly product when sold in the market is now worth less than the increased minimum wage. Many, if not most, such workers are teenagers, who because they are just beginning in the labor force are relatively unskilled and inexperienced. Because there are proportionately more teenagers in the low-wage category, any effect upon the employment opportunities caused by increasing the minimum wage falls disproportionately upon them. The average wage paid to an employed teenager during 1977 was $2.58, which was 28 cents above the 1977 minimum, but 7 cents below the 1978 minimum. Teenage unemployment during 1978 ran at better than 16 percent, and the jobless rate among minority youths was close to 35 percent. Teenagers are probably the only group in the economy that loses more to reduced employment opportunities when the minimum wage increases than it gains by higher wage rates.

One point often raised in support of the minimum wage is that it is a way of eliminating menial, "dead end" jobs. Employers, responding to an increased minimum wage by substituting capital for labor, eliminate these jobs. But the unemployment that results from the replacement of, for example, manually operated elevators with automatic elevators is not necessarily socially welcome. Menial jobs, such as elevator operator, provide employment opportunities for young people going to school, or to persons who are unable to obtain the basic educational skills or who suffer physical handicaps that keep them from holding jobs that require higher skill qualifications. Moreover, not all menial jobs eliminated by higher minimum wages are dead ends. Many newspaper reporters and editors began as copy persons, just as some business executives began as mail room and delivery clerks. These low-level jobs can provide an alternative to formal education as a way to develop the experience and skills to qualify for higher skilled positions.

Economists have long recognized that establishing a wage floor creates unemployment for some. The important social questions become: how much unemployment is created by increases in the minimum wage, who will be affected, and where will it occur? Economists have assembled a great deal of evidence on the extent to which legislated pay increases will affect unemployment, especially teenage unemployment. One study found that changes in the minimum wage occurring during the late 1960s, which raised the minimum by 26 percent, cost teenagers 225,000 jobs, or 17 percent of the youth unemployment total. Another study found that the 25 percent increase in 1974 increased teenage unemployment by 13 percent, which added two percentage points to the teenage unemployment rate. This study suggests that increasing the minimum wage to $2.65 per hour at the beginning of 1978 added 1 percent to the unemployment rate of teenagers reported above, and about 4 percent to the minority youth jobless rate. This is the effect of increasing the rate from $2.30 to $2.65; the contribution of the already existing wage floor to the high teenage unemployment is not reported. Another investigator reported an inelastic price elasticity of demand for teenage labor of −0.3. A price elasticity of this amount suggests that a 13 percent increase in the minimum wage, as occurred in 1978, would reduce teenage employment prospects by almost 4 percent.

The effect of the minimum wage upon employment opportunities would be expected to vary between industries. It will be lowest in industries (1) for which there are few possibilities for substituting other factors for labor, (2) for which substitutes are available but difficult to obtain, (3) for which the final product is not very responsive to changes in the product price because labor costs have increased, and (4) for which low-wage labor is a small part of the total costs of production; that is, industries in which the price elasticity of demand for low-wage labor is very low. It is unlikely that low-wage laborers employed in petroleum refining and computer manufacturing, which meet these criteria, would find their employment opportunities reduced very much by an increase in the minimum wage.

Unfortunately, such industries are not large employers of low-wage workers.

It is more likely that increases in the legal minimum wage will adversely affect employment (1) if it is easy to substitute other easily obtainable factors of production for low-wage workers, (2) if the price elasticity of demand for the final product is high, and (3) if the proportion of low-wage labor in the total cost of production is large. Industries that meet these specifications, such as textile and clothing manufacturers, are also potentially the largest employers of low-wage workers.

Most industries probably fall somewhere between these two extremes. Industries employing the greatest number of low-wage employees are retail sales (especially department, discount, and grocery stores), hotels and motels, service stations, cleaners and custodial services, and fast food restaurants.

The response of the fast food industry to increases in the minimum wage is probably typical of the responses of other major employers of low-wage labor. We saw above that the initial effects were not as severe as industry spokespersons would have had us believe. It is possible to some extent to substitute capital for labor. The introduction of slow cookers has already been mentioned. McDonald's employs smart machines to aid in preparing burgers, fries, and shakes. Partially in response to increases in the minimum wage, the firm recently introduced automatic cash registers that calculate the total bill, complete with sales tax, thus reducing the labor time in filling orders. Moreover, these machines can be connected to a computer that keeps track of sales so that labor hours can be better scheduled to meet demand. Other fast food chains have begun to employ a central commissary to prepare and freeze the food sold at local outlets, relying upon microwave ovens to heat the food piping hot before it is served. This changeover conserves on low-wage labor employed at the individual outlets.

There are several other ways of conserving on labor in the fast food industry. Besides directly substituting capital for labor, firms may close earlier or open later, eliminating marginally profitable hours of operations. It is perhaps more difficult now to buy a hamburger late at night than it used to be. Another possibility that fast food chains are exploring is to hire housewives rather than teenagers. Housewives generally demand more than the minimum wage, but don't come and go as fast as teenagers. The narrowing differential between what is necessary to pay homemakers and what must be paid teenagers, considering the savings in training costs, may render it advantageous to employ homemakers, further reducing the employment opportunities for youth in the fast food industry.

Initially the effect of the increased minimum wage upon the fast food industry's demand for labor was mitigated by the other forces that influence that demand. The price elasticity of demand for the final product of the fast food industry is probably close to 1, so that small changes in price will scarcely affect total sales revenue. Moreover, in the fast food industry labor accounts for about 25 percent of total costs, so a 13 percent increase in the minimum wage would, ignoring the possibilities for factor substitution, increase retail prices by only 3.25 percent, approximately the increase that took place in the fast food industry in early 1978. The unitary price elasticity of demand and the low proportion of total costs accounted for by labor are probably the major reasons that the predicted massive layoffs did not occur in the fast food industry when the minimum wage went up.

But it takes time for any firm to seek out all the possibilities for substituting other factors for labor. The quest for laborsaving devices continues. A McDonald's spokesperson quoted in the *Wall Street Journal,* December 15, 1977, stated:

Higher labor costs intensify the search for productivity, and we'll be putting more money into research. But I can't tell you that tomorrow we'll be installing machines that cook hamburgers without us having to turn them. It doesn't work that way.

So the full effects of increases in the minimum wage take time to develop, and the eventual result will be a further reduction of employment possibilities for low-wage workers in the fast food industry as well as elsewhere.

The current rate of joblessness among the young is unacceptably high and the minimum wage is a contributing factor. Furthermore, the official rate of unemployment probably understates the actual unemployment of the young. This is because a significant number of youths facing limited employment opportunities simply withdraw from the labor market. Such persons are no longer considered unemployed. Only 65 percent of white male youths and 40 percent of black male youths are in the labor force, a considerable decline from a generation ago.

Repeal of the minimum wage would seem an obvious solution and one favored by many, if not most, economists. But the minimum wage has broad-based political support, not only from union leaders, who see it as a substitute for immediate unionization of the unorganized sectors of the economy, but also from some business executives. A 1973 survey of 100 executives in as many industries reported that 53 percent supported the general idea of a minimum wage.

Given the political support that has kept a minimum wage on the statute books for more than 40 years, critics of the law seem to have turned from advocating repeal to proposing modifications that would eliminate some of the law's worst effects. One proposal to reduce the adverse effects of the minimum wage on teenage employment opportunities is to have a lower minimum wage for this age group. This is often referred to as the "teenwage." A study done by the chief economist of the U.S. Chamber of Commerce estimated that a teenwage 15 percent below the minimum wage for adults would have preserved 364,000 jobs for teenagers that were lost by 1978, and a teenwage 25 percent below the adult minimum would have saved 617,000 jobs, which amounts to 38 percent of the 1978 teenage unemployment.

The proposal for a teenwage has not been well received. Congress debated and rejected this idea in 1971, in 1974, and again in 1978. Opponents of the program point out that a lower wage for teenagers opens up possibilities for business to substitute lower paid teenagers for low-wage adult labor. It is thus possible that, with a subminimum wage, white teenagers from fairly well-to-do families might replace some low-wage black adult heads of families.

A second proposal is to subsidize on-the-job training to allow teenagers who do not qualify, or do not wish to pursue subsidized formal education, to choose subsidized on-the-job training instead. Under one proposal, the government would issue vouchers to young persons looking for jobs. Those who accept jobs at the minimum wage would give the voucher to an employer, who would turn it in to the government for a payment of between 30 and 40 percent of the minimum wage. The employer would be obligated to spend all, or part, of the subsidy training the young worker. The young worker would receive the minimum wage and on-the-job training. The training, by increasing skill levels, would presumably lead to higher paying jobs, stronger job attachment, and less teenage unemployment.

Critics of the program believe that if every youth were given a voucher, the affluent, who generally don't need the help, would also receive the training. Trade unions see the proposal as a disguised means of circumventing the minimum wage. If the employer did not provide the training but accepted the subsidy anyway, the effect would be the same as the teenwage, except that the teenager would receive the full minimum wage. The same potentially adverse substitution possibilities would exist as under the teenwage proposal.

The federal minimum wage has raised the incomes of millions of low-wage workers. But these benefits have not been obtained without social costs. The biggest social cost is the reduction in employment opportunities for the nation's youth. It is widely believed that the nation's poor should be helped, but it is questionable as to whether the minimum wage is an effective tool for alleviating poverty. The minimum wage is at best an imperfect tool for altering the distribution of income, since remedying the poverty of some of the poor through higher wages comes at the expense of others who were equally poor, but are now unemployed.

Additional Readings

Falconer, Robert T. "The Minimum Wage: A Perspective." *Quarterly Review,* Federal Reserve Bank of New York, Autumn 1978.

Gramlich, Edward M. "Impact of Minimum Wages on Other Wages, Employment, and Family Incomes." *Brookings Papers on Economic Activity*, 2, Brookings Institution, 1976.

Ingrassia, Paul. "Quick Adjustment." *Wall Street Journal*, December 19, 1977.

Mincer, Jacob. "Unemployment Effects of Minimum Wages." *Journal of Political Economy*, August 1976.

Ragan, James, Jr. "Minimum Wages and the Youth Labor Market." *Review of Economics and Statistics*, May 1977.

Preview

The superstars of the pop music field earn fabulous amounts of money annually. It is not unusual for a rock 'n roll star to earn more in a year than the average American worker earns in a lifetime. Such extraordinary incomes naturally raise the question: how could anyone be worth that kind of money? This chapter explores the answers to this question. First the reasons that society pays superstars so much money are explored. Then the question of whether or not this is too much is considered within the context of a discussion of the existence and function of economic rent in the economy as a whole and in the music business in particular.

Key Economic Points

Economic rent is defined.

The concept of economic rent is applied to the gains from trade in the market.

Do economic rents exist in the music business and, more generally, in the economy as a whole?

The usefulness of economic rents in the efficient allocation of resources is evaluated.

Economic Rent: Superstars of Rock 'n Roll

The fastest way to make a fortune today is to become a music superstar; it's better in some ways than just being a millionaire. The typical millionaire becomes one only after years of working, saving, and investing; a music superstar often makes his or her fortune almost overnight. There are at least seventy individuals and groups in the music field that make between $1 million and $12 million a year. A few of the music millionaires are older country and pop singers, such as Johnny Cash, Buck Owens, and Andy Williams, but most are young rock 'n roll stars.

Fantastic wealth comes early to the superstars of rock. Alice Cooper, the "freak" rock star of the early 1970s, was 24 when he drew his first million out of the bank in cash, to pose for publicity pictures of him playing with it in imitation of the Disney cartoon character Scrooge McDuck. That afternoon of fun and games cost Alice $3,270 in interest penalties. Consider the example of ex-Monkee Michael Nesmith. He was able by age 26 to accumulate over $1 million in his checking account. He actually was worried that he was going to run out of squares in his bank book to record his money. Unlike Alice Cooper, when Nesmith drew out his money, he spent it, which was not unusual for music millionaires. By the age of 29 he was broke. There are reports of top performers running through as much as $3 million in a single year. In the fickle world of rock music, a performer typically doesn't stay on top very long,* but even a short stay at the top is enough to make a fortune.

There are exceptions. The Rolling Stones were still on top more than a decade after their rivals, the Beatles, split up. Chicago, a group formed in the windy city in 1967, is also an exception. Initially called The Big Thing, the group became superstars after changing their name and moving to Los Angeles. Chicago has been at the top ever since. Each of the group's first twelve records sold over 2.5 million copies, worth over $300 million at retail. Chicago earns about $10 million a year, which when split among the band's eight members qualifies each performer as a music millionaire.

Most of the earnings of rock 'n roll stars come from record sales. During the 1970s record sales boomed. Every year more than seventy albums went platinum, selling over 1 million copies. Some records did so much better that it was necessary to coin new words such as "a monster" or "a gorilla" to refer to their "King Kong" sales. "Saturday Night Fever" sold over 15 million and Fleetwood Mac's "Rumors" sold 12 million copies. Other gorillas that sold over 6 million albums were "Songs in the Key of Life" by Stevie Wonder, "Come Alive" by Peter Frampton, and "Hotel California" by the Eagles.

The performers get a percentage of the price of each record sold. Beginners generally get 4 percent of list, about 30 cents on a typical LP after recording expenses are deducted. It takes sales of 100,000 just to break even. On sales of 1 million the beginning performer comes out with about $225,000. But that's just for performing. Most performers write their own songs, so they earn an additional royalty on the songs, about 15 cents a copy. Superstars do even better because they can command a higher percentage. Some command a so-called 16 percent deal which earns them about a dollar a record. The Beatles at their peak earned between $10 million and $20 million a year from their record sales.

Recording contracts typically call for twelve records or 5 years, whichever comes last. One rock manager calls the system "volunteered slavery" but the "slaves get to ride around in a Mercedes." In order to induce superstars to sign such long contracts, the recording companies often have to sweeten the deal. Guarantees abound and each superstar wants to have the biggest contract. The Rolling Stones demanded more than Stevie Wonder, and ex-Beatle Paul McCartney wanted one bigger than the Stones. McCartney reportedly signed for a guarantee of $20 million.

Records provide only part of the income of a superstar. Concerts can be very lucrative. The Rolling Stones every couple of years net several million dollars for a 3-month concert tour of the United States. During the 1978 tour, a Stones concert in the New Orleans Superdome grossed $1.06 million, and the show in Chicago grossed $919,000. The Stones netted more than half the gross for every night's work. Neil Young is perhaps more typical. Young cleared $2 million for a 3-month tour after paying his backup musicians $100,000 each. Other superstars easily do as well. Concert tours and record sales go hand-in-hand, complementing each other in creating music millionaires. Billy Joel reportedly earned $10 million from tours and record sales in 1978.

Observers are often incredulous when they hear of the money that superstars make in rock music. They ask themselves and others how anyone could earn that kind of money in such a short time. Moreover, how could anyone be worth that much? This view is also shared by some on the inside of the business. Singer Johnny Mathis, who himself made $1 million a year during the 1950s and still commands $500,000 a year, thinks: "It's ridiculous. Performers aren't worth this kind of money. In fact, nobody is."

Of course, Mathis is wrong. No one gives the superstars their money. They earn it in trade. Record companies and concert promoters are willing to make the deals that make music millionaires because they also expect to profit thereby. When people pay their hard-earned cash for an album or a concert ticket, it is because they expect to gain more satisfaction that way than from any other use to which they could put their funds.

But there is a sense in which Mathis is right. Rock superstars, or any other kind of superstar, are probably paid more than is necessary to keep them performing. If they were paid less, they would still compose and perform their music. The difference between what they now make as superstars and the earnings that would keep them in the music business is called in economics a "rent." A rent serves no allocative function, because the person would perform even if he or she didn't receive the rent.

One way of looking at the rents received by music superstars is to compare their current incomes, the highest valued use of their time, with their next best alternative. Their next best alternative is what they would do if they couldn't be performers. The late Elvis Presley, for example, was a truck driver before he became a music superstar. Before he died, he could command $150,000 in Las Vegas for 7 nights work. The difference between the two incomes is the rent he earned because of his special talent. It wasn't necessary for society to pay him that rent to ensure his performing music instead of driving a truck. A little bit more than a truck driver's wages could have accomplished the same thing. He was paid more because he attracted enough business to the casino for the owners to make money on the deal. If one casino hadn't paid him what he was worth in the entertainment market, another would have. Competition between hotels ensured that Presley received the full market value of his efforts.

The opportunity cost of Harry Nilsson, a composer and singer, was greater than Elvis'. Nilsson, before he hit it big with two smash albums and four hit singles in one year, worked for a bank during the early 1970s. In fact, he headed the bank's computer section at night and wrote songs during the day. "I loved the bank job," he said. "But I couldn't afford to stay. I was making twice as much in music." Nilsson went on to earn almost

$1 million during 1972. But it wasn't necessary for society to pay him that much to ensure his full time participation in music. Less than twice as much as he made at the bank would have sufficed. The rest of the $1 million was an economic rent.

Take the more recent case of Tom Scholz, the lead guitar player for Boston. Scholz was a 29-year-old senior engineer at Polaroid when Boston's first album took off toward the top of the charts. He had worked his way through MIT and was earning $25,000 a year in the conceptual products design department when he quit. As soon as album sales shot past the 100,000 mark, he gave his supervisor his notice. Here was a case of the leader of a then relatively unknown, unproven group burning his bridges. Scholz went on to become a music millionaire, but it wasn't necessary for society to pay him that much. A little more than he was paid at Polaroid, as his behavior demonstrated, would have been enough.

Rent, which we have considered to be the difference between the payment a factor of production receives and the minimum payment necessary to ensure employment in its highest valued use, is not unique to the music businesss. While it appears in magnified form there, it is present to some extent in almost all factor markets. The real income of college professors fell during the late 1970s as the result of inflation. College teachers' salaries generally did not keep up with inflation, so the purchasing power of their incomes fell. This is the same as taking a cut in pay. Yet few professors left the teaching profession for other occupations. Most professors were earning rents during the boom years of the late 1960s and early 1970s. At that time, relatively higher salaries were necessary to attract new teachers to the colleges and universities that were expanding to handle the "baby boom." The higher salaries required to attract newcomers had to be paid to existing teachers as well. If they hadn't received them, they would have left their old jobs and become some other school's new teacher. There simply was no way to discriminate between existing teachers who were willing to teach at the old salary levels and new teachers who weren't. Now that schools are contracting rather than expanding, the real income of teachers is falling. Some are leaving. Most are just receiving less rent.

Almost all occupations and most units of the other factors of production receive some rents as part of their factor incomes. Rent payments are unnecessary in the sense that the factor would remain in its highest valued use without them. But they are necessary in another sense. It is simply too costly for society to devise ways of eliminating them.

Nor would it necessarily be a good idea to try to do so. The rents that accrue to the owners of the factors of production are part of the gains from trade. Some economists have suggested that rents be taxed because rents are unearned increments and the tax would not alter the efficient allocation of resources. But it is no more legitimate to tax rents because they are considered unearned increments than it is to tax the benefits consumers receive for which they don't pay. Almost everyone when buying a good would be willing to pay more than the market price rather than do without altogether. Economists refer to this unearned increment as consumer surplus. The existence of consumer surplus, like rent, is not needed to ensure the efficient allocation of resources. It is the reward from efficiently allocated resources. Taxing rents would be taxing part of the gains from using the market to allocate resources. It is no more defensible to select rents for tax purposes than to tax the consumers' gains from trade.

Additional Readings

Drinkhall, Jim. "Are Mafia Mobsters Acquiring a Taste for Sound of Rock?" *Wall Street Journal,* January 29, 1979.

"The Gorillas Are Coming. *Forbes,* July 10, 1978.

"The Rockers Are Rolling In It." *Forbes,* April 15, 1973.

Preview

Million dollar employment contracts between star professional athletes and professional teams are becoming increasingly common. Are these contracts really as big as announced in the press? An analysis of several contracts reveals that they often are not. In some cases much of the reported salary is pure public relations hype. In another important sense, the contracts indeed call for the reported amounts, but are misleading because the payments are deferred until a future date. It is a basic principle of economics that money in the future is worth less than money today. In this chapter, the principle of present value is applied to determining the true value of two of the reportedly million dollar sports contracts.

Key Economic Points

The rate of interest plays a crucial role in determining the current value of a future payment.

The application of the concept of present value can determine the value today of a future payment.

23

Present Value: "Million Dollar" Sports Contracts

It is sometimes difficult to distinguish the sports pages in today's newspapers from the business section because of the extended coverage given to the contract negotiations between professional athletes and the teams that employ them. While sports fans have always been interested in the salaries of big league players, this interest, as judged by the space devoted to the subject, has risen with the substantial reported increases in athletes' pay. A little more than a decade ago it was front page news when Joe Namath signed a $400,000 contract with the New York Jets football team. In 1979, when Dave Parker signed a $6.75 million contract with the Pittsburgh Pirates baseball team, it was reported as a regular sports story. Multimillion dollar contracts are no longer big news; dozens of athletes now have them. Parker's contract was merely the biggest at the time.

The salaries of professional athletes have risen dramatically during the past two decades. The rapid increase has been the result of the formation of rival leagues, now mostly gone, the demise of the reserve clause which bound a player for life to the team that originally signed him, and the sports boom in general. There is no doubt that the salaries of professional athletes have increased more rapidly than that of any other professional of late. The average salary of a National Basketball Association player, for instance, is over $100,000 a year, double what it was prior to the formation of the rival American Basketball Association.

Nevertheless, a large portion of the fantastic contracts that have been negotiated in professional sports is public relations hype. Consider the 1975 contract of baseball pitcher "Catfish" Hunter. Hunter became the most valuable free agent in baseball's history when his employer, the Oakland Athletics, failed to live up to terms of his contract. A court of law declared Hunter's contract with the A's null and void, and he was free to negotiate with any team interested in his services. Hunter was at that time one of the best pitchers in baseball. Taking advantage of his opportunity, Hunter negotiated with several clubs to sell his services before agreeing to terms with the New York Yankees. The Yankees announced that they had agreed to pay Hunter $3.75 million for a 5-year exclusive services contract. Catfish Hunter thus took his place with Rembrandt's painting of "Aristotle Contemplating the Bust of Homer" as one of New York's most valuable possessions.

But did Catfish Hunter cost the Yankees as much as Rembrandt's painting cost the Metropolitan Museum of Art? In truth, Hunter cost a great deal less. Much of Hunter's contract called for deferred payments, while the painting cost cash up front. Money to be paid later is worth less than money now. In this chapter the concept of present value will be applied to determining what Catfish Hunter's $3.75 million contract was actually worth.

Hunter, it was reported, would receive $750,000 per year for his efforts. The purported details of his contract were leaked somewhat later to the press. Supposedly he received $1 million as a bonus for signing and a salary of $200,000 per year for 5 years for another million, a deferred salary of $500,000, a $1 million life insurance policy, $200,000 for attorney fees, and a $25,000 life insurance policy on his children. That these amounts total $3.725 million, $25,000 short of the announced figure, went unnoticed, perhaps because the shortage was such a small percentage of the total.

But, more to the point, the contract as reported did not cost the Yankees anywhere near $3.75 million, nor was it worth that much to Hunter when he signed. A paid-up insurance policy of $1 million face value probably costs less than $150,000 for a man like Hunter, who was then in his late 20s. Furthermore, the cost in 1975 of a salary payment that is deferred to sometime in the future is much less than the face amount, as discussed below.

It turned out that the fabled $3.75 million contract was just that—a fable. When a newspaper reporter was allowed to do a story on the finances of the Yankees, among the information he was fed was the Yankees' salary schedule. Catfish Hunter's name appeared third on the list, with a scheduled payment of $260,000 a year, which was clearly inconsistent with the previously reported sum of $750,000 annually. Eventually the details of another contract were published. According to this report, Hunter's contract called for the following total payments equaling $2.892 million:

PRESENT VALUE

	Payments	Actual Value
Salary for 5 years	$500,000	$364,000
Cash bonus for signing	100,000	100,000
Deferred bonus (1985)	250,000	115,750
Deferred salary (1985–2000)	1,500,000	862,400
Insurance policy	500,000	75,000
Scholarship for children	36,000	11,340
New Buick	6,000	6,000
	$2,892,000	$1,554,490

Even if this report is accurate, the actual value of these payments to Hunter when he signed the contract is considerably less than the reported amount (a little more than half). The reason for this is that money delivered in the future is worth less than money today. In order to understand how this could be so, consider how the Yankees could arrange to pay Hunter. Suppose the $250,000 deferred bonus was to be paid in 1985, 10 years after signing the contract. How much would the Yankees have to invest in 1975 in order to have $250,000 in 1985? If the Yankees could receive 8 percent interest on the money they invest, they would have to invest only $115,750 in 1975. This sum earning compound interest would increase to $250,000 in 10 years. The reason a relatively small sum, only 46 percent of the amount owed in 1985, increases so fast is that the interest earned the first year, $9,260, itself earns interest the second year and each year thereafter. Furthermore, the interest earned on the interest will in turn earn interest, and so on. It all sounds more complicated than it is. The rapid growth of the principal is the result of the compounding of interest. Therefore a promise to pay $250,000 in 10 years costs only $115,750 when the promise is made.

The lesser amount is also the value to Hunter of his promised future bonus. The value of an asset is what you can sell it for. If Hunter had tried in 1975 to sell his deferred bonus to a financial institution, how much would they have been willing to pay him for it? The most a bank would be willing to pay is the present value of the $250,000 bonus. The present value is the amount a person would be willing to pay for a certain amount delivered in the future. Since the bank has the alternative of loaning its money at 8 percent a year, the most it would be willing to pay for Hunter's bonus would be the sum that when earning 8 percent interest for 10 years would equal $250,000. This sum is also $115,750. Therefore the present value of the deferred bonus is the value of the bonus to Hunter when he signed his contract in 1975, not the $250,000 promised future amount.

The same principle applies to the deferred salary. Salary payments of $100,000 a year were to begin in 1985 and run to the year 2000. The Yankees would have had to invest $46,300 in 1975 to pay Hunter $100,000 in 1985 and only $14,600 to pay him the sum promised in the year 2000. The total investment in 1975 required to meet the annual deferred salary payments from 1985 to the year 2000, which totals $1.5 million, is only

$384,000. It is possible to employ a formula to calculate these amounts, but tables are available that are much easier to use, or a pocket calculator already programmed to figure both present values and future compounded amounts can be used.

The important point is that as long as interest rates are positive, money promised in the future is worth less than the same amount of money available today. A sum of money to be delivered in the future is worth the amount that when invested at the current interest rate would grow to the future amount in the time specified. This relatively simple concept would have saved numerous college athletes thousands of dollars had they known about it. This was especially true in the days before star athletes started hiring agents who receive 10 percent of the athletes' earnings for knowing about the concept of present value, taxes, and other things needed to negotiate contracts.

Jim McDaniels is a case in point. McDaniels is unique only because the details of his contract with the Carolina Cougars of the American Basketball Association (ABA) became public knowledge. McDaniels in 1970 was a senior at Western Kentucky and heavily involved in extracurricular activities—he played basketball. McDaniels, who reportedly stands over 7 feet tall, was the star center for his team, which finished second in the NCAA national tournament. McDaniels became an All-American and signed a $1.5 million contract with the Carolina Cougars. McDaniels thought he would receive over $100,000 a year, but his paychecks amounted to much less than that.

Most of his payments, he discovered to his sorrow, were to come later; they were deferred over a 25-year period. Professional athletes came to refer to these contracts as the "dog-out" plan, which meant that once the player was no longer on the team, it probably would be difficult to collect the deferred payments. McDaniels jumped the newly formed ABA for the established NBA to escape his dog-out contract. In the resulting lawsuit his contract with the Carolina Cougars became public knowledge. McDaniels was to be paid $40,000 for his 1971 season; $65,000 a year for the years 1972–1977; $55,000 for the years 1978–1982; $50,000 a year for 1983–1994; and $70,000 for 1995. The payments totaled almost $1.5 million, but the current value at 8 percent in 1970 was only a little more than $600,000.

McDaniels was fortunate because he could prove that he had been deceived. In fact, he had signed not one but seven separate contracts with the Cougars. His contract with the Cougars was legally voided, and he subsequently signed with the NBA Seattle Supersonics in 1972 for $267,000 a year for 6 years. He did not do well in the NBA and was released a few years later. But his contract was guaranteed, so he collected his salary, or most of it. McDaniels was lucky; others were not so fortunate. A knowledge of the concept of present value would have saved them thousands of dollars. Money in the future is simply worth less than money now. How much less depends upon the rate of interest and how far into the future the promised money is to be delivered.

There are signs that professional athletes are learning about the concept of present value, but newspaper people still have a long way to go. Before the 1979 season, basketball center Marvin Webster became a free agent. Webster had led the Seattle Supersonics into the NBA championships the previous year. Even though the Sonics lost the championship, Webster demonstrated his abilities sufficiently to impress the New York Knicks. The Knicks offered Webster $600,000 a year— $500,000 in cash and $100,000 deferred—to sign with them. The Sonics' president at first agreed to match the offer, but later reneged after discussing the matter with his financial vice-president. The Sonics' president instead offered Webster $300,000 in cash and $300,000 deferred, which the Sonics argued still totaled $600,000 and matched the Knicks' offer. The press swallowed that line, but Webster didn't. He signed with the Knicks.

Additional Readings

Kennedy, Ray. "For the Athlete, How Much Is Too Much." *Sports Illustrated*, July 24, 1978.

Kennedy, Ray. "Money, the Monster Threatening Sports." *Sports Illustrated*, July 17, 1978.

"Success Can't Stop Steinbrenner." *New York Times*, October 24, 1977.

V

CURRENT MICROECONOMIC PROBLEMS

Preview

Rent controls have been spreading throughout the country as local political solutions to rising rents. New York City has had a rent control ordinance since World War II. This chapter explores the experience New York has had with rent controls. This experience corresponds so well with what economic theory would predict that it deserves to be a textbook example.

Key Economic Points

If the price system is not allowed to allocate scarce resources, some other nonprice means must be used.

How have apartments been allocated under rent controls?

The shortages initially created by a rent control program are not eliminated in the long run.

Why are rent controls, despite the social costs, politically popular?

24

Rent Controls: Who Would Want to Own New York?

John Jacob Astor, the nineteenth century fur baron, died bemoaning that he had not, as a younger man, purchased every square foot of Manhattan Island. Actually, he had bought enough land to become America's first real estate multimillionaire. The land he had acquired for $2 million was worth $20 million when he died in 1848. His son carried on the tradition, increasing the family's real estate holdings to $80 million in 1875. By 1920 these holdings were reportedly worth $450 million. In the 1940s, the Astors and other smart businessmen began to get out of New York real estate. Today the Astors own only four properties worth less than $6 million.

It used to be, and the Astors' fortune testifies to it, that if you owned a chunk of Manhattan you had it made. Not so anymore. The largest land-owners in New York City, Penn Central and the City of New York itself, are either bankrupt or close to it. Everyone knows that New York City is the largest, wealthiest city in the world. There's more of everything in New York—more theaters, more art, more business, more addicts, and more crime—and less repair and maintenance than anywhere else. Abandoned stripped automobiles line the freeways, the garbage may or may not be picked up, the streets are maintained like Oklahoma country roads. Perhaps most striking of all, thousands of abandoned buildings line the cityscape while a severe housing shortage exists.

People line up to obtain the early editions of the city's newspapers to read the obituaries and classified ads for indications that an apartment may soon be available. Striking contrasts exist in the quality of the available housing. The housing of the poor and middle class is generally in a shabby state of repair while that of the rich or owner-occupied (whether rich or poor) appears well maintained.

New York landlords do not appear to have profited from the decay of their properties. New York City has become the largest landlord in the city, not by design or purchase, but by default. The city in 1970 owned 13,000 buildings that had been abandoned since the mid-1950s and another 13,000 that were acquired via condemnation proceedings. In Manhattan, 21,500 of the 48,000 buildings on the tax rolls were in arrears on tax payments. By 1975, 33,000 apartment buildings were in tax arrears, another 6,000 buildings were foreclosed by the city during the year, and 35,000 to 50,000 individual apartment units were lost by owner abandonment. During the last 20 years more money probably has been lost than made in New York real estate. New York real estate evidently has gone from being a golden nest egg to a rotten apple in a few decades.

This turnabout is primarily the result of New York City's rent control program, which dates from 1943 and has been frequently revised, and to the 1970 rent stabilization program. The federal government initially imposed rent control as a temporary measure during World War II, but when the war ended New York City continued rent control. In 1978, out of 2.2 million housing units there were approximately 400,000 rent-controlled and 800,000 rent-stabilized apartments. Basically all the large apartment buildings are covered by one type of control or the other. Single-family dwellings and owner-occupied housing (such as coops and condominiums) and luxury apartments are not covered by rent controls.

The purpose of a rent control program is to reduce the price of housing to tenants below what they would have to pay with a free housing market. Rent controls, if they are enforced, do accomplish this. But there are side effects, not all of which are fully appreciated by supporters of price controls. Holding the price of housing below the market equilibrium price immediately increases the quantity demanded, creating a housing shortage. Individuals seeing the lower rent-controlled price demand more housing than they would at the market price. Apartment owners respond to the lower rents by supplying fewer units. In New York City they responded by converting some apartments to business offices and warehouses or to owner-occupied cooperative apartments that were not subject to regulation. A situation of excess demand was created where not all potential renters could find suitable apartments to rent.

The available apartments in New York, given the shortage, had to be allocated in some nonprice fashion. Waiting lists were created, landlords discriminated among the several prospective renters for each available apartment according to their own particular biases; race, sex, religion, pets, children, and marital status became important in deciding who obtained apartments and who didn't. Money payments were not entirely eliminated in housing allocations. Bribes enabling a person to move to the top of the waiting list were not unknown. The common practice of paying "key money" was created whereby a prospective tenant negotiating to pay the controlled rent also had to pay a substantial sum to purchase the key to the apartment. During the 1970s a tenant giving up a three-room apartment renting for $60 a month could secretly sublease it for as much as $5,000 in key money. Substantial damage deposits, which turned out to be nonrefundable in practice, were required of new tenants.

Often the law was just ignored. More than 25 percent of renters were voluntarily paying more than the legal rent, according to one report. Bribes, key money, large nonrefundable damage deposits, and voluntary overpayments occurred because the available housing was worth more than the legal maximum to many buyers, some of whom were inclined to pay more illegally rather than do without altogether. When both buyers and sellers find it in their interest to disregard a law, the law becomes difficult to enforce. New York City found it necessary to constantly revise its rent regulations to outlaw new practices designed with the consent of both landlord and tenant to circumvent the law.

The long-term consequences, if the law is enforced, are perhaps more serious than short-term disobedience because they involve the deterioration of the urban environment. Landlords facing rising costs and fixed rents responded by reducing their operating expenses. Taxes were paid late or not at all. Mortgage defaults became common. Fuel bills were not paid, and repairs and maintenance outlays were deferred. Almost one-half of the apartments in Manhattan, as we have already seen, are currently in tax arrears. Fuel suppliers cut off the credit to 10,000 residential buildings in 1975 for slow payment or nonpayment. Violations of health and building codes reached epidemic proportions due to lack of general maintenance and repairs. Eventually thousands of buildings were simply abandoned. It was estimated that New York City lost 33,000 housing units as the result of abandonment in 1970 and from 35,000 to 50,000 in 1975. In the midst of a worsening housing situation, block after block in New York stands vacant, abandoned, and in an advanced state of decay.

After almost four decades of rent controls, New York City bears sad witness to the full effects of such regulatory acts. Price controls have destroyed the incentive for entrepreneurs to provide adequate housing. Almost no new housing subject to rent controls has been built by private enterprise for over 40 years. Net additions to the housing supply averaged only 7,500 per year during 1963–1973, and almost all of these were luxury or owner-occupied units. The housing of the rich, which is generally not subject to controls, remains in good repair in stark contrast to surrounding deteriorating rent-controlled units. As a foreign scholar has observed:

In fact, next to bombing, rent control seems in many cases to be the most efficient technique so far known for destroying cities, as the housing situation in New York City demonstrates (Assar Lindbeck, *The Political Economy of the New Left,* p. 39.)

Except for luxury housing, rent controls have effectively thwarted the growing demand for housing by New Yorkers. In a free market, an increase in demand for housing would lead to an increase in the price of apartments, increasing in the short run the profits of landlords. These growing profits would attract new construction as would-be landlords attempted to share in the higher returns offered in housing. The price and profitability of housing would then decline somewhat as the increased supply of housing entered the rental market. Prices and profits thus serve as a signal to producers that consumers desire more housing. Business persons respond by offering more housing in an attempt to share in the higher profits. As more housing becomes available, rents and profits fall until the amount of housing available at the market price just equals the amount demanded.

Price controls place a "blackout" on these signals. Since prices are not allowed to increase in a reflection of consumer desires, these desires are not transmitted to business firms, and no incentives are created to increase the housing stock. In fact, just the opposite effect is observed. In the long run, less housing is available as existing owners cut their losses and leave the industry. Price controls, which immediately create shortages, cause these shortages to worsen over time, as demand and supply conditions change.

If price controls are causing the destruction of New York's housing and neighborhoods, why do the citizens not demand repeal of the law? Certainly there has been ample time to remedy the problem, yet with three decades of experience with rent controls, New York in 1970 actually extended, in modified form, rent regulation to another 650,000 units.

There are several possible reasons for the city government of New York, despite the ample evidence of the destructiveness of rent controls, to actually extend rather than repeal the regulation. One is mass innocence: the citizens and city leaders are not associating progressive neighborhood decay with continued rent controls and/or not believing their economists. This is possible but not very likely. A second possible explanation is that imposing, retaining, and extending rent controls gains more voters than it loses in the political marketplace. If individuals vote in accordance with their immediate self-interest, those persons who are already tenants in rent-controlled or stabilized apartments will support the system that gives them housing at less than the market price. These fortunate persons thus receive a gift of subsidized housing. In New York City, 76 percent of the voters are tenants, not owners. Thus tenants with a direct interest in rent controls make up a majority of the voting population.

In order to identify potential opponents of rent controls, let us consider which groups are directly damaged by the regulation. Obviously, landlords are hurt by the act, as are the persons who cannot obtain housing because of the shortage and all citizens who must live in a decaying urban environment. Landlords are directly damaged, suffering a loss in rental revenues and, correspondingly, in the value of their assets. However, landlords are relatively few in number in comparison with tenants. Prospective tenants who cannot find the housing they want are also harmed by rent controls. Often these persons already live in rent-controlled housing and desire a bigger or better apartment; they are subsidized by lower housing costs while they search the obituaries and classifieds. Or the people affected by the shortage are newcomers to the city or live in the suburbs and are not voters in city elections. It appears that the housing shortage that results from rent controls does not generate sufficient political pressure for repeal of the laws.

Finally, the resulting deterioration of the city harms everyone. Those with rent-controlled apartments share in these social costs, but while they gain all the benefits of rent controls, they do not bear all the costs of the urban blight rent controls cause. This condition means that for a substantial group of voters the private benefit of rent controls exceeds the private costs, but when New York is considered as a whole the social costs clearly exceed the social benefits. Politicians attempting to win or to stay in office have found it necessary to pay attention to the private interests of tenants even at the cost of continued urban decay.

Additional Readings

Aaron, Henry. "Rent Controls and Urban Development: A Case Study of Mexico City." *Social and Economic Studies,* December 1966.

Cheung, Stephen N.S. "Roofs or Stars: The Stated Intents and Actual Effects of a Rents Ordinance." *Economic Inquiry,* March 1975.

Crampp, William D. "Some Effects of Rent Control." *Southern Economic Journal,* April 1950.

Lindbeck, Assar. *The Political Economy of the New Left.* Harper and Row, 1971.

Olsen, Edgar O. "An Economic Analysis of Rent Control." *Journal of Political Economy,* December 1972.

Rand Corporation. "The Effects of Rent Control on Housing in New York City." Condensed and reprinted in *Contemporary Issues in Economics: Selected Readings,* R. W. Crandall and R. S. Eckaus, eds. Little, Brown, 1972.

Preview

During the Great Depression many Americans lost faith in the ability of the competitive market to allocate resources in the public interest. This led to the establishment of numerous government regulatory agencies mandated by law to improve the economic performance of the industries supervised. The Civil Aeronautics Board was entrusted in 1938 with regulating the airline industry. During the 1960s, economic studies of the effects of airline regulation revealed that significant social costs, not benefits, had resulted. Regulated airlines charged significantly higher prices and had higher costs and lower profits than nonregulated airlines. This chapter examines the economic performance of the airlines prior to and after deregulation in 1978. Particular attention is paid to the nature of airline competition under regulation. This examination suggests that there are significant social costs of monopoly that have been neglected by economists.

Key Economic Points

How can regulation result in the lessening of competition?

The economic performances of the airlines prior to and after deregulation are compared.

Why does nonprice competition lead regulated airlines to have higher costs than nonregulated airlines?

Traditional economic calculation of the social costs of monopoly may understate the true social costs.

25

Deregulating the Airlines: Avoiding the Social Cost of Monopoly

During 1978 the real price of airline tickets fell 11 percent, the first decline in prices in the industry in a decade. A price war broke out in the industry late in 1977 when American Airlines offered Super Saver discounts. These lower fares were generally matched as the rest of the industry sought to remain competitive. Prior to this time, price competition had been absent from the industry. All fares and schedules were regulated by a government agency, the Civil Aeronautics Board, which for all practical purposes refused to allow price competition. During the middle 1970s a movement began to deregulate the airlines. Air freight operations were deregulated in 1977. The Airline Deregulation Act, which did the same thing for passenger service, was passed and signed into law in October, 1978. The Air Cargo Act and Airline Deregulation Bill represent the first instances of the reversal of the trend toward increased government regulation of the private sector.

In order to show how the inefficient behavior of the airlines led to deregulation, we investigate the performance of the airline industry while it was strictly regulated by the Civil Aeronautics Board. We also examine the behavior of the airlines themselves under regulation, which suggests that there are social costs of monopoly that economists have neglected until recently. When these social costs are taken into account, monopoly is seen as a much more serious social problem than it has recently been considered.

During the Great Depression of the 1930s, many Americans lost faith in the free market as a mechanism to efficiently handle economic matters. In the field of airline transportation, this led the federal government to pass the Civil Aeronautics Act of 1938, which established the regulatory agency later called the Civil Aeronautics Board (CAB). The CAB was charged with regulating, in the public interest, air fares and schedules for interstate flights. Thereafter, no interstate airline could fly or set rates without prior CAB approval.

The public expected the regulatory agency to improve the performance of the industry. Throughout the 1950s, both economists and policy makers maintained their faith in regulation. As defects appeared, efforts were made to find ways of improving regulatory practices. However, during the 1960s economic studies of the CAB and the airline industry began to reveal the extent of the social costs imposed by regulation and the lack of economic justification for regulation in the first place. During the 1970s many economists reversed their earlier opinion and openly called for deregulation.

One economic study concluded that the air transport industry had market structure characteristics that would produce economic performance of reasonable quality without regulation. Furthermore, the performance of the CAB was judged to be severely defective. The board appeared to have been concerned primarily with maintaining the profitability of its principal clients, the domestic trunk airlines, and not with the service of any higher social goal, such as the public interest. The CAB, in short, had been captured by the firms it was supposed to regulate and had been used to form a legal cartel whose function was to maintain prices above the competitive rate.

The board succeeded in creating and maintaining monopoly prices for air travel. A direct comparison of the ticket prices charged by regulated interstate airlines with the rates charged by substantially unregulated intrastate airlines in California and Texas revealed that unregulated air fares were 30 to 50 percent below the fares charged in regulated markets. An early study estimated the social costs of the airline industry's legal cartel at $1 billion annually. Another study found that the regulatory price increase was 66 percent higher than a competitive rate would be and that the social cost of maintaining the cartel price was between 19 and 60 percent of the total revenues of the regulated airlines. This translates into an increased air travel cost of between $3.25 billion and $10 billion a year.

As the evidence of the substantial social costs of regulation mounted, President Ford and his successor President Carter became interested in deregulating or at least improving the performance of the airlines. The first step was the appointment of new members to the CAB who were interested in promoting price competition in the industry. The airline price war of 1977 was the result of this new policy.

Next, Congress passed the Deregulation Act of 1978. The Deregulation Act, ending the CAB's powers over routes and fares by 1983 and abolishing the agency entirely in 1985, allowed airlines to immediately cut fares by half or raise them by 5 percent without the board's prior approval, and to add and drop routes more easily than was previously possible. Each airline may add one new route a year without approval and more if they can show that they are "fit, willing, and able" to serve the market. Moreover, they can drop unprofitable routes after giving 90 days notice. The Deregulation Act substantially freed the airlines to compete against one another. The results were as expected when a cartel is turned into a competitive industry, that is, lower prices and increased output.

The history of the CAB points out a potential social loss due to monopoly that has often been ignored by economists: the tendency for a cartel or monopoly to convert potential monopoly profits into social costs. Despite the willingness of the CAB to allow prices substantially above the competitive rate, the airlines never were able to earn large profits. Prior to deregulation, the airlines generally earned rates of return below the average return of all industries, perhaps 25 percent lower. The first year after the introduction of price competition, the average return in the airline industry was 40 percent greater than the all-industry average. While regulated as a cartel, the airlines were never able to earn more than a normal return on their investment, but they did succeed in increasing costs until they were significantly higher than the minimum attainable.

Although the CAB was able to block the use of lower prices to attract passengers, it was unable, despite unceasing efforts, to stop nonprice competition. In a cartel each member has an incentive to increase sales relative to other members to gain a larger share of the monopoly profits. When price competition is impossible, each firm attempts to attract more customers by spending resources to make its output more valuable to customers than the output of fellow cartel members.

The airlines spent resources to offer more and better service than their rivals: more flights at convenient departure times, more attractive airport facilities, better meals and drinks, more comfortable passenger accommodations, quicker baggage handling, and large advertising budgets to spread the word. This process of nonprice competition continued until the potential profits of the cartel were translated into costs, as the historically low profits of the industry while regulated testify. These higher costs must be considered a social cost of monopoly.

Although improving the quality of service is of some economic value to consumers, the increase in value in such a situation is less than the added costs. This was demonstrated when deregulation occurred and lower prices became the main competitive weapon. Airlines reduced frills, installed smaller and more seats in each plane (reduced the quality of the service), and still attracted more customers. Under regulation, nonprice competition had proceeded to the point where the costs of improving the quality of service exceeded the value to passengers. The result was to convert the potential cartel profits to costs, wasting scarce resources in the process.

Traditionally, the economic analysis of monopoly has assumed that a profit-maximizing cartel or monopoly would always produce its restricted output at the minimum cost. The traditional analysis associated the social cost of monopoly with the reduced output a monopolist produces in order to obtain the higher, profit-maximizing monopoly price. The price customers pay is greater than the marginal cost of producing the good, which imposes a social cost on society. The social cost of monopoly, therefore, was confined to the output the monopolist did not produce. Because it is always less costly to misallocate resources than to waste time entirely, empirical estimates of the social cost of monopoly have always been small, suggesting that monopoly was not a serious social problem.

The quantitatively much larger monopoly profits were not considered a social cost but a transfer of wealth from consumers to the owners of the monopoly, which supposedly involved no misallocation of resources. This is because the losses of consumers are exactly offset by the gains to the monopolist; society as a whole neither gains nor loses. Therefore, the traditional analysis ignored monopoly profits and calculated the social costs of monopoly on the assumption that monopolists always allocate resources as efficiently as firms in a competitive industry are forced to do.

The performance of the airline industry as a cartel reveals the deficiency of this approach. The possibility of obtaining or sharing in a monopoly profit will attract resources as would any other profitable activity. This opportunity will provide the incentive for individuals and groups to spend resources in attempts to create a monopoly and for purchasers of the product to spend resources to keep this from happening. The resources spent attempting to create a monopoly and to resist its formation are social costs of monopoly just as are the costs of restricting output. These resources have productive alternative uses which are wasted in attempts to create and resist the establishment of socially undesirable monopoly profits.

The airlines, for example, lobbied hard to obtain regulation in the first place, wasting, from society's point of view, valuable resources to create a legal cartel. The airlines then agreed to various inefficient practices to maintain the good will of the regulators. The most obvious was their agreement to fly to cities where the demand was insufficient to cover the operating costs. This was demonstrated by the airlines' rush to drop unprofitable flights and to replace them with profitable new routes once the deregulation bill was passed. Cities such as Providence, Chattanooga, Shreveport, Norfolk, Charleston, and Yuma suffered reductions in airline service whereas Reno, Seattle, Tampa, Pittsburgh, Kansas City, and St. Louis benefited from increased service. The airlines responded to deregulation by allocating their resources according to consumer demand rather than bureaucratic decrees.

DEREGULATING THE AIRLINES

Most airlines resisted the drive to deregulate the industry, as did organized labor. Supporting the bill was an unlikely assortment of organizations representing conservative Republicans, liberal Democrats, Naderites, retailers, retired persons, students, and a few airlines (United Airlines and Pan American Airlines being the biggest). The resources spent attempting to preserve and to eliminate regulation could be considered a social cost of monopoly. At the very least, the resources expended to maintain the cartel were wasted. The resources spent by both sides on such political activities were considerable, and the costs did not stop there. In order to placate organized labor, the Deregulation Bill contained a provision that all employees laid off by any airline that cut its work force by 7.5 percent or more in a year because of the impact of deregulation would be reimbursed by the U.S. Treasury for up to 6 years or until the laid off employees could find comparable jobs..

An analysis of the performance of the airline industry under regulation is instructive to anyone interested in assessing the social cost of monopoly. Despite a "captured" regulatory agency willing to prevent entry into the industry and to allow a monopoly price, the firms in the industry failed to profit. The potential monopoly profit was dissipated by competition to share in or maintain the monopoly. Airlines, in their efforts to increase their individual share of the potential profit, turned to non-price competition, which increased costs, and agreed to fly some unprofitable flights. Furthermore, they had to spend resources in lobbying to maintain and deal with regulation, which in the end they lost anyway. The end result of the legal cartel was not higher profits but higher costs of production. This example suggests that the social cost of monopoly is not confined to the cost of reduced output but may also be found in the higher costs of production inevitably brought about by socially unprofitable competition attempting to create, share, or resist the formation of a monopoly. The airline industry under regulation demonstrated that it is quite possible for society to suffer the costs of monopoly without any of the overt signs predicted by the traditional economic analysis, such as large profits and a price that exceeds the incremental costs of production.

Additional Readings

Caves, Richard. *Air Transport and Its Regulators: An Industry Study.* Harvard University Press, 1962.

Caves, Richard. "The Kennedy Subcommittee's 'Civil Aeronautics Board Practices and Procedures.' " *The Bell Journal of Economics,* August 1976.

Harris, Ray J. "Airline Regulation Causes Anger and Joy at Nation's Airports." *Wall Street Journal,* March 5, 1979.

Jordon, W. A. *Airline Regulation in America: Effects and Imperfections.* Johns Hopkins University Press, 1970.

Moore, Thomas. "Deregulating Transportation." *Regulation,* March–April 1978.

Posner, Richard A. *Antitrust Law.* University of Chicago Press, 1976.

U.S. Senate, Committee on the Judiciary, Subcommittee on Administrative Practice and Procedure. *Civil Aeronautics Board Practices and Procedures.* Committee Report, 94th Congress, 1st Session. U.S. Government Printing Office, 1975.

Preview

The dispute between the Amalgamated Clothing and Textile Workers Union and
J. P. Stevens, the nation's second largest textile firm, illustrates the social costs
involved in the attempts to establish labor unions. The struggle at J. P. Stevens has
become the modern symbol of the struggle to extend union membership in the
United States. The goal of union organizers and the workers they enlist is to win
the monopoly right to supply labor to the firm. Unions hope to use this right to
win higher wages, which provides the incentive for firms to attempt to resist the
establishment of unions. This chapter explores the social costs and benefits
involved in forming unions and examines the private costs and benefits of union
membership.

Key Economic Points

The process of establishing labor unions is not free to society.

Have unions been successful in increasing the wages of organized workers relative
to nonorganized workers?

How were gains made at the expense of some nonorganized workers and all
consumers?

What function do work rules perform in a unionized firm?

The threat of unionization may provide the incentive for nonunionized firms to
provide many of the benefits a union would win, especially a personnel
department.

26

Social Costs of Unionization: The Union Versus J. P. Stevens

The Amalgamated Clothing and Textile Workers Union (ACTW) spent 17 years, thousands of manhours, and millions of dollars in its successful attempt to organize the J.P. Stevens and Company. J. P. Stevens, the nation's second largest textile company, employed a battery of lawyers and a seemingly endless variety of tactics to thwart the union. The union countered with lawyers of their own. As a result, J. P. Stevens has been convicted in sixteen separate cases of refusing to bargain, or of illegally firing and intimidating workers. A nationwide consumer boycott was called against Stevens products, which was supported by the NAACP, the National Council of Churches, and three major Protestant denominations. J. P. Stevens became the modern symbol of the struggle to extend union membership in the United States.

The battle between the ACTW and J. P. Stevens provides a good illustration of some of the social costs that have been created by the union movement. Unionism in the United States has been quite secure since the early 1950s. But union membership has been declining since 1975, both in absolute numbers and as a percentage of the work force. Furthermore, organized labor has been losing more certification elections, which are called to determine whether the workers in a company want a union or not, than they have been winning. Organized labor has responded to its declining membership by lobbying hard to obtain legislation that would make organizing easier. The proposed labor law reform bill, for example, has been nicknamed the J. P. Stevens bill by union lobbyists in their attempt to persuade Congress that the proposed law is necessary. So far, despite persistent efforts by organized labor, Congress has been reluctant to enact the legislation.

This chapter concentrates upon examining the larger social interests that are exemplified in the struggle to unionize J. P. Stevens. The issues involved are similar to those encountered in the examination of the costs of any monopoly because, whatever else a union is, it is an agreement among workers not to compete for jobs, and to bargain with the employer as a group rather than as individuals.

It is only relatively recently in U.S. history that this has been possible. For example, it wasn't until 1914 that the Clayton Act stated: "The labor of human beings is not an article of commerce." The purpose of this historical declaration was to exempt labor unions from prosecution under the Sherman Antitrust Act. Prior to passage of this legislation, traditional union activities, such as strikes and picketing, had been prosecuted as anticompetitive behavior. Full immunity from the antitrust laws was finally obtained in 1932 in the Norris-LaGuardia Act, which removed the court's power to intervene in labor disputes unless violence and property damage occurred. The New Deal also passed other legislation that made it legally possible to form labor unions and provided a procedure for doing so. The mechanism for legally establishing a union was the National Labor Relations Board (NLRB), which would call and oversee a certification election whenever 30 percent of a firm's employees petitioned for one. If 50 percent of the workers voted in favor of a union, the employer became legally bound to recognize and bargain with the union.

This legislation created the opportunity for workers to join together and establish a monopoly of the right to supply labor to a business firm or even to a whole industry, an opportunity that is generally denied to the business sector by the antitrust laws.

The question of whether organized labor attempts to exercise its legal privileges to behave as a monopolist is hardly worth asking, since the answer is obvious. The purpose of a labor union is to exercise its power to deny the employer access to workers, via the strike threat, in order to increase the wages of union members above the level a competitive market would establish. Unions also use their power to improve or maintain working conditions and to establish a system of industrial jurisprudence that guarantees workers certain rights on the job.

The economics of labor monopoly is straightforward. Labor unions, backed by the threat of a strike, are able to negotiate wages that are higher than the competitive wage rate. The result is higher production costs and product prices and corresponding reductions in the quantities of goods sold by firms whose labor force has been organized. The reduced output requires fewer workers to produce, so that the total amount of labor employed by a unionized firm or industry is less than it would be in the absence of a union.

The most comprehensive study of the effects unions have had on the relative wages of labor examined the labor market during the 1950s. During the 1950s the average union wage was 10 to 15 percent higher than the average nonunion wage. This difference was made up of a union wage that was 7 to 11 percent higher than the competitive wage and a nonunion wage that was 3 to 4 percent lower than it would have been in the absence of unionization. Industries that are unionized hire fewer workers than they would if labor were supplied competitively. These excess workers are forced to compete for jobs in the nonunion sector, increasing the supply of labor and driving down the wage rate. In a real sense, the gains of unionized workers were purchased at the expense of unorganized workers.

More recent studies have found the union/nonunion wage differential to be even greater than initially reported. A study using 1967 data found union wages to be 15 to 25 percent higher than nonunion wages. A still more recent study determined that in 1973 the wages of union workers exceeded those of nonunion workers by more than 25 percent. Craftspersons, for example, earned 29 percent more than nonunion workers, factory operators 23 percent more, truck drivers 44 percent more, and laborers 36 percent more. Unions, on average, have succeeded in using their monopoly power to increase the wages of their members. The higher union wages are raised relative to the competitive level, the greater the social cost of reduced employment in the organized sector of the labor market.

The existence of labor unions whose members earn more than the competitive wage also imposes another cost upon society. As long as union jobs, when available, are open to the first applicant, there will always be excess labor available to fill them. A successful applicant, however, will obtain a job that is worth tens of thousands of dollars more over a lifetime of work than a job in the nonunion sector. It is thus worthwhile for a young worker to spend time searching for a union job. If union wages were just 10 percent greater than nonunion wages, it would pay for a recent high school graduate to spend up to 1 year searching for a union job. But a graduate who spends a year searching before finding a union job will, because of the value of the time spent searching, over his or her lifetime do only as well as if he or she had accepted a nonunion job immediately. But if all youths search for a union job, only a small portion of them will find one, and the rest will have invested in costly job searches for nothing. The limited availability of union jobs thus imposes costs on society in the form of excess and unproductive job searches. Indeed, once the initial generation of union workers has retired, it is even possible that new union members will not gain over their lifetimes from union membership. The higher union wages will have been dissipated in the time spent initially searching for the union job.

But not all unions have succeeded equally in winning pay increases for their members. The findings of the initial study on the effects of unions on relative wage rates is instructive on this point. About one-quarter of all union members, this study reports, belonged to unions that had succeeded in increasing the wage rates of members by 25 percent. Half of all union members belonged to unions that had won relative increases of 10 percent. However, the remaining one-quarter of union members had failed to gain any increase from membership over what they would have earned in the absence of the union.

It is to be expected that unions would first have been organized where the potential gains were greatest. The firms and industries that remain to be organized are unlikely to afford much chance of increasing wages significantly, in comparison with what unorganized workers are currently receiving. It is thus uncertain as to whether the ACTW could deliver on a promise of significantly higher wages if textile companies finally organized. The textile industry is highly competitive and currently besieged by competition from imports. Significantly higher wages would probably make firms uncompetitive, significantly reducing sales and employment. A union has the best chance of increasing wages when the demand for the firm's product is price-inelastic and the opportunities to substitute other factors for labor are expensive. Neither is the case for textiles.

The struggle between J. P. Stevens and the ACTW also points out another social cost involved in the union movement. It is expensive to organize workers into a union. Even though the law of the land makes it possible, it does not compel either workers or business firms to accept a union. The possibility of higher wages provides an incentive for workers to organize, but the prospect of paying higher wages gives employers an equal incentive to resist the organizers' efforts. Both activities require real resources that have productive alternative uses.

A brief history of the attempts by the ACTW to organize the textile industry prior to taking on J. P. Stevens in 1963 illustrates the potential social costs involved in union-organizing activities. The union first lost a battle with Deering-Milliken, which closed a plant in South Carolina rather than negotiate. The union was then defeated after a long strike at Harriet and Henderson Mills, and was subsequently beaten off by Cannon Mills, and again by Burlington Industries. Organizing efforts were met everywhere in the textile industry with equally organized opposition. All of this illustrates the social costs involved in attempting to organize a labor monopoly.

Then in 1963 came the union's fateful decision to attempt to organize J. P. Stevens. When union organizers first appeared in Roanoke Rapids, where Stevens has a seven-plant complex, they found that they had a war on their hands. Employees were notified that the company was opposed to a union and that it believed that a union would operate to the serious disadvantage of the employees. Supervisors got tough on suspected union sympathizers. Three new union members were actually fired 2 days after joining the union.

The central institution in labor relations is the National Labor Relations Board (NLRB). Charges of violations of labor law are filed with NLRB, cases are prosecuted by NLRB lawyers and judged by administrative law judges of the NLRB, and the first appeal is before the full board of the NLRB. Only then can an appeal go before a circuit court judge.

The union brought before the NLRB a series of charges of unfair labor practices against Stevens. Besides accusing the company of illegally intimidating and firing workers for joining the union, the union also accused Stevens of refusing to bargain. In one case, when a rump union that had not been elected sought to negotiate a contract, the company closed the plant. In another case, where the union was elected, it was not successful in negotiating a contract. The company offered the same wage increase that it granted its nonunion plants and refused to institute a mandatory check-off of union dues or to set up a grievance procedure.

As a result of such actions, the NLRB found the company guilty of sixteen separate charges of refusing to bargain and of firing and intimidating workers. The company was also subsequently found to be in contempt of court, was found liable for millions of dollars in fines, and its chief executives have been threatened with jail sentences.

The union spent large sums on its organizing efforts, succeeded in imposing a nationwide labor boycott of Stevens products, and finally applied pressure through a major lender of Stevens, Metropolitan Life Insurance Company. Stevens has matched the union's efforts by unilaterally increasing nonunion employees' wages, by closing a plant, by firing and intimidating workers, and by generally operating at the limits of legality. The results: after two decades of organizing efforts, the ACTW had succeeded in organizing only 3,000 of Stevens' 44,000 employees until Stevens agreed to sign labor contracts with the union in 1980.

While the ACTW–J. P. Stevens contest is exceptional in both the length and the vehemence of the struggle, it does illustrate that it is not costless to form unions. A union that meets considerable resistance from business may well find that the total gains to union members and union officials from creating a union are smaller than the return that could have been obtained if the same effort had been expended for productive purposes. The ACTW–J. P. Stevens struggle, from society's point of view, certainly involved a substantial loss of resources: both the firm and the union have spent resources that have alternative productive uses in an effort to gain or resist the creation of a monopoly rent for labor.

The potential social costs from unions do not stop their formation. Once a firm has been successfully unionized, it is often necessary for the union to insist upon stringent work rules to protect the gains made at the bargaining table. These work rules limit the flexibility of management to efficiently allocate resources and often stand in the way of technological progress. Nevertheless, such rules are necessary from the union's point of view. An employer who has grudgingly granted his or her employees a wage higher than the competitive rate has an incentive to reduce labor costs in any way possible. Besides laying off some workers, the firm could attempt to increase productivity by forcing employees to work harder. Speeding up an assembly line and pressuring supervisors to obtain more work from the employees are ways to do this. Or the employer could reduce expenditures on employee amenities, scrimping on rest rooms and toilet facilities, and even on safety precautions. A union employer could provide poorer working conditions than a nonunion employer and still retain its labor force because of the higher union wages paid. Unions realize this and insist on specifying in great detail work rules to deal with these situations. Furthermore, unions insist upon a grievance procedure to protect the workers' rights as specified in the contract.

Work rules are also sometimes used to require more union workers than are required to do the job. Union contracts with the airlines specify that three pilots be hired to fly planes designed to be operated by two pilots. The railroads are required to hire a rear brakeman for each train when there are no brakes to operate, a practice known as "featherbedding." The costs of restrictive work rules to the economy have not been conclusively estimated, but they are undoubtedly substantial.

Many of the most progessive firms in the economy have succeeded in remaining unorganized. IBM, Kodak, and Xerox, for example, have rewarded their employees sufficiently to remain unorganized. The threat of unionization and the potential costs involved may have provided the incentive to treat employees as well or better than they would be treated if unionized. In part, these firms have succeeded in avoiding unionization because they have provided personnel departments that defend both the employee and the long-run interests of the firm from arbitrary actions by subordinate supervisors. This function in companies with strong unions is provided by the union in the form of a formal employee grievance procedure. This protection, whether given by the firm or by the union, has become an established feature of American industry and is the great positive contribution of the union movement.

This contribution has been won at some social cost. Labor monopoly has imposed costs on society by restricting employment in the organized sector of the economy to gain higher wages. The results of this restriction are to reduce the wages of nonunion workers and to create an inefficient allocation of labor resources. Perhaps an equally important social loss is the waste of resources that occurs in the attempts to form and resist the creation of labor unions. The example of the ACTW–J. P. Stevens struggle suggests that these costs are not insignificant. The existence of labor unions that have succeeded in raising the wages of labor above the competitive rate also creates the incentive for young workers to search for a union job. The results of competition to obtain union jobs both reduces the benefits of higher union wages to the successful seekers and imposes uncompensated costs on the unsuccessful. Finally, restrictive work rules, often necessary from the union's point of view to protect their wage gains, reduce the ability of business to allocate resources efficiently.

These are some of the costs that have stemmed from granting organized labor a legal monopoly by exempting unions from antitrust laws. The public should recognize that a contradiction exists in public policy between the antitrust laws, which seek to promote competition, and the labor law, which has the opposite effect. Granting organized labor a legal monopoly has imposed costs on most workers and on all consumers.

Additional Readings

Boskin, W. J. "Unions and Relative Wages." *American Economic Review,* June 1972.

"A Gathering Momentum Against J. P. Stevens." *Business Week,* March 20, 1978.

Guzzardi, Walter, Jr. "How the Union Got the Upper Hand on J. P. Stevens." *Fortune,* June 19, 1978.

Hutt, W. A. *The Strike Threat System.* Arlington Howe, 1973.

Lewis, H. Gregg. *Unionism and Relative Wages in the United States.* University of Chicago Press, 1963.

Ryscavage, P. M. "Measuring Union-Nonunion Earnings Differences." *Monthly Labor Review,* December 1974.

Stafford, E. P. "Concentration and Labor Earnings." *American Economic Review,* March 1968.

Preview

Everyday product advertising invades all of our lives. What is uncertain is whether advertising serves a useful social function or not. The economics profession is divided on this issue. A decade ago many, perhaps most, economists viewed advertising in a negative light, but recent research based upon the economics of information places advertising in a more favorable perspective. In this chapter, three questions that lie at the heart of the debate over advertising's economic impact are considered. Does advertising provide useful information or create wants? Does it increase the efficiency of resource allocation or waste resources? And does it promote competition or protect monopoly?

Key Economic Points

Information about products and services is a scarce good that is costly to obtain.

The question of whether advertising creates wants or simply provides useful information is weighed.

Does advertising increase the efficiency of resource allocation or is it a waste of resources?

Does advertising promote competition or foster monopoly?

Should government regulate product advertising?

27

Imperfect Competition: The Economic Impact of Advertising

It is almost impossible to spend a day in modern America and not be subjected to some form of product advertising. The average American experiences more than 40,000 television and radio commercials during a year. The newspapers and magazines we read contain between two-thirds and three-quarters advertisements. Business firms spent over $33 billion in 1976 to advertise their wares, which amounts to over $150 for every person in the country. Business persons are satisfied that these expenditures are warranted by their ability to attract customers and sell merchandise.

The economics profession and government officials are not so sure. While business persons believe that advertising is profitable, which is their criterion for value, economists concerned with the efficiency of resource allocation are not convinced that all advertising is in the social interest. And government officials at the Federal Trade Commission (FTC) act as if they believe that some advertising is socially damaging. The doubts of economists stem from the fact that a purely competitive industry has no need to advertise, since each firm can always sell all it desires at the market price without advertising. A firm that advertises must, therefore, be price searching and exist as a monopoly, an oligopoly, or in a monopolistically competitive industry. The relevant question is: does advertising increase competition or enhance the monopoly position of these firms? The professionals are divided in their judgment on this issue. A decade ago most economists viewed advertising in a negative light, but recent research based upon the economics of information places advertising in a more favorable perspective.

The FTC evidently is uninfluenced by these new findings, as it recently proposed sweeping new bans on television commercials aimed at children, similar to the ban on cigarette advertising that took effect in 1971. The FTC's proposal is rooted in the proposition that advertising creates wants in children that parents cannot resist. Earlier, the FTC sued the ready-to-eat cereal industry, alleging that intensive advertising resulted in barriers to entry that made the industry less competitive.

The controversy over the effects of advertising is very wide ranging indeed; therefore, it is necessary that we direct our discussion to three of the most important areas of contention: (1) Does advertising provide consumers with useful information or does it attempt instead to persuade consumers to buy things that are not really needed? (2) Does advertising increase the efficiency of resource allocation or actually waste resources? (3) Does advertising promote competition or produce the opposite result by creating and protecting monopoly?

One of the most basic, yet elusive, views about advertising is that it persuades consumers to buy unneeded goods. This position is perhaps distilled from the views of economist John Kenneth Galbraith. According to Galbraith, a modern economy requires that individuals covet the goods produced by an industrial system in order to ensure that individuals spend their incomes in a predictable manner and work reliably because they are always in need of more. Advertising is the tool that ensures this outcome. Galbraith in *The New Industrial State* (p. 201) states: "In the absence of the massive and artful persuasion that accompanies the management of demand, increasing abundance might well have reduced the interest of people in acquiring more goods. They would not have felt the need for multiplying the artifacts—autos, appliances, detergents, cosmetics—by which they were surrounded." Galbraith's views can be summarized in one sentence: advertising persuades people to buy things they do not need. Galbraith is not alone in this view. Noneconomists such as Vance Packard and Ralph Nader agree: consumer demand in an economy is managed by advertising.

It is difficult to come to grips with this proposition precisely because no one knows what "need" means. Needs originate inside people's minds where they are inaccessible to measurement by outsiders. Any behavior can be explained on the basis of need. A man sells an automobile because he no longer needs it or does not sell it because he still needs it. Whether he sells it or not, need provides an explanation. But needs are not an acceptable explanation because the explanation can never be wrong. Economists avoid the term entirely, employing the more testable term "want," which can be defined as the willingness to sacrifice to obtain a good, a behavior that can be observed. Needs simply cannot be defined in a way that allows the testing of propositions. Therefore, the evaluation of the Galbraith proposition that advertising causes people to buy things they do not "need" must be left up to the individual.

Galbraith's proposition, however, does suggest that advertising expenditures should be greatest for the goods least needed by the American people, since it surely must take more resources devoted to persuasion to convince people to prefer the things they need least to the goods they need most. Yet if the advertising expenditures of the 100 largest advertisers in the country for 1975 are grouped into 11 product categories, food is by far the most heavily advertised item. The next heaviest advertised product was medicine, followed in order by automobiles (including gas and tires), cleaning products, liquor and soft drinks, cigarettes, cosmetics, consumer electronics (such as TV and hi-fi sets), photographic equipment and film, paper products, and finally, chewing gum (Does Advertising . . . ., p. 239).

If Galbraith's proposition is correct, then food, which is the most heavily advertised product category, is the least needed; candy and paper are more needed because they are less heavily advertised. You will have to form your own opinion, of course, but if you feel that food, drugs, and personal transportation are more "needed" than candy, paper, and photographic equipment, you also do not believe that advertising causes people to buy what they do not "need."

The opposite view suggests that advertising actually helps people to buy the goods they want by reducing the information costs of buying consumer products. Consumers require information about what products are available at what price, where they are sold, and how substitutes compare in quality. Advertising, by reducing search costs, helps consumers buy the right product at the lowest available price. Some advertising is directed toward informing people of the availability and price of goods offered for sale. The weekly supermarket newspaper ads and the classified ads serve this purpose. Much advertising, however, is used to inform consumers of the quality of differentiated products. How valuable is this kind of advertising in providing information? Because the purpose of advertising is to sell goods, the advertiser has an incentive to provide biased information.

Of course, people do not rely exclusively upon advertising for information about the quality of rival products; they also rely upon personal experience and the recommendations of relatives and friends and consumer magazines. Because business firms depend upon repeat customers for the bulk of their business, they also have an incentive to advertise their products truthfully. If a product can be tested before purchase, it would be foolish to mislead the customer. Polaroid has every incentive to truthfully represent the qualities of its sonar rangefinder cameras. Levi Strauss will factually advertise the color, style, and quality of its pants. With products such as these, potential customers would detect misleading claims prior to purchase, and sales and reputation of the company would suffer.

A substantial number of goods, however, cannot be tested prior to purchase. Bubble-Yum must be chewed, Pepsi and Coke must be tasted: these goods must be experienced to be judged. The advertising for these products carries no direct information about product quality. Slogans such as "It's the real thing" or "Join the Pepsi generation" tell absolutely nothing about the product except that it is available. This fact alone, according to one view, is valuable information to the consumer. Advertising is not randomly distributed over the millions of products in the market, but allocated to those goods that the advertiser feels best meet the demands of consumers. Business firms, by merely spending money to advertise, are informing consumers that they believe their product is of high quality and worthy of consideration. The fact that heavily advertised products sell more than less advertised ones implies that consumers in general feel that they are of higher quality. The consumer, according to this view, is probably right because business will advertise products that are winners, not losers. It would not be profitable, except in rare circumstances, to pay to induce people to try a product that they will be dissatisfied with and never purchase again.

If consumers learn quickly, and that's a big *if*, in order to reduce search costs, it may be a good consumer rule of thumb to buy the least expensive of the name brands, but this rule assumes that consumers as a group can substantiate advertising claims easily and cheaply. Some goods, such as nonprescription drugs, may require extensive testing by the individual. Furthermore, for consumer durables (such as automobiles and stereo equipment), the past experience of consumers, because purchase is infrequent, may not be a good check on advertising claims. Under these conditions the heavily advertised brand may not be the best buy. A clear exception to this rule is that a consumer should be very wary of purchasing heavily advertised goods that are once-and-for-all sales. Movie and record ads may be an attempt to sell you a turkey. Hit records and movies do not require advertising to sell.

It is possible, of course, to accept the fact that advertising provides factual information and that the advertiser is trying to promote the better product without accepting the proposition that all advertising is useful to the consumer. After all, 80 percent of all new products introduced each year fail the market test and disappear, some of which have been heavily advertised (such as the ill-fated Tramp cigarette). Business firms, it would appear, are not perfect judges of consumer tastes. Furthermore, believing that advertising is an effective purveyor of information may be a good reason to oppose its unrestricted use. It may, after all, be against society's best interest to have people smoking cigarettes, and reducing information about cigarettes by banning cigarette ads on radio and television may reduce the amount of smoking. Or a ban on advertising sugared cereals to children may reduce tooth decay.

The second question about the economic effects of advertising is: does advertising increase the efficiency of resource allocation or waste resources? Persons who believe that advertising wastes resources see most of advertising as competitive in nature. The television rivalry between the Hertz and Avis Rent-a-Car agencies probably does not significantly increase the number of automobiles rented by the industry but merely keeps the market share of each firm constant. The net result of this advertising expenditure, if this is so, is to raise costs and prices of renting cars, hence to waste resources.

The fact that Bayer aspirin costs more than three times as much as Safeway aspirin in Washington, D.C., even though both kinds are therapeutically the same, is reported by Ralph Nader as an example of the social costs of advertising. The slogan "Bayer is better" evidently works because Bayer, the most advertised aspirin, is also the best-selling brand.

Persuasive evidence that larger expenditures on advertising lead to higher prices was offered at a U.S. Senate hearing on the advertising of proprietary medicines. Bayer aspirin for adults had higher advertising expenditures and charged higher prices than rival St. Joseph's. Bayer in 1 year spent $15.6 million advertising its adult brand, whereas St. Joseph's spent only $700,000. Bayer aspirin sold for between 60 and 75 percent more than the aspirin offered by its rival. At the same time, Bayer and St. Joseph's spent about the same amount advertising their children's aspirin ($2.3 and $2.1 million, respectively), and both products sold for the same price.

Critics of the view that advertising is wasteful are not persuaded by this evidence. They point out that there is considerable room for variation among the nonaspirin components of the pain-killing tablet, components which may affect the quickness of pain relief and the occurrence of side effects. Probably more important, the statistics do not reveal what the price of St. Joseph's aspirin would be in the absence of Bayer's advertising. Bayer and St. Joseph's are generally located next to each other on market shelves, so if Bayer's advertising effectively increases the demand for aspirin, the demand for St. Joseph's may also increase. St. Joseph's, in this case, would enjoy a "free ride" on Bayer's advertising expenditures. Thus, while Bayer's prices are higher because of advertising expenditures, St. Joseph's are lower precisely because of their rival's expenditures. Whether or not advertising increases aspirin's prices is an empirical question that the statistics presented above do not fully answer.

It is also possible that the higher price for Bayer aspirin may actually lower the total cost to consumers. This apparently paradoxical result can be resolved if the search costs of consumers are considered. The total cost to the consumer is the price of the good purchased plus the costs of obtaining information about the price and quality of rival products.

Bayer's advertising, by informing consumers that "Bayer is better," may reduce the search costs of consumers enough to lower the total cost of consuming Bayer aspirin below the costs of searching out and purchasing a substitute pain killer. A few years ago, fifty tablets of Bayer cost 63 cents, whereas the same quantity of St. Joseph's cost 39 cents; the 24-cent difference would not pay for much consumer research by an individual purchaser.

It is also conceivable that advertising reduces both search costs and product prices. One study compared the prices of eyeglasses in states that allowed optometrists to advertise with those that prohibited such advertising. The study reported that in states that prohibited advertising, the average price of glasses paid by consumers was $37.48. Where advertising was permitted, the average price was $17.98, or almost 50 percent less. This study has the advantage in that the "free rider" problem is absent because all eyeglasses in an entire state are included, and because differences in the quality of glasses purchased by persons in California and those in New York should not be enough to account for the big difference in price.

The average price of eyeglasses was lower in states that permitted advertising because low-price sellers require large sales volumes, which means that they must draw from a wide geographic area. Advertising allows them to convey the information about their lower prices to persons located in a large area. In the absence of this information, it is not possible to sell in enough volume to reduce prices significantly. The result is more smaller firms, but higher costs and consumer prices.

The final question that we will consider is whether advertising increases competition or fosters monopoly. This is a question of whether advertising erects barriers to new firms that prevent the firms from entering an industry when economic profits appear. The FTC alleged that this was the case in the ready-to-eat cereal industry. If no barriers exist whenever economic profits appear, then new firms will enter the industry, increasing the quantity supplied and lowering both product prices and business firms' profits. Does advertising create a barrier to entry, which protects existing firms, granting them a form of monopoly?

Again, as you might expect, the evidence is contradictory and expert opinion exists on both sides of the question. The argument that advertising creates a barrier to entry generally revolves around the effect that product advertising has upon brand loyalty. If advertising commits consumers to a particular brand, a new entrant would have to either offer lower prices or spend more on advertising, hence have higher costs than established firms. If this is the case, established firms can charge somewhat higher prices and earn higher profits without attracting rivals into the industry. In order for advertising to create a significant barrier to entry, a new entrant would have to spend more than a dollar on advertising to counteract a dollar spent by an existing firm to maintain brand loyalty;

hence advertising must be more effective for an entrenched firm than for the new entrant.

The measurement of advertising effectiveness is generally very imprecise. An often quoted statement by the advertising manager of a firm illustrates this difficulty: "We know that half of our advertising is wasted, but we don't know which half." To avoid this problem, economists have chosen indirect ways to measure the effect of advertising on the barriers to entry. If the economy is competitive, then in the long run profit rates among industries should be about the same, adjusting for risk. A high-profit rate will attract rivals, which will force the rate down to that earned in other industries. When the profit rate between industries is examined, as the FTC and others have done, those industries that engage heavily in advertising, such as the drug, soap, cereal, grooming supplies (razors), and soft drink industries, tend to consistently earn higher-than-average profits. This suggests to the FTC that advertising does create barriers to entry.

Such studies are not without their critics, who claim that the researchers failed to make the necessary adjustments to adequately reflect investment in advertising by an industry. When advertising is considered a capital investment rather than a current expense, the excess profits disappear. Furthermore, when firms, not industries, are compared in the same way, scholars find no statistically significant relationship between advertising expenditures and profit rates. These studies conclude that advertising does not create barriers to entry.

The evidence on the influence of advertising upon the condition of entry is thus indirect and contradictory. A possible reason for these results could be that the effect of advertising upon the ease of entry into an industry may vary between industries. Advertising may ease entry if it increases brand switching, but it may make entry more difficult if it increases brand loyalty.

We have heard arguments that advertising raises prices, reduces competition, and wastes resources; and arguments that advertising lowers the total costs to consumers by providing information that promotes competition and efficient resource allocation. Either view might be correct in a particular situation. It would appear that judging the economic effect of advertising must be done on a case-by-case basis.

Additional Readings

Ayanian, Robert. "Does Advertising Persuade Consumers to Buy Things They Do Not Need?" *The Attack on Corporate America*, M. Bruce Johnson, ed. McGraw-Hill, 1978.

Bloch, Henry. "Is Corporate Product Advertising a Barrier to Entry?" *The Attack on Corporate America*, M. Bruce Johnson, ed. McGraw-Hill, 1978.

Brozen, Yale. "The FTC's Outmoded Campaign Against Advertising." *Reason*, June 1973.

Galbraith, John Kenneth. *The New Industrial State*. Houghton-Mifflin, 1967.

Nader, Ralph, Mark Green, and Joel Seligman. *The Taming of the Giant Corporation*. Norton, 1976.

Preview

The Environmental Protection Agency is searching for new, low-cost ways to control pollution. The rising costs of environmental protection have generated political demands to modify pollution standards. There are two basic ways for the government to control pollution. The first is to directly prohibit the behavior that causes pollution. The second is to create the incentives that would cause people to behave differently in a way that eliminates the social problem. Until recently, Congress and the Environmental Protection Agency have chosen the first approach, but the rising number of complaints about the cost of this approach have caused the Environmental Protection Agency to recently consider other, potentially lower cost, means of accomplishing the task. Among the alternatives being considered is a proposal to allocate pollution rights by using a market. This chapter considers the virtues of this proposal and explores a case history in which a price system has been successfully employed to control pollution.

Key Economic Points

A resource held as common property lies at the heart of most environmental problems.

A price system could be used to control pollution.

The costs of controlling pollution by direct regulation are compared with the costs of using a price system.

28

Environmental Problems: A Novel Way to Control Pollution

The Environmental Protection Agency (EPA) is looking into the possibility of establishing a market to sell the right to pollute. It is considering creating an auction market that would allow companies to buy and sell the right to discharge specified quantities of pollutants into the environment. Under this proposed system, the existing emissions limits already in existence for an area would determine the amount of pollution "rights" that would be put up for auction. Business firms would be able to bid against one another to determine how much pollution each would be allowed to emit. The experimental use of a pollution market is being considered specifically to control the emission of fluorocarbons used widely in refrigeration and air conditioning. A future market in pollutants to regulate air pollution in the Ohio Valley is also under consideration. If the experiments are undertaken and prove worthwhile, the use of a market to control pollution could have wide applicability in the nation's fight against pollution.

The potential use of a market to control pollution represents a major change in policy for the EPA, which has up to now relied mainly upon direct regulation and controls to reduce air and water pollution and to control pesticides, noise, and radiation. The EPA or appropriate agency currently sets standards for the maximum allowable amounts of discharge for particular pollutants, and the administrative agencies and the judicial branch of government enforce these standards. This approach has yielded important gains in the struggle against environmental damage. The trend toward increasing environmental harm has been slowed or, in some places, such as Los Angeles, actually reversed.

Environmental regulations, however, have also proven costly and cumbersome, and contain defects that promise to forestall further significant reductions in environmental damage. The regulations have been criticized as being too rigid, too costly, and too restrictive of economic growth. Many people fear that the considerable costs of abating pollution will cause the federal and state legislators to weaken or abandon some regulations altogether. Recently, even the EPA proposed to slacken certain water pollution rules because compliance would be "unreasonably costly."

The pressure to reduce the costs of direct regulation has caused the EPA to consider less costly ways of accomplishing its goals. The creation of a market in pollution rights is the most promising of the alternatives. Economists have been arguing for this approach for more than a decade. This chapter considers the advantages of a market to reduce pollution compared with the existing system of direct regulation.

It is vitally important to reduce the cost of controlling pollution whenever possible because the amount of resources required for the task is staggering. Although there is probably no good estimate of the total costs involved, all existing estimates suggest that the costs are very large. The Commission on Water Quality, for example, has estimated the capital costs of meeting the statutory water quality requirements by 1983 to be $43 billion, or over $200 for every person in the United States. Estimates of the total capital cost for controlling all forms of pollution (air, water, noise, solid waste, and pesticides) run as high as $100 billion, with estimates of annual operating costs of up to $20 billion. No one knows the total costs for certain, but all estimates agree that the opportunity cost of completely controlling pollution is high. Since society has alternative uses for scarce resources, if we insist on employing a system of pollution control that is more expensive than necessary, we jeopardize achieving the goal of controlling pollution. When faced with excessive costs, society may choose less pollution control and more of other things, a choice that could be unnecessary if the most efficient methods of controlling pollution are employed.

The costs of regulating pollution by using a market compare so favorably with the costs of direct regulation that the proposal deserves serious consideration. The market is the major social institution used to allocate scarce resources in the United States. Under certain conditions, competitively determined market prices provide all the information consumers and producers need to make optimal economic decisions. As long as private costs and benefits are identical to social costs and benefits, the market will allocate resources efficiently. This condition suggests what would make a pollutant discharge market different from other kinds of markets. The environment as a vessel to absorb waste products is not priced, even though it has become a scarce resource. A pulp and paper mill, for example, contracts with labor and the owners of capital and resources, and pays the market price to obtain the factors of production it requires to produce paper. Because the firm must sacrifice by paying a price to obtain these inputs, it has an incentive to conserve on each resource and to use it efficiently.

But a paper mill does not bargain or contract with anyone to use the rivers and atmosphere to dispose of its waste products. The right to use the environment freely has historically been theirs and everyone else's. The environment has been held as common property, with everyone having an equal right to use it. Because everyone already has access to as much of the resource as desired, it is used as if it were a free good. If everyone uses it as such, its capacity to absorb waste will eventually inevitably be exceeded and a pollution problem created.

The existence of a common property resource lies at the heart of every pollution problem. The relative scarcity of the environment is not reflected in its cost to users because no market exists to trade rights of access. No market exists because no one can be excluded from using the resource; hence there is nothing to trade or exchange. As a result, the resource is overutilized because all the benefits of discharging waste products into the environment accrue to the polluter, but the costs are shared equally among all users of the environment. Therefore, the polluter receives all the benefits but pays only a small part of the costs involved in overusing the environment. The harm caused by the overuse of a common property resource is called a "negative externality" because the cost falls upon society as a whole and not on the individual user.

The solution to this problem may appear extremely simple: create private property rights over the environment. Then potential users would have to bargain with the owners of the resource to obtain its use, just as the paper mills bargain with the owners of other resources held as private property. However, in practice it is not physically possible to separate air, water, and silence into ownership units in the way land and labor are divided. Government has therefore turned to the most obvious way of limiting use of the environment—direct regulation of access.

This is the approach employed under the Clean Air Act and Water Pollution Control Act. Agencies set standards for the total amount of pollutants that can be released into the environment, and the states enforce these standards. Two types of standards are typically employed: the ambient standard and the effluent standard. The ambient standard is the legal specification of minimum conditions that must be met for some indicator of environmental quality. The ambient standard may state, for example, that the amount of nitrous oxide in the atmosphere may not exceed 2 parts per million at a specified place more than 1 day a year. The effluent standard specifies the maximum amount of permissible discharge of a pollutant from a single source.

The use of direct regulation, especially the effluent standard, encourages the inefficient allocation of resources because direct regulation does not encourage the marginal cost of pollution abatement to be the same everywhere. Suppose existing atmospheric conditions in a region require emissions to be reduced by 10 percent. A direct governmental order for all emitters to reduce their discharges by 10 percent is almost certain to be inefficient.

Consider the not unrealistic case of two factories, a steel mill and a copper smelter, that discharge equal amounts of pollutants, but the costs for each factory of reducing emissions are different. Suppose it costs the steel mill $500,000 to reduce its emissions by 10 percent, and twice as much, or $1 million, to reduce emissions by 20 percent. It would cost the copper smelter $5 million to reduce its emissions by 10 percent because of its different technological process, and $10 million for a 20 percent reduction.

But it is possible to accomplish the same goal at a much lower cost. The steel mill could reduce its emissions by 20 percent, which would meet the region's requirements, for a cost of $1 million. Thus the control of pollution could be accomplished for less if some mechanism existed that would concentrate all abatement controls in the steel mill.

An auction market would accomplish this task. Suppose the pollution control agency auctioned off the right to continue discharging as before. The bidding would quickly go to $1 million, at which point the steel mill would drop out of the bidding, choosing instead to install the necessary pollution control equipment. The copper smelter would obtain the right to continue discharging as before for the payment of a little more than $1 million. The pollution control agency could then pay the steel mill the $1 million as a subsidy. The result: emissions in the region would be reduced by 10 percent at a total cost of a little over $1 million, a saving of $4.5 million over the cost of direct regulation.

Another defect inherent in relying exclusively upon regulatory standards to control pollution is that they often discourage economic growth. The Clean Air Act of 1970, for example, barred further industrial expansion in areas that did not meet standards by 1975. A majority of the nation's air quality districts (156 out of 247) failed to meet this goal, legally halting further growth until the standards were met. But few existing industrial firms had any incentive to reduce their emissions to make it possible for new factories owned by others to be built. The Ford Motor Company was able to expand in Louisville, Kentucky because the firm was able to reduce emissions in its painting plant enough to offset the pollution from the new facilities. But Ford would have had no incentive to do the same so that General Motors could build a new plant.

This led the EPA to adopt its "emissions offset" rule. If a firm wants to expand in an area that does not meet the environmental quality standards, it can do so if the company cleans up a greater amount of pollution than its new facility will create. This policy has allowed General Motors to build a plant in Oklahoma, Volkswagen to construct a facility in Pennsylvania, and several refineries to expand in Texas. Standard Oil of Ohio (Sohio), for example, was able to meet California's rigid standards for its Long Beach terminal to unload Alaskan oil, partly by installing, at its own expense, $78 million worth of pollution control equipment for the Long Beach power plant owned by Southern California Edison. The emissions offset rule thus allowed Sohio to search out the least costly way to reduce pollution to meet the standards. The offset rule is, in effect, the first step taken by the EPA toward using a price system as the lowest cost means of controlling pollution. But this approach involves higher transaction costs in seeking out and negotiating with rivals to achieve the necessary pollution reduction than using a market directly would entail.

The best argument for the use of a market to control pollution is found in the actual practices that control pollution in Germany's Ruhr River Valley. The Ruhr is the sewer of one of the world's most concentrated industrial areas. The Ruhr Valley contains 40 percent of German industry, including 80 percent of the coal, iron, steel, and heavy chemical output. It is a small river about half the size of the Potomac. The volume of waste discharged into the river is large, actually greater than the natural flow of the river during the dry season. Yet the Ruhr is clean enough for people and fish to swim unharmed.

This amazing accomplishment is the result of using prices or charges to control emissions into the river. The goal is to maintain the quality of the water at minimum cost. The authorities calculate the amount of pollution the river can carry and then put a price on discharges. Once a price is set, each business is free to adjust its operations any way it chooses as long as it pays for the pollutants discharged. Each source of pollution under this system decides how much to control its discharges on the basis of its own costs. Those with costs of cleaning emissions lower than the price set will comply, and those with higher costs will clean up to the point at which the costs equal the price charged and discharge the rest. The result is that the cost of controlling pollution is lower than it would be under direct regulations, which do not allow this kind of private decision making by business firms. If the authorities find pollution levels exceeding the standards, they raise the price and business firms respond by voluntarily reducing their discharge (treating more of the effluent) rather than paying the higher price.

Although water management in the Ruhr is not a complete market system (authorities set the price rather than let the market do it), the system does rely more on prices to control pollution than most other methods. The system is also more successful than others presently used elsewhere. In both theory and in limited applications, then, the market or price system so far has proven to be an attractive, relatively low-cost way to control pollution.

Another advantage of creating a market to control pollution lies in the low cost of administrating environmental protection. Under a market system, the EPA would have only to establish the permissible level of discharge and then arrange an auction. Thereafter, the authorities would need to be concerned only with monitoring the quantity and quality of the pollutants discharged. This would be a highly favorable turnabout. Currently, under direct regulation, environmental protection agencies must not only set the overall standards but are charged with seeing that industries use the best practicable control technology available. Thus the agencies must master the technologies of production in each industry in order to determine the best available techniques for controlling pollution. They must do this as well as monitor the behavior of thousands of firms affected by the regulation for compliance. It is simply too much to expect any government agency with limited resources to be able to meet these requirements. It is much more reasonable to expect the EPA, or state agencies, to become experts on monitoring procedures than to expect them to become knowledgeable about every industrial process and pollution control technique currently in use or forthcoming.

The advantages of creating a market to control pollution are substantial for many of the areas now governed by direct regulations. This is not to suggest that there is no place for direct regulation. A price system is probably not suitable for some environmental problems. The control of highly toxic substances, for example, is probably better handled by direct regulation because the goal is zero discharge.

There are a number of objections that have been raised to creating a market in pollution rights. Many objections are common to any kind of pollution control, but some are specifically aimed at a market system. One such objection is that a market in pollution rights would lead to speculation. No doubt speculation would occur, but it is not apt to create any more problems in this area than in any other area where the price system is used. Another objection is that environmentalists could also buy, and hoard, pollution rights in order to keep pollution below the administratively desired level. But this would only happen if the value of reduced pollution was higher to environmental groups than the value of polluting was to industry. If so, then the highest valued use, as determined in the market, is a cleaner environment, and that is a virtue, not a defect, of the proposed market system.

Creating a market in pollution rights has so many advantages over direct regulation in many areas that it should certainly be tried on an experimental basis. The main advantage is that a price system would bring about environmental repair at the lowest possible social cost. Not only would business firms have an incentive to minimize the cost of achieving the socially desired level of emissions, but the EPA could administer the program at much lower cost than the present system of direct regulation. Creating a market in pollution rights would remedy the main cause of pollution; namely, that the environment currently is a scarce good that is not priced. A market that establishes the price of using the environment as a waste receptacle overcomes this defect and allows the overall price system to function efficiently. This is not to suggest that a system of direct regulation could not accomplish the same thing, only that a market for pollution rights would do it more efficiently.

Additional Readings

Anderson, F. R., A. V. Kneese, P. D. Reed, Serge Taylor, and R. B. Stevenson. *Environmental Improvement Through Economic Incentives.* Resources for the Future, 1978.

Dales, J. H. *Pollution, Property and Price.* University of Toronto Press, 1968.

Martin, Douglas. "Building Blocks: Curbs on Construction Where Air Is Dirty Rankles Businessmen." *Wall Street Journal,* December 17, 1977.

Martin, Douglas. "EPA Ponders Letting Concerns Buy and Sell 'Right' to Pollute Air." *Wall Street Journal,* December 15, 1978.

Ruff, L. E. "The Economic Common Sense of Pollution." *The Public Interest,* Spring 1970.

Preview

Ocean oil spills are becoming an increasing world problem, but so far human achievement and nature have succeeded in significantly reducing environmental damage from this source. With oil tanker traffic expected to increase with time, the potential damage to both fishing grounds and ocean beaches is considerable. This chapter explores what can and should be done to minimize the social costs from ocean oil spills. There are reasons to expect that environmental damage to the oceans will be much higher than it should be because oil tanker owners are not responsible for all the damage their vessels might do. Two possible approaches to solving this problem are considered.

Key Economic Points

Limited liability for the owners of oil tankers creates a negative externality for the world.

Changing the existing property rights with respect to legal liability is required to eliminate the externality.

The benefits and costs of creating unlimited liability are compared with the benefits and costs of raising minimum standards of tanker safety to solve the oil spill problem.

29

Altering Property Rights: Dealing with Oil Spills

On December 15, 1976, the oil tanker Argo Merchant ran aground 27 miles southeast of Nantucket, breaking up and spilling its cargo of 7.5 million gallons of thick, gummy residual oil into the Atlantic, creating an oil slick that at it peak covered 12,000 square miles. The spill threatened the beaches of Nantucket, Martha's Vineyard, Cape Cod, and Rhode Island, and the fish in the Georges Bank, which produces about 10 percent of the world's catch. Fortunately, these disasters were averted as the slick drifted out to sea. Not so fortunate were the consequences of the 1967 Torrey Canyon spill in the English Channel. The slick from that spill spread along the coast of England and France, and cost $22 million to clean up. Ten years later the Amoco Cadiz broke up off the coast of Brittany, polluting 110 miles of coastline and raising fears of damage to nearby fishing grounds. The damage was less than initially expected, partly because of the ability of the marine environment to absorb oil spills and to regenerate itself, and partly because of massive efforts mounted by the French to contain and clean up the mess.

The initial fears of massive environmental damage from oil spills were based upon the belief that oil is not biodegradable, a belief that appears in retrospect to have been exaggerated. Oil does evaporate. It is oxidized by the sun, and some ocean fauna and microorganisms are able to "eat" at least some of its components. This natural cleansing action of the sea has been sufficient to deal with most oil spills so far.

The damage of recent oil spills has been reduced by improvements in the techniques of cleaning up spills. New chemical detergents and absorbents have been developed, and new and better methods of sweeping up spilled oil are being employed. The improved techniques, equipment, and skilled personnel are now on standby to be employed whenever an oil spill occurs.

The fact that the combined efforts of the ocean and human beings have been able to contain the damage of oil spills to date does not mean that oil spills will never be a serious threat to the environment. The worst possible spills involve refined products within sheltered waters that are not fully subject to the wave and storm activity of the open seas. The increasing dependence of the world on oil from the Near East means increasing tanker traffic and, with it, the likelihood of more frequent accidents. The number of tankers entering U.S. waters increased almost 90 percent between 1970 and 1976, for example. What can and should be done to minimize the social cost of the oil spills, both minor and major? Editor Phillip H. Abelson of *Science* magazine summarized the matter succinctly in an article on the subject of oil spills: "Incidents of this kind should be avoided, and the perpetrators should be forced to pay any demonstrable damage" (p. 145). To understand what Abelson meant by this statement, we need to first know something about the economics of oil spills.

Oil spills present an economic problem to society because they involve a negative externality. When the owner of the oil tanker and the owner of the oil itself contract with each other, they do not have to consider all the social costs. They can ignore the cost of potential damage resulting from oil spills. When a spill occurs, the owners lose their ship and the owner of the oil the cargo. However, the oil may also damage marine life, so that fishermen and consumers lose, and beaches may be ruined for recreation. Fishing grounds and most ocean beaches are held as common property. Everyone has the right to use them, but no individual owns them, so the individuals affected by oil spills cannot sue to recover their losses. The private costs of transporting oil, therefore, are less than the social costs, hence the contractually determined price for chartering an oil tanker is too low and too much oil is transported by tanker.

Furthermore, because they ignore the social cost of environmental damage, the tanker owners devote too few resources to ship safety. The Argo Merchant, for instance, was over 26 years old and ready for the scrap yard when it ran aground. It had been involved in eighteen previous accidents, including two groundings. In its final mishap the ship was 24 miles off course because of a faulty gyrocompass and an inexperienced crew. Spectacular improvements in oil tanker construction have been made in the past two decades, but almost all efforts have been devoted to building bigger, rather than safer, vessels. The average size of oil tankers has increased from less than 30,000 tons at the end of World War II to more than 200,000 tons. Vessels of more than 750,000 tons have been built; they are the largest ships afloat. Yet these ships generally have only single-plated hulls and one propulsion system and one rudder. There are no safeguards against grounding should engine or steering problems develop, nor against spills during grounding caused by the rupture of a single hull.

Had tankership owners been forced to bear the full cost of any oil spills caused by their vessels, they would have insisted that their ships be made safer. They would have insisted, for instance, on double hulls and twin propulsion and steering units, even if these improvements meant that the ships had to be smaller. It would have been in their economic interest to do so.

There are two ways that society could require ship owners to consider the social cost of oil spills. The government could make the owner liable for all damages, as editor Abelson suggests, or it could legislate minimum tanker safety standards for vessels entering U.S. territorial waters. If the tanker owner was legally liable for all damage done by an oil spill, and insurance or a security bond was required in advance, the owner would have to consider the potential costs of an oil spill when setting shipping rates. The social cost of oil spills thus would become a private cost, providing a strong incentive for owners to take safety precautions

With increased liability, insurance rates would vary significantly with the safety of the insured vessel. Double-hulled vessels with two engines would pay lower rates according to their loss history, and owners would have a stronger incentive to employ them. Imposing unlimited liability upon vessel owners would create the incentive for owners to do all that was economically feasible to avoid oil spills and ensure that cleanups would be paid for and compensation paid for all damages.

The second approach would be for the government to establish and enforce minimum standards for tanker safety. A list of safety regulations pertaining to vessel construction, crew training, and required navigation aids would be developed, along with a schedule of mandatory inspections and a system of fines for violations. In principle, this procedure would work as well as establishing unlimited liability. But in practice it is more difficult to enforce compliance because public authorities are responsible for detection and enforcement. One advantage of the unlimited liability approach is that the costs of enforcement are shifted to the tanker owner, who would decide which improvements were economically feasible and be held responsible if the precautions taken proved inadequate.

The U.S government has moved toward adopting both approaches since the Argo Merchant spill. In 1978, Congress passed the Port Safety and Tank Vessel Safety Act, which established a variety of new standards for tanker construction. Among other things, new tankers must now have double bottoms and improved navigation and safety equipment. Many of the new features are costly, but the industry, under intense public pressure since the Argo Merchant wreck, has accepted the most important ones. The Coast Guard has stepped up its program of boarding tankers to check for deficiencies in ventilation, electrical systems, and fire prevention equipment.

The House of Representatives in 1978 also passed the Oil Pollution Liability Compensation Act, designed to increase the shippers' liability, but the Senate took no action and the bill died at adjournment. The bill would have raised the legal liability of tanker operations from $160 a ton to $300 a ton. Thus, a supertanker of 200,000 tons would be liable for $60 million. Even more important, the law would extend the rights of injured parties to collect damages, overcoming some of the common property problems. Under the proposed law, a hotel owner would be able to collect if a spill damaged a beach and affected the hotel's bookings, and a fisherman could collect for a declining catch resulting from a spill.

This bill, even if eventually passed by Congress, would not completely solve the externality problem. While the limits of liability would have paid for the $22 million cleanup of the Torrey Canyon spill, for example, it would not fully compensate for the damages of future large spills in confined waters. A spill of distilled product in Puget Sound or Chesapeake Bay would easily exceed the limit of liability. The French government is suing Amoco International Oil Company for $300 million in compensation for the Amoco Cadiz incident, and eight French communities in Brittany filed suit in U.S. Federal Court for $435 million in damages. Neither suit has much chance of full success because of the limited liability law now in effect. But even given the plaintiff's incentive to overstate actual damages, the Amoco Cadiz incident demonstrates that a bad spill can cause damages in excess of the liability limits of the proposed law.

In order to deal with this possibility of damages in excess of the liability limit, the proposed act calls for a $200 million fund to be raised by a 3-cents-a-barrel tax on all oil entering the United States. This fund would be drawn upon to pay damages in excess of the legal liability of the spill, or damages when the source of the spill is unknown. The purpose of this provision is to overcome the defects of limited liability and the problems of detecting the actual violator, since many spills are small and the violator escapes detection. The incentives produced by this provision, however, would discourage investment in safety since both safe and unsafe vessels pay the same tax.

Despite its defects, the proposed Oil Pollution Liability and Compensation Act would be a step in the right direction. It would internalize most of the externalities currently existing in the oil tanker industry. It would be noted that whichever direction the government takes to deal with this externality—imposing safety regulations or extending liability—a modification of property rights is required. The externality originated because existing property rights did not require oil tanker owners to consider all the social costs of transporting oil. Any solution will require existing property rights to be modified so that tanker owners have an incentive to minimize the possibilities of an oil spill.

Additional Readings

Abelson, Phillip H. "Editorial Commentary," *Science.* January 14, 1977.
"Oil Spills: How Much Real Damage." *Dun's Review,* December 1978.

Preview

American cities offer many advantages to their residents. The main virtue of living in a city is the variety of alternatives available to a resident. However, the obvious urban problems that burden many American cities significantly increase the costs to a city dweller of enjoying this variety. Unfortunately, many urban problems either are made worse or are the result of ignoring the role that the incentives created by public policy play in determining behavior. Local governments, by ignoring or refusing to explicitly employ the price system, have created in its place a perverse price system that was never intended. One of the unintended effects was to actually reduce the variety of alternatives available to residents. This chapter investigates several specific urban problems to discover their causes and explores some potential solutions that involve explicitly employing a price system.

Key Economic Points

The first step toward solving any urban problem is to identify the incentives that cause people to behave in the way that causes the problem.

Employing a policy of zero pricing for publicly supplied goods means that some other nonprice way of allocating resources must be substituted.

Some of the social costs involved in employing nonprice mechanisms to allocate scarce publicly supplied goods are identified.

What are the incentives created by the property tax?

Three functions of publicly provided goods and services are reviewed, as well as whether a zero price is always appropriate for these goods and services.

30

Urban Problems: The City as a Perverse Price System

No one needs to be told that urban problems exist. Most people experience every day some of the frustrations of dealing with congested streets and roadways, an unresponsive educational system, the sight of urban blight and sprawl, the dangers of pollution, and inept and insufficient public services. These problems are not new; they have been with us as long as cities have existed. However, they are more important today than ever before because of the mass migration of Americans to urban areas during the last century.

Cities also offer some significant advantages to their residents. Because of their large concentrations of people, cities provide a large market that supports a wide variety of consumer attractions. Large cities simply have more of everything, more goods to choose from and more services to enjoy. Urban problems, however, increase the cost of taking advantage of this pluralism. The mass flight to the suburbs to avoid the problems of the central city has reduced the welfare of both the suburban dweller and the residents left behind in the cities. The suburban dweller bears higher commuting costs and reduced access to the city's attractions. The remaining city dweller enjoys less pluralism and directly suffers from the deterioration of the urban environment caused in part by the financial pinch resulting from a dwindling tax base. It's a vicious circle: the worse the plight of cities becomes, the more the middle class moves to the suburbs; the more that move, the worse the urban problems become.

The root of many urban problems is the failure of city, state, and federal governments to consider the incentives current public policy provides individual decision makers, and to explicitly use the price system to allocate scarce resources. Prices in the private sector ration the use of existing facilities, signal the direction for new investment, and influence the distribution of income. Whereas prices perform such a function in the private sector, they have been virtually eliminated in the public sector. The goods and services produced by the public sector are generally allocated on a nonprice basis. The result is widespread inefficiency, which wastes valuable resources and affects the distribution of income in our cities in unexpected ways.

Much of economics deals with the problem of how a decentralized decision-making system can be made to provide the proper incentives, so that individuals acting in their own best interests collectively behave in a way that furthers the public good. Most of the major urban problems require solutions that channel the decisions of millions of individuals toward socially desirable objectives. Currently, the incentives provided by existing laws, institutions, and government practices provide incentives that guide individual decisions in perverse directions, actually causing some of the problems for which we now seek solutions. A price system allocating urban resources is not absent, but is present in a distorted and, until relatively recently, unanalyzed form.

The beginning step toward any solution to a particular urban problem is to identify the incentives that channel people to behave in the way that causes the problem. What incentives, for example, cause a neighborhood to decay, a school system to become unresponsive, either to the pupils or to the parents it is supposed to serve, or the streets to be filled to capacity with traffic jams during rush hours?

Consider the traffic congestion that chokes the entrances and exits to the downtowns of our cities during rush hour. A motorist, under our existing tax structure, is subject to the same license fees and gas taxes to pay for the very expensive streets, freeways, bridges, and tunnels whether he or she drives at rush hour or not. In order to facilitate rush hour traffic, multiple lanes must be provided that are empty of motorists during off-peak hours. Thus drivers at off-peak times subsidize the rush hour commuters, paying for facilities they do not use. Because rush hour drivers do not pay the full cost of traveling during this time period, too many choose to travel during peak hours.

If all motorists had to pay the true cost of their rush hour travel, some drivers would voluntarily switch to public transit or car pools, or elect to travel during off-peak times. A tax on rush hour driving would accomplish this. Moreover, such a tax is relatively easy to administer. The city of Singapore has instituted an entry-to-the-city tax for motor vehicles. A fee must be paid to drive into the city between 7 and 9 in the morning. After the tax was imposed, congestion in the city was substantially reduced, as many former rush hour drivers switched to alternative means of transportation. The entry tax thus became a price that rationed existing scarce facilities to those persons who valued their use enough to pay the tax. Those who did not selected another alternative.

Equally important, the entry tax, by reducing the number of cars entering the city during morning rush hour, delayed or eliminated the costly investment required to increase the capacity of the city streets. Resources that would have been channeled into this program were freed for alternative uses. Given the severe budget constraints placed on our nation's cities, with many of them on the brink of bankruptcy, the opportunity cost of resources freed by explicitly using price to allocate scarce existing resources is very high indeed. It is sometimes difficult to realize that the opportunity cost of maintaining and expanding municipal streets is to have fewer other urban goods and services, but it is. If a city has to increase its street maintenance expenditures, it cannot use the same funds to hire police, buy library books, or purchase a kangaroo for the children's zoo. The opportunity cost of providing too much of one good or service is the provision of less of other goods or services.

The use of prices to allocate scarce resources serves another important function; it acts as a guide for further public investment. If the demand for driving into the city employing an entry tax increases, it will be reflected in increased toll revenues, signaling to the city planners that the effective demand for transportation facilities has increased. Political decision makers are thus provided with excellent evidence that more social investment in this area should be considered and may be desirable. Furthermore, the revenues from the tax provide the means of financing the investment. Because the tax is paid only by persons who desire and would benefit from the new facilities, it becomes a user tax par excellence. Those who benefit also pay.

In Singapore, a money price in the form of the entry tax replaced a nonprice means of allocating scarce resources. Space on the city's streets prior to tax had been allocated on a first-come, first-served basis. Commuters paid with their time for the congestion that free access caused. The tax substituted money for time. Another advantage of the tax is that the city collectively (politically) decided to ration scarce street facilities in this way. Prior to that no one had agreed to use time as a rationing device. It just happened as over time traffic density had increased.

It would perhaps have been even better had Singapore instituted an entry tax on one or more roads into the city, leaving some alternative routes for free access. In that case a commuter could choose to pay with either time or money, whichever he or she had more of. One of the problems of unthinkingly offering public services at zero price is that the diversity of options that are a city's great attraction is reduced. Using prices that can be varied to allocate scarce urban resource potentially allows a much wider range of public services to be offered.

Other urban problems are made worse by not recognizing the incentives that existing costs and prices create. A tax is, after all, a cost to the person who must bear the tax and provides incentives for behavior just as powerful as those market prices provide.

Consider the influence of taxes upon another serious urban problem, the decay of neighborhoods in the central city. Urban blight is the consequence of the independent decisions of thousands of landlords to let the buildings they own deteriorate. The incentives that led to these decisions are many and varied, but among them is the property tax. The property tax is levied on the value of real estate, the land and the building. If a landlord remodels the building, installing up-to-date heating, plumbing, and sanitation facilities that are socially desirable, rents must increase to pay for the investment. But the increase in rents must not just cover the costs of the improvement, but also must cover the resulting increases in property taxes. Remodeling the building increases the assessed value, hence the property taxes go up, and rents must rise by more than the value of the newer facilities. The property tax is in this sense a tax levied on improvements, a tax on socially desirable behavior.

The property tax, by creating incentives to allow buildings to deteriorate and reducing the supply of housing in general, has contributed to the current housing plight in the United States. The poor have been left behind to inherit the decaying central city, while the more affluent have escaped the problem by moving to the suburbs. This flight of the middle class has created another problem, known as urban sprawl. The migration of the middle class has even been subsidized by the persons left behind. The price that has been set for using urban fringe space has been too low, that is, below the full cost of extending utility, transportation, and fire and police protection. Ordinarily a flat charge is imposed for extending water, sewer, gas, and electricity to a new suburban development regardless of the actual cost of extending the services. An incentive is thus created for developers to skip over contiguous expensive vacant land and develop instead the less expensive, more remote parcels. The pricing of utility and public services thus creates some of the incentive that results in urban sprawl.

The flight to the suburbs has reduced the tax base of cities. While the financial condition of cities has declined, cities have continued to extend "free" public access to an increasing number of activities, with serious consequences for the allocation of scarce urban resources. There are very good reasons for some goods to be publicly supplied at zero price, but these reasons do not extend to all publicly supplied goods and services. Some services must be collectively consumed in one indivisible amount. Once such services are produced, everyone consumes them, and no one can be excluded. Goods with these characteristics are termed public goods. Justice and air pollution control are examples. When the air improves in quality as the result of pollution control, everyone benefits and no resident can be denied the benefits. Once an urban area provides cleaner air through an air pollution abatement program, the clean air is there for all to enjoy. Public goods cannot be left to the private sector to provide because not enough will be produced. Because no one can be excluded from enjoying the good once it is produced, few persons will voluntarily pay for what can be obtained for free. Therefore government must provide such goods and impose taxes to pay for them. But compare the provision of pollution control with the provision of a city-owned free public library. Although no resident can be excluded from enjoying the benefits of cleaner air, any potential user could easily be excluded from using the library. Thus price could be used to ration library services, charging users to check out books. The public goods that cities must produce include local law, police and fire protection, and a system of legal courts.

But this is not all the goods that cities provide for free. Cities also provide a range of goods and services at zero price, or below the full cost of operation, that, like libraries, are not public goods. These goods are called "merit goods," and are collectively provided or subsidized because their consumption is believed to be particularly meritorious. Basic education is a merit good. It is provided free, not because students couldn't be locked out of schools, but because of the widely held belief that none should be denied an education and the equality of opportunity that results. The range of merit goods offered by cities is large. A partial list would include, besides basic education, public parks, stadiums, arenas, libraries, museums, and perhaps golf courses, garden patches, boat marinas, and urban expressways.

A third function of government is to alter the distribution of income. Welfare payments are an example of one group receiving income supplied by taxes on another group. Cities often provide the merit goods listed above at zero price in order to provide the "poor" with equal access.

Public goods, merit goods, and the distribution of income provide the rationale for free or subsidized publicly produced goods. Unfortunately, this rationale has become entrenched in the belief that all local public services should be provided at zero cost, even if they do not meet any of these criteria. The provision of free public expressways for automobile movement through the crowded cores of our urban areas cannot be defended on the ground that (1) motorists could not be excluded if they refused to pay a toll, (2) the private automobile is an especially meritorious way to travel, or (3) private motorists cannot afford to pay the full social costs of driving. Neither do golf courses, tennis courts, or boat marinas meet any of these criteria. The extension of publicly supplied goods at less than full cost has effects upon the distribution of income that run counter to the general public belief that more equality is desirable. Taxing the poor so that the more affluent may drive their automobiles, play golf, and moor their boats at less than the full cost of providing these facilities does not promote more equality of income.

Attempts to alter the distribution of income provide another example of the danger of ignoring incentives. When we collectively decide that we wish to provide a good or service to one group and charge another, we do so because we feel the recipients to be particularly "worthy" or "needy" of our collective aid. Even here incentives matter. If aid to dependent children is available only to single-parent families, an incentive for family disintegration is created. If all income from work efforts is deducted from welfare payments, little incentive remains for recipients to work to supplement welfare income. Welfare payments may, depending upon how they are administered, reinforce the root causes of poverty.

Sometimes, in a collective concern over the distribution of income, cities have attempted to regulate the private sector—often without full knowledge or consideration of the effects of the regulations imposed. The housing sector has been particularly prone to local regulation. New York City's rent control legislation is infamous. Despite the deterioration of the cityscape that is a direct result of rent controls, other cities are still experimenting with such legislation. Los Angeles recently imposed temporary rent ceilings. Seattle and other cities have legally halted the conversion of apartments to condominiums.

Cities have been particularly active in regulating or operating public transit. Policy in this area has generally been to create monopolies and cartels. Hitchhiking, for example, is often illegal, as is carrying passengers for a fee in a private automobile (the latter law despite government efforts to encourage car pooling). The average rush hour automobile contains 1.7 passengers, but it remains illegal to fill up the remaining 3.3 seats at a price by bargaining with strangers. This situation was not always the case. Between 1914 and 1915, private automobiles, called jitneys, were allowed to carry passengers for fares. During peak usage the number of jitneys operating in the country was estimated at 62,000. Seattle, for example, had 518 vehicles that managed to carry 49,000 passengers a day. The jitneys, because they threatened the existing electric streetcars, were legislated and regulated into taxicabs.

Since that time, in most cities drivers carrying passengers for a fee must have taxicab licenses, which are strictly limited in number. The taxi medallion, the required license to operate in New York City, sells for more than $50,000, reflecting the monopoly profits inherent in operating a cab in the city. In addition to the restricted number of cabs, present policy often causes a perverse allocation of taxicabs during rush hour. Cabs typically operate at a regulated, metered rate with a high initial charge increased by a time and distance meter. This rate is often inadequate to compensate drivers for driving during the slower rush hour traffic, so that drivers have an incentive to sit out rush hour over leisurely meals. In addition, drivers are usually prohibited from accepting another passenger after loading the first one. So taxis during rush hour haul even fewer travelers per vehicle than do private automobiles. The absence of higher rush hour cab fares and the limitation on the number of passengers carried make inefficient use of the restricted number of cabs that are allowed to operate. The legislation of the return of the jitney by removing taxicab licensing would in many cities go far toward solving the existing public transportation problem.

When governments in general and cities in particular undertake to directly provide their citizens with goods and services, the incentives to provide them efficiently are often missing. Efficiency in the private sector is ensured by competition. The most efficient firm will win the business, and less efficient rivals must improve or withdraw. Often the goods and services provided by our cities are local monopolies exempt from competition.

The reason that publicly owned facilities are less efficiently operated than private facilities is not that publicly employed persons are "dim" or "nasty," but that they are simply confronted with different incentives than exist with competition. The income, job security, and fortunes of public employees do not depend upon efficient behavior in the same way that those of employees of private industry do. The public school system, for example, is widely believed to be inefficient and unresponsive to its clients. Student test scores have been declining for a decade. When the incentives that have been created for administrators and teachers in the public schools are examined, their implications provide substantiation of the general belief that public education is ineffectively supplied.

The publicly owned and supported basic education system is run by professional administrators and teachers supervised by a handful of generally unpaid elected officials. The public schools are essentially a monopoly, providing education at zero cost to a captive consumer forced by law to attend. This service is paid for not directly by the parents of the students but most often by property tax. The amount an individual pays for support of the schools is dependent not upon the number of school age children in the family but on the value of the property he or she owns. Private schools do exist, but parents pay twice to educate their children if they elect to send them to private schools, once for tuition and again with their property tax.

Consider the incentives facing local school administrators. Their clients, the pupils and parents, have no choice but to attend school through the eighth grade, nor do they have a choice of which school to attend. Administrators will not lose pupils if they do not provide an adequate education, nor will their schools suffer a financial loss, since the appropriations are provided by the school board, not the parents. The teacher receives tenure after a probationary period. The salaries of teachers are not dependent upon the achievements of their pupils but on length of service and educational attainments. If he or she survives for 20 years and attains a master's degree, a teacher will make it to the top of the salary scale. Nor is the level of the top salary based upon merit; it is determined by negotiation between the school board and the teachers union. There is little incentive, aside from professional pride, for either the administrator or the teacher to provide a quality education.

The plight of our system of basic education suggests the danger in relying exclusively upon professional pride to provide quality work. Imagine what would happen to the level of performance of local school systems if the education system involved the following incentives instead. Individual parents would be allowed to choose the school their children attend and to pay the tuition with vouchers provided by the government. The salaries of school administrators and teachers would be paid entirely out of voucher receipts, and merit raises would be based upon the increased competence of pupils in standardized pre- and post-test results.

The change in performance is readily imaginable. Schools would compete among themselves by offering a variety of programs designed to attract and maintain student interest. Predictably, schools would specialize in their scholastic offerings. Each program would be designed to attract students and convince them that their time in school is well spent. Individual teachers, if their income were dependent upon the educational attainments of pupils, would have an incentive to create an atmosphere conducive to learning. Much less time would be spent babysitting and assigning make-work projects and much more time spent on productive educational endeavors. The current plight of public education, like many urban problems, is more the result of inappropriate incentives than anything else.

A price system interpreted in its broadest sense is nothing more than a set of incentives. When a social problem exists, it is most probably due to a perverse set of incentives that encourages the behavior which creates the problem. The city as it is administered today is often governed by a perverse price system that provides the wrong signals to the city's inhabitants. There is a need, it would seem, not only for a knowledge of the economy of the city and the price system that prevails, but for some knowledgeable city economists as well.

Additional Readings

Cohen, David K. and Eleanor Farrar. "Power to the Parents—The Story of Educational Vouchers." *The Public Interest,* Summer 1977.

Eckert, Ross D. and George W. Hilton. "The Jitneys." *Journal of Law and Economics,* October 1972.

Hirsch, Werner Z. *Urban Economic Analysis.* McGraw-Hill, 1973.

Thompson, Wilbur. "The City As a Distorted Price System." *Psychology Today,* August 1968.

Vickrey, William. "Pricing As a Tool in Coordination of Local Transportation." *Transportation Economics.* National Bureau of Economic Research (NBER), 1965.

The growth of the governmental sector in the United States has expanded over the century at a rate two-thirds greater than the growth of the private sector. The rapid expansion of government has led to proposals to limit the growth of government by a constitutional amendment. The increasing popularity of these proposals suggests that the public believes that government is now larger than is desirable. This chapter explores the factors that have led to the rapid expansion of government. First, the extent to which the growth of government is due to the same forces of supply and demand that lead to the expansion of any industry in the private sector is investigated. Then two hypotheses that have been proposed to explain that portion of the growth of government not explained by conventional economic tools are examined.

Key Economic Points

The conventional tools of economic analysis explain only part of the rapid relative growth of government during this century.

The law of demand can be used to explain why government may well be too large.

What effects has extending the vote to a larger number of persons had on the rate of growth of the governmental sector?

Is a constitutional amendment necessary to halt the rapid growth of government and, if so, what form should it take?

31

Government: Why Does Government Grow?

The United States may see its first constitutional convention some day soon. The Constitution states that Congress "shall call a convention for proposing amendments" when requested by two-thirds of the states. The issue that has aroused a large number of states to call for a convention is the rapid growth of government spending. There are two proposals to limit the growth of public spending being considered. The first is to pass a constitutional amendment requiring the government to annually limit expenditures to revenues received, which means to balance the budget; the second, also in the form of a proposed constitutional amendment, is to limit the percentage increases in government spending to the percentage increases in gross national product.

Although a constitutional convention to limit government spending may never come to pass, it is fairly certain that some political action will be taken to reduce the rate of growth of government expenditures. Government has for several decades been the fastest growing sector of the economy. If government spending at the federal, state, and local levels continues to grow at its present rate, it will absorb over half of national income by the late 1980s.

The expenditures of the federal government are fast approaching $0.5 trillion, up from only $0.5 billion in 1900. During this century, government spending in real terms has increased at an average annual rate of 5 percent, doubling roughly every 14 years, while national output has grown about 3 percent a year, doubling every 23 years. In 1902, government expenditures absorbed 2.4 percent of the nation's output, and state and local governments spent another 4.4 percent. By 1970, government spending at the national level accounted for 21.3 percent of national income, and state and local government 12.8 percent.

Why has government grown so rapidly relative to the private sector during the twentieth century? It is possible that the same forces that would account for the expansion of any other sector in the economy could also account for the growth of government. In fact, these forces do account for part of the growth of government, but not for all. In this chapter the forces that have affected the demand and supply of government services are first considered; then two hypotheses that have been proposed to account for the unexplained portion of government growth are examined.

The rapid growth of government expenditures could have resulted from an increase in the public's demand for services due to increases in per capita income and a growing population, or due to the social problems that have accompanied America's economic development—urban problems, environmental decay, mutual interdependence—or because the relative costs of providing services have risen much more than the cost of providing goods.

Economists have considered these possible sources of government growth. Increases in the demand for government services due to increases in consumer incomes and population growth have been found to be quantitatively the most important causes of the measurable increases in government spending. As incomes increase, people desire to consume more of most goods, including government services. The increase in the public demand for government services due to higher incomes may account for over 25 percent of the increase in government expenditures.

A growing population might be expected to lead to a proportional increase in spending. However, if some of the activities of government involve the production of public goods, it will cost less on a per capita basis to provide these goods as population grows. A public good is one that, in benefiting one person, does not decrease the amount available for other persons. National defense and justice are examples of public goods. The cost of defending the country is the same no matter how many or how few persons live in it. If it costs $100 billion to defend the United States, it will not cost more if population grows. The per capita cost of some government services, that is, those that are public goods, will decline with increasing population. It has been estimated that population growth coupled with the provision of public goods has accounted for no more than one-fifth of the total growth in public expenditures. Therefore, increases in demand are responsible for a little less than one-half the growth of government.

The relative cost of providing services, as opposed to goods, has increased with time. The rate of productivity increase in the service sector of our economy has not grown as rapidly as in the manufacturing sector, causing the relative price of services to increase with time. Since government is principally a service industry, it has cost relatively more over time for government to function. This source of increase in government expenditures turned out to be of minor importance, accounting for slightly more than one-tenth of the increase.

As population and income in the United States have grown, the degree of economic interdependence has increased. The United States has become highly urbanized and some undesirable side effects that are not easily handled by free markets have arisen. Problems of environmental decay and urban deterioration have led to increased demands for government action. Surprisingly enough, little evidence exists that these concerns account for much of the increase in government spending. The costs of cleaning up the environment, for example, have been accomplished by regulation, not by government spending, and are mainly borne by the private, not the public, sector.

In summary, the rapid expansion of government due to increases in demand caused by increased affluence, a growing population, the provision of public goods, and growing economic interdependence, along with the added costs of providing services, account for a little more than half of the rise in government expenditures.

A substantial portion of the expansion of government thus remains unexplained by the standard analytical tools of economics. Part of the unexplained rise in government expenditures may be the result of the unique economic nature of providing government services. The consumption of government services, unlike the consumption of goods provided by the market, is separated from the cost of acquiring the goods or services. A person who acquires an apple, or an automobile, in the market pays for it directly, sacrificing the opportunity cost of the purchase. A person who consumes a government service, such as defense, rapid transit, or education, does not pay for it directly, but shares the cost with all other taxpayers, who pay whether they benefit or not. Almost all citizens can list some government services that benefit them and some that do not, but everyone jointly, to the extent that they pay taxes, pays for them all.

The separation of benefits from payment encourages people to demand more government services than they would if they had to pay for them directly. A group that benefits from a government action that is mostly paid for by others receives the benefits at less than its costs society. This group of beneficiaries, call them a special interest group, will, according to the law of demand, actively seek more government services than they would if they had to pay the true cost.

It is not difficult to discover existing special interest legislation. The U.S. government provides subsidies to the merchant marine, railroad passenger travel (AMTRAK), and farmers, to name a few. The federal government subsidizes tobacco farmers, for instance, at the same time warning that cigarette smoking is dangerous to the consumer's health.

Special interest groups win favors from government because it pays politicians to grant them and does not pay the general public to oppose them. Consider the farm price support programs. The farm population constitutes only a small part of the general public, less than 4 percent of the total. In 1976, the 8.3 million persons living on farms received $764 million from price support payments, or $92 a person. The average farm received $264 in benefits, but only 4 years earlier each farm on average received $1,380.

Why should this group be politically favored at the expense of the general taxpayer? Farmers, although they make up only a small part of the voting public, are strategically placed politically. Farmers are the political balance of power in several midwestern states. It is difficult to be elected President of the United States without carrying some of these states. Furthermore, each of these states has two senators, which gives farmers more than proportional representation in the U.S. Senate. In order to receive the support of the senators from farm states for other legislation, the senators from nonfarm states often find it politically advantageous to support a farm bill.

Why would nonfarm senators risk supporting legislation that means higher taxes and higher food prices for their constituents? The explanation lies in the low cost of farm price supports on a per capita basis. Farm price supports in 1976 cost each citizen $3.50, and even in 1972, when the farm bill cost a record $3.96 billion, the direct cost was only $19 a person. This of course neglects the higher cost of food that inevitably resulted. Because of low per capita cost, it simply doesn't pay any one individual or group to be informed of and to actively oppose farm price supports. The nation's farmers represent a special interest group par excellence. The perennial farm bill represents substantial benefits for a few at a small cost to everyone else.

However, when the special interest bills for farmers, teachers, industry, the poor—almost everybody—are added up, the small cost of each would account for a large part of the unexplained increase in government spending. The separation of benefits from costs of government service opens up the public treasury for raids by special interest groups, which are not always small minorities of the population.

In fact, there are reasons to expect that middle class citizens, who form a majority of the nation's voters, receive more benefits from public expenditures than they pay for in taxes. Studies of the burden of taxation have found that the middle class pays a lower proportion of income in taxes than does either the upper or the lower class. It would not be surprising to find that the middle class receives more than its proportional share of the benefits of public expenditures. Consider the public's support of higher education. State universities and colleges are heavily subsidized out of the public tax monies. Persons who attend these state-supported schools are mainly the children of the middle class. The children of the rich often go to private schools, and the children of the poor are less likely to attend college at all. Thus the rich, the poor, and the middle class are taxed to pay for part of the college education of the children of the middle class.

Or consider the use of tax monies to support our national parks and wilderness areas. Surveys of park users have found that it is the middle class that visits the parks and mainly the upper middle class that enjoys the wilderness areas. Neither the rich nor the poor avail themselves of these services to the same extent.

A large portion of the expenditures of government are not for public goods that benefit all, but for services that benefit identifiable groups but are paid for by the public as a whole. Each of these groups, like the middle class in general, because they receive services at less than their true social cost, has the incentive to demand more than if they were required to pay the full cost of the benefits received.

When the total costs of providing the services demanded by each successful special interest group are calculated, the resulting increase in the cost of government apparently appalls the individual taxpayer. A Harris Survey found that Americans favored a major cutback in federal spending by a 68 to 24 percent margin. They also favored an amendment to the Constitution that required a balanced budget by an identical 69 to 23 percent. But when specific cuts to accomplish this goal were suggested, American voters opposed them all. A majority would oppose major cuts in welfare (78 to 19 percent), cuts in health programs (75 to 20 percent), cuts in education (73 to 24 percent), cuts in defense spending (62 to 31 percent), reductions in the budget for environmental protection (57 to 36 percent), or similar cuts in aid to the unemployed (54 to 39 percent). In terms of specifics, a majority ranging from 54 to 78 percent opposed specific cutbacks. Such polls obviously provide little guidance for our elected representatives.

In fact, such polls reflect the major problem of government. Everyone is in favor of more goods and services. Reality, however, forces society to pay the bills, and when costs are separated from benefits, as they are in the provision of public services, too much will be demanded. This explanation suggests that government will always be too large, but it does not explain why government has grown so rapidly.

An alternative explanation that does explain the growth of government focuses upon the provision of government services only to the extent that they represent a redistribution of income. Indeed, the government activity that has grown most rapidly during the last half century has been in the areas of transfer payments (social security, welfare, veterans' benefits) and personal services (education, health, housing, and community redevelopment).

This explanation points out the decisive difference between the political and economic processes. The market system generates a distribution of income that is more unequal than the distribution of political power (basically one person, one vote). Politicians seeking to be elected offer programs that provide net benefits for the median voter whose income is also below the average income. These programs will be paid for by all voters, but those with higher incomes will pay more. Thus government will grow as long as the distribution of income is less equally distributed than the distribution of political power.

The extension of the voting franchise during the last century in the United States thus accounts for the rapid growth of government. Historically, the franchise has been extended from propertied men to all men 21 years or older, and then to all men and women over 21, and then to all persons 18 years or older. Each step gave the vote to groups whose income was lower than the average income of voters had previously been. Politicians sought the votes of each new group by offering programs that provided the new group of voters with net benefits. The result was the growth of government.

According to this explanation, government will continue to grow as long as the distribution of income differs from the distribution of political power. A constitutional amendment requiring a balanced budget will not stop the growth of government as its supporters suggest. Almost all states are required by their constitutions to balance their budgets, and this limitation has not stopped the rapid growth of state government. The proposal to limit increases in federal government expenditures to the rate of growth of national output would accomplish this goal, reducing the rate of expansion of the governmental sector to the pace of the economic growth of the private sector.

Additional Readings

Borcherding, Thomas E. "One Hundred Years of Public Spending, 1870–1970" and "The Sources of Growth of Public Expenditures in the United States, 1902–1970." *Budgets and Bureaucrats: The Sources of Government Growth,* Thomas E. Borcherding, ed. Duke University Press, 1977.

Buchanan, James M. "Why Does Government Grow?" *Budgets and Bureaucrats: The Sources of Government Growth,* Thomas E. Borcherding, ed. Duke University Press, 1977.

The Budget of the United States Government. U.S. Government Printing Office, annual.

Meltzer, Allan H., and Scott F. Richard. "Why Government Grows (and Grows)." *The Public Interest,* Summer 1978.

Pechman, Joseph A. "The Rich, the Poor and the Taxes They Pay." *The Public Interest,* Fall 1969.

Setting National Priorities. Brookings Institution, annual.

Preview

According to the public opinion polls, most Americans believe their government to be inefficient, and they single out for blame the bureaucracy that is in charge of the day-to-day operation of the public sector. When asked to compare the relative efficiency of business with that of government, the vast majority of Americans believe that business, especially big business, is more efficient. Furthermore, this belief is supported by several empirical investigations. Yet both big business and government are operated by bureaucracies, so that form of organization cannot be responsible for the relative inefficiency of government. This chapter investigates the causes of government's relative inefficiency by considering the incentives that influence bureaucratic behavior in government and how these incentives differ from those present in big business.

Key Economic Points

How do the incentives that influence the behavior of government bureaucracy differ from the incentives used by the bureaucracies that operate big business?

The incentives that influence government bureaucratic behavior often do not promote the efficient allocation of resources.

The concept of consumer surplus can be applied to explain the behavior of government bureaucracy.

Should the government encourage the duplication of efforts between agencies in order to encourage competition?

32

An Economic Theory of Bureaucratic Behavior: Government Inefficiency

Americans, if the polls can be believed, widely believe that their government is inefficient: 80 percent of the persons polled believed the government wastes tax dollars. When the Roper Organization asked Americans to compare business competence with government competence, nearly everyone believed that business, especially big business, was more efficient. When asked specifically which is run more efficiently, the persons polled chose business by a margin of 8 to 1. Almost every major survey on the topic reveals the exceptional emphasis that voters place on bureaucratic waste and inefficiency. Starting with California's Proposition 13 and spreading to other states, voter response has expressed the view that taxes can be cut without reducing public necessities by simply reducing waste.

There are both theoretical and empirical reasons to suspect that the American public is correct in the perception that government is wasteful and inefficient. This chapter explores this issue, employing economic theory to develop a theory of bureaucratic behavior and then presenting some of the results from empirical studies that support the theory. This investigation suggests some surprising remedies for inefficiency in bureaucracy.

A bureaucracy is a way of organizing an institution. It can be defined as the administration of a business or government through departments and subdivisions (bureaus and agencies) managed by officials who follow an inflexible routine and have little personal stake in the results of their efforts. Both government and the large corporations are run by bureaucrats and differ only to the extent that the incentives facing the bureaucrat are directly tied to the promotion of organizational efficiency, which is more direct in business than in government. A recent secretary of the treasury came to office after serving as president of a large corporation. While he was president of the corporation, he had the authority to hire and fire the employees of the firm, to transfer them, and to reward efficiency with higher salaries and bonuses. When he became secretary of the treasury, he was able to select only 25 of the 120,000 employees, Furthermore, he had virtually no control over the other 119,975. He could not transfer them, nor could he discriminate by granting higher pay to the more efficient. It also turned out to be virtually impossible to fire anyone. The self-interest of the government bureaucrats is almost totally divorced from contribution to the government's output.

Economists think that differences in incentives are crucial for understanding differences in behavior. Consider the public's widely held belief that business is more efficient than government even though both big business and big government are run by bureaucrats. The difference in behavior stems directly from the different incentives facing the bureaucrats in business as opposed to those facing government employees. If an employee in business behaves inefficiently, placing the interests of the firm behind those of personal preference, he or she will be warned by a superior, who has the power to fire or transfer the employee, to promote, or to give a bonus. The ability of the superior to reward efficiency and to punish inefficiency provides a strong incentive for employees to perform. If the government bureaucrat does the same thing, the employee will be warned and will know that that is probably all that will happen. It is not the difference in people that causes the observed different behavior of business and government bureaucrats; it is the system of incentives. Given the present system of lifetime employment offered by government, inefficient performance is to be expected. So far we have considered the lack of incentives for efficient behavior on the part of the government employee. But what are the incentives influencing the behavior of the managers of government agencies and departments, not the appointed officials, but the career civil servants who are actually in charge of the day-to-day operations of government?

A good rule of thumb is that the larger the appropriation a bureau or agency receives, the better the life of the bureaucrats. The larger the agency, the more opportunities there are for advancement. The higher the salary schedule, the better the working environment, and the more power and influence the managers possess. Since these benefits increase with the size of the agency's budget, let us assume that the persons in charge attempt to maximize the agency's appropriation from the legislative and executive branches of government.

The desire to maximize the bureau's appropriation does not preclude the efficient operation of the agency. Suppose the public's price elasticity of demand for the agency's services is elastic. Then any cost reduction will increase both the quantity demanded and the total appropriation for the bureau. But this possibility is not comforting because studies of the price elasticity of demand for public services have found them to be inelastic, so that increased efficiency will be rewarded with a less than proportional increase in the public's demand for the service and, more important, in an actual reduction of the bureau's budget, hardly the outcome the bureaucrats would desire. Increasing efficiency in many, if not most, cases runs counter to the self-interest of civil servants. Consequently, a bureau will have an incentive to hide the minimum cost of providing services from the executive and legislative officials when bargaining for next year's appropriations.

The agency will have a fairly good idea of the legislature's demand for its services because this demand is derived from the voters' demand. The bureaucrats can devote resources to monitoring and encouraging this demand. Each agency has access to the media and to public opinion polls. The agency also has a constituency that directly benefits from the services provided by the agency. The Defense Department, for example, has the military-industrial complex; Health, Education, and Welfare has the poor and the educational community; and Social Security has the retired. The agency can mobilize these groups to pressure their elected representatives to support the appropriations for the agencies that directly benefit them.

If the bureau has a good idea of the legislature's demand for its services, then the legislature has difficulty in determining the minimum costs of delivery for the services of government agencies. In fact, the legislature, because the agency is generally the sole source of supply, often has to rely upon the bureau to supply the information. The agency obviously has little incentive to reveal the true minimum costs of production. In fact, agencies have an incentive to ask for more than they hope to receive, to allow the legislature to look good politically by cutting the proposed appropriations. This process does not, of course, lead to the revelation of the true minimum cost of providing the service.

The legislative and the executive branches are at a disadvantage when bargaining with the bureaus over their appropriations. The bureau knows the legislature's demand for its services, but can hide the true minimum cost of production from the legislature. By overstating the costs of production, the bureau can capture at least part of the citizen's benefits, which correspond to the economic concept of consumer surplus. The agency can increase costs to just below the point where the legislature would choose to do without rather than pay the asking price.

The agency thus acts as a monopolist making an all-or-nothing offer after having calculated the demand for its product or service. A monopolist would calculate how much consumers would be willing to pay for the product rather than do without altogether. The amount that consumers would be willing to pay is the total value of the satisfaction the product provides. A monopolist, by asking for a little less than this amount, sells output for a total amount that captures almost all of the consumer surplus. Because almost all government agencies are the sole supplier (a monopolist) of the services they provide, they are in a position to try to extract as much of the citizens' consumer surplus as they can when bargaining with elected officials over appropriations.

What does the bureau do with the extra appropriations that, unlike a monopolist in the private sector, the bureaucrats cannot take in the form of profits? The agency can absorb the surplus in any of several ways. A larger appropriation means that a higher grade of civil service employees are required at correspondingly higher salaries, working in better offices. More employees may be hired, less work can be required of each employee, new services can be offered, more conferences can be held in attractive places, and better capital equipment can be purchased. A bureaucracy, like anyone else, will have little trouble spending more money, even if it cannot directly use the added funds for personal consumption.

There are a number of empirical studies of the proposition that government provides services at more than the minimum cost of production. One of these studies is remarkable because it makes a direct comparison of a private firm with a public bureau providing virtually identical services in the same market. In Australia there are two local airlines: Trans-Australian, which is government-owned, and Anset Australian National Airways, a private firm. The two airlines fly the same routes, charge identical prices, use similar aircraft, and have similar airport facilities. Yet their performances differ. The private airline is twice as productive in carrying freight and mail, and 22 percent more productive in transporting passengers. The study found that if the private airline took over the public airline, the total cost of running Trans-Australian would fall by at least 13 percent.

Closer to home, a study was made of the costs of publicly provided fire protection in comparison with the costs of employing a private firm. Data were gathered in the Seattle–King County area of the State of Washington, which relies on publicly operated fire departments. An empirical cost equation was developed. Per capita cost was a function of quantity variables, such as population and geographic size, and quality variables as represented by fire insurance rates. The equation was used to estimate the cost of providing the same quality public fire protection for Scottsdale, Arizona, which uses the privately owned Rural/Metro Fire Department instead of a municipally owned one. The estimated cost of using a public fire department, such as that in Seattle, rather than the private firm would be twice the actual cost charged by the private fire department.

Another study dealt with the costs of garbage collection. A survey of eighty-five cities, some of which used private firms and some of which used public bureaus, found that the private firms were significantly more efficient than the public agencies. Private companies not only succeeded per employee in serving more residences, but did so at lower cost. Whereas private firms succeeded in collecting 9.6 tons per man-day, public bureaus collected only 4.3 tons. The private firms succeeded in picking up 216 tons of garbage for each $1,000 spent, whereas the public bureaus collected only 104 tons for the same expenditure. Another study of the same activity found that the average per capita costs of garbage collection were 70 percent higher if public agencies were employed.

Studies of other organizations such as educational institutions, hospitals, and municipal utilities all find the same thing: the costs of providing services by government bureaus are higher than if private firms are employed. The significant disparity between the costs of public bureaus and private firms has caused some municipalities to turn to the private sector to provide such services as building and vehicle maintenance, street repair, security, and computer services. In 1978, Los Angeles voters approved overwhelmingly an amendment to facilitate the city's contracting with private firms to provide any service as long as city officials can prove that the private contractor can do the job for less money. The most widespread use of the private sector by cities has been to subcontract garbage collection, and even some police forces are contracting with private firms. Some have employed two private firms, NET Inc. and Rent-a-Narc, for undercover work, and Guardsmark Inc. rents police officers to small towns when extra security is required.

Government inefficiency is caused not by public employees doing the work, but by public bureaus generally having no competition. They are monopolies that can hide the true minimum cost of providing the service from elected representatives. The solution is to encourage competitive bids. Oklahoma City, for example, has established five garbage collection zones. City crews do the work in one zone, and a different private firm has the contract for each of the four other zones, each of which is periodically put up for bid. In this way the city can obtain information about the costs of garbage collection. Periodical open bids are vital to keeping the private firms from becoming a monopoly and increasing the city's costs in the same way as the public bureau they replaced. Competitive bidding reveals to officials the minimum costs of providing the service.

One way, then, to increase the efficiency of government is simply to subcontract, via competitive bids, as many services as possible. But this is not always possible. It is possible to introduce competition between bureaus. Government officials could make certain that there are always several agencies that provide the same service. A government service, such as Medicare and Medicaid, could be administered regionally, with the most efficient regional administrator being rewarded or promoted. Congress could use the costs of that region as a basis for setting the next year's budget for all regions. Perhaps we could even let the regional administrators bid for their authority to administer other regions, using something like the takeover bid system in the corporate sector. Clearly, this recommendation flies in the face of the recommendations of most efficiency studies that suggest that government eliminate "costly and wasteful duplication" and concentrate all authority in one agency. The effect of these recommendations is to root out all competition between government bureaus, allowing them the opportunity to effectively disguise the true minimum costs of their operations.

The problem stems from the inability of elected officials to determine the minimum costs of production. In a market economy, competitive bids reveal this information. Part of the solution to this problem is to allow private firms to bid on government services, as they are now allowed to do in Los Angeles, and to encourage competition the way Oklahoma City does in providing garbage collection. Even when it is not desirable for private firms to provide government services, competition between agencies could be encouraged. This recommendation runs counter to most government efficiency studies that recommend the elimination of duplication in government. If all government activities are carried on as inefficiently as the services that have been studied, the gains from competition would almost certainly exceed any waste involved in duplicating efforts.

The widely recognized inefficiency of government is not the result of bureaucratic waste, but rather the lack of incentives for efficient performance. The individual government employee is isolated from both reward for efficient behavior and penalties for inefficient performance. Everyone in an agency benefits if the appropriation is increased, and in most cases the best way to obtain a bigger appropriation is for the agency to disguise the true minimum costs of production and to overstate costs. Because elected representatives have no inexpensive way to determine the minimum costs of a bureau, this unequal bargaining situation puts the agency in the position of extracting part of the citizens' consumer surplus in the form of an appropriation that exceeds the minimum costs of providing the service. The result is waste and inefficiency.

Additional Readings

Ahlbrandt, Roger. "An Empirical Analysis of Private and Public Ownership and the Supply of Municipal Fire Services." *Public Choice,* Fall 1973.

Davies, D. G., "The Efficiency of Public Versus Private Firms." *Journal of Law and Economics,* April 1971.

"More Clout for Tax Dollars." *Dun's Review,* February 1979.

Niskanen, William A. *Bureaucracy and Representative Government.* Aldine-Atherton, 1971.

Orzechewski, William. "Economic Models of Bureaucracy: Survey, Extensions and Evidence." *Budgets and Bureaucrats: The Sources of Government Growth,* Thomas E. Borcherding, ed. Duke University Press, 1977.

Tullock, Gordon. *The Politics of Bureaucracy.* Public Affairs Press, 1965.

Preview

Since the middle of the 1960s the United States has attempted to eliminate poverty and increase the proportion of total income going to the poor. In order to do this, the government has transferred income from persons who are better off to the poor. Welfare expenditures have increased substantially, and currently more than 20 percent of gross national product (GNP) is transferred. An effort this extensive should have substantially improved the economic condition of America's poor, and that improvement should show up in the official statistics. But it doesn't. Either the United States' antipoverty program has been a failure or the official statistics are woefully inadequate. This chapter explores the adequacy of the official income statistics in measuring the distribution of income and in determining the numbers of America's poor.

Key Economic Points

The proper measure of the distribution of income is total after-tax income.
Not all income is money income.
The adjustment of money income to exclude tax payments and to include in-kind transfers can alter the distribution of income statistics.
It is difficult to obtain a set of basic facts about the distribution of income that all economists will accept.

33

Distribution of Income: Trying to Determine the Extent of Poverty in the United States

Official statistics on the distribution of income show that income is and has been very unequally distributed in the United States. In 1962, for example, the lowest 20 percent of income earners received only 5 percent of total money income, while the top 20 percent received more than eight times as much, or over 40 percent of total money income. Since then the United States has taken extensive measures to redistribute income and combat poverty. Social welfare expenditures have increased during the period from less than $100 billion to almost $400 billion, or from 10 percent of GNP to almost 21 percent. Despite these efforts, the total money income received by the lowest 20 percent has not increased significantly. The share of the lowest 20 percent in 1977 was only 5.2 percent, or scarcely different than it was before the government began its "War on Poverty."

It is possible that these expenditures, although not altering the distribution of income, have succeeded in reducing the extent of poverty in the country. Poverty, unlike the distribution of income, is not a relative matter. Poverty exists when a person does not receive a sufficient income to purchase the goods and services that would allow a minimum standard of living. In 1965, the Social Security Administration estimated that an annual income of $3,165 was necessary to permit a family of four a nutritionally adequate diet and minimum standards of clothing and shelter. A family whose annual income was below this poverty level was defined as living in poverty. This minimum annual income had increased to $6,500 by 1979, basically because of inflation.

When President Lyndon Johnson started the War on Poverty, 33 million Americans had incomes below the poverty line. By 1977 there were still 25 million persons living in poverty in the United States. The percentage of Americans living in poverty had fallen from 22.4 percent to 12.6 percent in 1970, but because population has grown, the absolute numbers of the poor have not declined as much as would be expected. Moreover, since 1970 the percentage of poor Americans has not changed appreciably, despite the rapid growth in welfare expenditures.

These results, on the face of it, suggest to many that the antipoverty effort has been a failure. Despite the annual transfer of more than 20 percent of GNP to the poor, the relative position of the lowest 20 percent of money income earners has not improved. Nor has the percentage of our population living in poverty declined significantly since 1970.

Failure would be the inescapable conclusion if the official figures accurately reflect the situation. But not every economist agrees that they do. Recent research has cast doubt on the accuracy of the official statistics. In this chapter we first consider what information would be required to measure the ideal distribution of income and the extent of poverty in the United States and the extent to which the official statistics meet the ideal. Then the results of several attempts to adjust the existing official statistics to more closely approximate the ideal are considered. Finally, it is noted that not all economists agree that these revisions are improvements on the official estimates.

The first step in evaluating the official estimates is to consider the appropriateness of money income as a measure of the total income received. First, the Census Bureau's money income statistics are before-tax figures. Thus, to the extent that higher income earners pay a larger proportion of their income in taxes than do lower income earners, the Census Bureau figures will overstate the extent of inequality in the society. The statistics that are more accurate are total income after taxes.

There is also a difference between total income and money income. We must take into account the production of goods and services by the household for its own consumption. In almost every family some food preparation, cleaning, and household maintenance takes place that could have been purchased but was domestically produced instead. Thus, to the extent that poorer families do relatively more of these activities, money income will not accurately represent the distribution of income.

Second, not all income is reported. There is a growing subterranean, or underground, economy whose transactions are designed to escape taxation. These activities take the form of either barter or nonreported cash transactions, as well as illegal activities, such as gambling, smuggling, prostitution, and drug sales. It has been estimated that the size of the underground economy has grown from 9 percent of GNP in 1970 to at least 15 percent of GNP in 1978. It is probable that proportionally more persons with low reported money incomes are engaged in these activities than persons with high reported money incomes. Therefore, to the extent that this is true, the money income statistics do not accurately reflect the distribution of income.

Finally, some income, particularly that of low-income earners, is received not as money but in kind. During the 1970s, when the percentage of families living in poverty was not declining significantly, the fastest growing transfer payments were in-kind transfers–Medicaid, food stamps, and public housing. In 1977, in-kind government transfers totaled $41.3 billion, which was $1,685 per person for the officially poor. Transfers of these kinds are not reflected in the official poverty statistics.

In order to decide whether the distribution of income has equalized or not and to determine the extent of poverty that exists in the United States today, we need not the money income statistics that are officially used but the total income after taxes. Even if we had this information, some economists would argue that these statistics should be adjusted further. It has been argued that total after-tax income should be adjusted for the number of workers in the family. Increasingly, wives have joined the labor force; therefore, the distribution of income will be considerably different if we consider the income of households rather than the income of individuals. The same argument is used to justify the suggestion that size of family should be considered, as should number of families headed by a retired person, and that income should be adjusted for the age of the wage earner. Moreover, this is only a partial list of the adjustments that have been suggested, but it should be sufficient to demonstrate that it is a difficult, perhaps impossible, task to obtain all the information about the distribution of income and the extent of poverty that would settle the issue to the satisfaction of most economists.

Nevertheless, there have been several attempts to make some of these adjustments, the results of which are very instructive. One of the first economists to attempt some of these adjustments was Edgar Browning. Browning added the in-kind transfer and subtracted income and social security taxes. By adjusting the data for family size, he measured the income per person. The effect of these adjustments on the distribution of income was striking. Instead of receiving 5.0 percent of income, the poorest 20 percent of wage earners in 1962 received 8.8 percent. Moreover, by 1972 the share of the lowest 20 percent of income earners had increased to 11.7 percent. Given the increase in in-kind transfers since 1972, it follows that this share has increased even more today.

The Congressional Budget Office (CBO) a few years later studied the effect the inclusion of in-kind transfers would have on the percent of the population living in poverty. The official poverty figures were adjusted for the benefits of food stamps, day-care service, public housing, school lunches, Medicaid, and Medicare. On the basis of these adjustments, the percentage of American families living below the official poverty level was less than half the official estimate, or 6 percent rather than 12 percent. The CBO concluded that the nation has come a lot closer to eliminating poverty than most people realize.

In a still more recent study Morton Paglin refined the CBO estimates. Paglin calculated that only 3 percent of Americans were poor in 1976. He found that the size of the poverty population declined by 80 percent between 1959 and 1975. According to Paglin, economic growth and government programs have gone far toward winning the War on Poverty with only 6 million Americans still living in poverty.

Not everyone agrees with these estimates. Among the telling criticisms that have been made is the point that the studies count in-kind transfers as the equivalent of cash transfers. In-kind transfers do not allow individuals a choice as to how to spend the additional income. Valuing in-kind transfers as equal to cash is to make the unrealistic assumption that, if given money instead, each person would have chosen to purchase the goods and services that were transferred. As this is very unlikely, valuing in-kind transfers at their cost overstates the value of these transfers to the individuals. There have been several attempts to estimate how the poor value in-kind transfers. These estimates generally fall in the 50 to 75 percent range depending on the type of transfer. If the in-kind transfers are valued not at cost but at the estimated value the poor attach to them, the decline in the income equality and in the number of poor would not be as dramatic as the above studies report.

Other critics question whether Medicare and Medicaid benefits should be counted as income. The logical conclusion of counting these benefits as income is that the sicker a person becomes, the more medical benefits he or she receives, and the less poor the person becomes. If a person becomes sufficiently ill, the illness could even lift the person out of poverty altogether! It is ridiculous, according to these critics, to suggest that a serious illness could be a cure for poverty.

So where does this leave us? The critics of the official estimates clearly have a point, but so do the critics of the estimate revisions. Probably the official money income estimates overstate the degree of income inequality in the United States and the amount of poverty, but these overestimates are not as great as the critics reported above suggest. No one knows for sure. The extent of income inequality and poverty in the United States is one of the questions about basic facts on which economists disagree.

Additional Reading

Arnold, Mark R. "We're Winning the War on Poverty." *National Observer*, February 19, 1977.

Browning, Edgar K. "The Trend Toward Equality in the Distribution of Net Income." *Southern Economic Journal*, July 1976.

Browning, Edgar K. "How Much More Equality Can We Afford?" *The Public Interest*, Spring 1976.

Congressional Budget Office. *Poverty Status of Families Under Alternative Definitions of Income.* U.S. Superintendent of Documents, January 1977.

Paglin, Morton. "Poverty in the United States: A Re-evaluation." *Policy Review*, Spring 1979.

Index

DATE DUE

NOV 17 '87			
DEC 1 '87			
5/3/88 ILL			